Lessons from the porch

Lessons from the porch

A Gathering Place For Telling Our Stories

Ed Poole

STEC Publishing
Naperville, Illinois

Published by STEC Publishing
P.O. Box 3972
Naperville, Il 60567-3972

Publisher's Cataloging-in-Publication Data
Poole, Ed.
Lessons from the porch: a gathering place for telling our stories / Ed Poole.
Naperville, IL : STEC Publishing © 2003.

p. ; cm.

ISBN 0-9720740-0-7
1. Poole, Ed. 2. Self-actualization (Psychology)
3. Self-Perception. 4. Happiness. I. Title.

BF637.S4 P66 2003 2002108688
158.1--dc21 0210

Project coordination by Jenkins Group, Inc. ❖ www.bookpublishing.com
Cover design by John Cassano
Interior design by Mike Dudek

Printed in the United States of America

06 05 04 03 02 ❖ 5 4 3 2 1

For more information and to order
Lessons From The Porch, A Gathering Place for Telling Our Stories
please visit www.lessonsfromtheporch.com

Dedicated to Ruth and Harley Poole

As Willie Nelson says, "You were
always on my mind," and I
know I was always on yours.
Thank you for your permission
to sit on the porch and
tell my story.

...With Gratitude...

Many people have joined me on the porch, helping me tell my story. They have been on the porch both as individuals and as groups. Some stayed for a long time, and some came and went rather quickly. While there, they listened to my story and shared with me parts of their own journeys. Every person who joined me on the porch has contributed to my story and my journey. Without their presence, guidance, insights, and encouragement, I would not have seen the importance of the porch, and my story would never have been told.

Ruth and Harley Poole were on a journey, and my path crossed with theirs when I was born. I'm grateful for that intersection, and for the intentions Mom and Dad had as they raised me. My sister Mary Belle and her family have their own journeys, and when our paths cross, I am the better for having experienced those crossings.

I am grateful to have married Bonnie, and we have been blessed with two children –Tracie and Eric, and now their spouses, Chris and Stacy. I am able to write this book because these five have always loved me and been so very supportive of whatever I wanted to attempt in life. My family, even in ways I still do not understand, has blessed me.

One long weekend in 1997 I was visiting with my friend and former pastor, Bob Baggott. As I spent many hours over that weekend beginning to tell Bob what at that time I understood as my journey, he said to me, "Ed, you've got a book here." No one had said that to me before. Thank you, Bob, for planting a seed that has finally come to life in *Lessons from the Porch*. I truly believe my path and Bob's path have crossed many times in our lives. Many of his struggles have been mine and mine his. Bob's words and thoughts, through his sermons and our conversations, are found throughout the book. Thank you, Bob.

I first learned of Greg Asimakoupoulos from my sister Mary Belle. In one of her Christian publications, *The Lookout*, she read an article by Greg in which he described his own journey through depression and his survival of that illness. The article was titled "I Survived the Depression Wilderness." She noticed Greg lived in the same community as I, so she sent me the article. I read the article and then said to myself, "Wow, if a minister can bring his depression out into the open and talk about it, this is someone I need to meet." I called Greg, we had breakfast, and we've been friends ever since. Greg is an extremely talented writer. Throughout the book, you will find special thoughts Greg has shared with me, written for me and about me, as he watched me on my journey. Greg also read a draft of this book and provided me helpful feedback. Thank you, Greg, for sharing your talents in this writing and with me.

Others have also read various drafts of the manuscript and provided meaningful feedback including Dr Ronald Banaszak, Edna Groves, Bill Hall, Denise Hatcher, Diane Herr, Ellen and Dale LaGow, Steve Mangrum, and Dr. Salina Shrofel.

What can I say about John Cassano? I have known John and the Cassano family for over twenty years. John is an extremely gifted graphic artist. After I shared some of my story with John, he created the line drawings that are attached to each of my twenty-two lessons. He also created the design for the cover of the book. John, thank you for sharing your talents with the readers of this book – and with me – and for helping to bring new meaning to my lessons. You helped breathe life into those lessons.

The members of the first doctoral cohort in The College of Education at Aurora University have encouraged me throughout the writing and have read parts of different drafts of the manuscript. It was not uncommon for one of them to ask from time to time, "Ed, how's the book coming?" I cannot name one without naming all, so thank you to: Anne Becker, Kari Brandstedt, Ann Butcher, Ken Carlson, Moses Cheng, Peter Clabough, Diana Harris, Kim Heinberg-Paulus, Ed Howerton, Dan Kallenbach, Pat La Bouff, Janet Lueck, John Lund, Brenda McKinney, Crysta Morrissey, Linda O'Connor, Rachel Overton, Minerva Perez, Olive Poliks, Mike Popp, Ann Riebock, Kathi Robinson, Jaime Sanchez, Sally Sover, Candace Thompson, Brian Tucker, Melanie Unterman, and Jim Varney. You took a risk, got off your porches, and became involved in a brand new doctoral program. You are finding paths for others to follow.

During the fall term, 2002, members of the second doctoral cohort at Aurora University read a galley copy of the book. They were taking a course with me on organizational change, and I wanted them to read *Lessons from the Porch* and discuss ways in which the twenty-two lessons can be applied to organizational settings. Their insights were invaluable and I want to thank them. As the second cohort they are following the paths discovered by the students in the above paragraph, and they are creating new paths of their own. Thank you: Robert Bell, Tatiana Bonuma, Vicki Childs, Marge Eskey, Daryl Fitts, Peggy Manville, Duane Meighan, Kathy Parge, Carla Peters, John Petzke, Joyce Powell, Tom Rogers, Lisa Smith, Tom Stiglic, Todd Stirn, Janet Stutz, Raquel Walker, and Pat Wernet.

Finally, I want to thank my Higher Power. You have sent me message after message. You have loved me enough to allow me to make my mistakes and learn from them – sometimes trying Your patience, I'm sure. Your unconditional love and forgiveness have allowed me to make decisions that were not always in my best interest or the best interest of my family. Again, You hoped I would learn and grow. About ten years ago You finally got my attention, and I have felt Your presence as I've sat on the porch, thinking and writing.

Ed Poole
Naperville, Illinois
June 6, 2002

- Contents -

Few people nowadays know what man is. Many sense this ignorance and die the more easily because of it, the same way that I will die more easily once I have completed this story...Each man's life represents a road toward himself, an attempt at such a road, the intimation of a path. No man has ever been entirely and completely himself. Yet each one strives to become that – one in an awkward, the other in a more intelligent way, each as best he can...We all share the same origin, our mothers; all of us come in at the same door. But each of us – experiments of the depths – strives toward his own destiny. We can understand one another, but each of us is able to interpret himself to himself alone.

Hermann Hesse, ***Demian***

But when the people gathered once again around the fire telling the story of all that had happened, something new came to mind. "We have overcome the strength of the elephant," they said, "and our fear of Shark and Hawk. We have done this by sitting by the fire and telling stories of what has happened to us, and learning from them. Only we, among all the creatures, have the gift of story and the wisdom it brings." From this day on the people held their heads high, never forgetting to sit by the fire and tell their stories. Never forgetting that in the stories could be found wisdom and in wisdom, strength.

African Folk Tale

In the long journey out of the self,
there are many detours, washed-out
interrupted raw places
where the shale slides
dangerously,
and the back wheels hang
almost over the edge
at the sudden veering,
the moment of turning.

Theodore Roetke, ***Journey to the Interior***

I was at a professional high.
I was out of touch with myself.
I fell hard.
But I survived.
And this book is about the lessons I learned.
Hopefully you can learn about your own journey as you read.

Ed Poole

The fall in the Midwest had been particularly splendid that year. It was mid-September; the leaves were beginning to turn their brilliant fall shades of reds, yellows, and oranges; the weather was warm; and the crisp days of fall were just around the corner. As I drove my car along the countryside, I could see the geese gathering, forming their V's, and preparing for their annual trip to warmer weather. Their long lines were majestic in their dipping down and rising up. I was reminded of the concept of teamwork we find with flying geese. The front goose is working the hardest, facing into the wind. The other geese honk encouragement, until the lead goose falls back in line, to take advantage of drafting on other geese, and another goose flies to the lead position.

The sunsets are beautiful this time of year, casting their long fall shadows over all of creation. I love sunsets in the fall. The shadows seem longer, and the daylight more precious. This year, as I experienced the fall, I was feeling the long, cold winter in my heart. Although I didn't know it yet, I needed to fall back in the pack and draft off others for a while.

Amidst all nature's beauty and serenity, the pieces of my life were falling apart around me. My journey along fall's amazing landscapes would soon take an unanticipated turn – one I had not planned, and for which I was totally unprepared.

After thirty years as a professional in the field of education, I found my job unbearable. Due to a wide array of circumstances at work, I was promoted to an interim position I didn't want, under conditions I felt were untenable. Because of these strong feelings, I submitted my resignation, which was made public at a highly charged meeting of staff, the governing Board, and the press. Resigning my position was the most difficult professional decision I have ever made. Though it was the very best decision. I was no longer functioning effectively in my interim position. I felt I had let my job down, and I felt my job had let me down. My motivation was gone. I decided it was better for me to resign on principle than to be fired for the wrong reasons.

One week later, after my resignation but while I was still in the interim position, I was walking out of a late-night meeting around 11:30 p.m. I noticed a car sitting next to mine in the parking lot – a car that looked like the one owned by my daughter and son-in-law. Before that meeting, I had called home to talk with my wife Bonnie. When she didn't answer, I left a depressing message on the answering machine, indicating, among other things, that I didn't see any way out of my pain.

Before leaving that statement on the answering machine that evening, I had spent some time on the one-hour commute back and forth between work and home looking at cement mixers and eighteen-wheelers coming at me, thinking if I would just make a slight shift to the left with the steering wheel, get up speed, and leave my seat belt off, I could surely bring a swift end to my misery. I found out later I had been depressed for some time, and was conscious of neither my depression nor its worsening state.

The last person in the world I would have thought would become clinically depressed was me. After all, I had been living "the American dream" – a very comfortable living, all the material comforts I needed and wanted, and a wonderfully supportive family. What went wrong? Why wasn't I happy?

As I approached the car on that September night, the windows came rolling down, and there sitting in the car were my wife, daughter, and son-in-law.

"What are you doing here?" I asked.

"I listened to your message on the answering machine," Bonnie responded. "I talked with Tracie and Chris, and the three of us didn't want you to drive the hour home alone after the meeting."

Having company on the drive home that night was probably one of the most fortunate happenings in my life. There wasn't much conversation during the drive. For my entire life I had kept my feelings to myself, operating my life mostly "from the neck up." I used my head both to think and to feel, so therefore I didn't "feel." Part of my story is how I have begun to realize the importance of living "from the neck down" – recognizing and valuing what my heart has to say. I kept my thoughts and pain bottled up inside me, and I had my secrets. At this time, I was reluctant to open up to anyone, even my wife, but I was very happy to have Bonnie's company on the ride home.

The next morning I told Bonnie if I didn't get some help I wouldn't make it through the day. This was an astounding admission for me because most of my adult life I have lived out the words in an Anne Murray song: "You'll take the sun for granted if you run from every storm." When life got rough, Ed got goin'. Very seldom had I stood still and faced my adversity. Flight was easier for me than fight. But as you can imagine, shortly after I took flight and found myself in a new situation, the old problems and issues resurfaced. This time there was no escape. I had no "back-up" plan. I had to surrender to what my heart and soul were saying to me: "Ed, you do need help, and you're the only one who can do this work." But I had no confidence in what I was about to experience.

There is an awkward moment at the top
of a ferris wheel when, having come up
the inside curvature, where we are facing
into a firm structure of confident girders,
suddenly that structure disappears, and we are thrust
out into the sky for the outward curve down.
Such perhaps is the present moment.

Julian Jaynes, ***The Ferris Wheel***

I had never felt like that in my life. The past few weeks had been pure hell. I considered suicide but was afraid to turn the car's steering wheel. I just didn't see a reason to continue living but was fearful of dying. My appetite had left me, as well as my ability to concentrate and focus. I couldn't read more than a paragraph in a newspaper article without getting distracted and quickly losing attention. I couldn't watch television, and I couldn't listen to music – two activities I have enjoyed all my life. Why did I feel this way? I had lost my smile, and co-workers were asking me what was wrong.

I found out later that day: I was clinically depressed, and the process had been going on for some time.

Through a series of phone calls and visits with doctors, I was admitted that day to the psychiatric care unit of a local hospital. I was a patient there for almost four months. I had been forced to call a time-out in my life.

Only after a lot of time in the hospital did I realize my depression was a gift from God. And God had been trying hard to get my attention many times over the past several years. I came to realize that life sends us messages, and if we don't hear them, other messages come along. If we don't hear those messages and keep ignoring subsequent pieces of information, eventually life sends us messages in the form of problems. When we ignore those problems, which I had been very good at doing throughout my life, the problems turn into crises. I have also come to realize, however, that just as we eventually have to confront the crises in our lives, our Higher Power also provides a breathing space – that time when, perhaps for the first time, we are able to see ourselves clearly.

I was definitely facing a crisis. The important word here is "facing" – a new experience for me. For the first time in my life, I had to reflect on my personal meaning of the beautiful line in the movie *The Natural*, when the Glenn Close character says, "I believe we have two lives: the life we learn with and the life we live with." Until my hospitalization, I had not gotten the message that all my attention had been focused on the life I learned with. It was time for me to pay close attention to the life I live with. Sure, I have learned much but not what I most needed to learn – how to live my life with personal meaning, self-reflection, unconditional love, and forgiveness.

As Gregg Levoy said in his book, *Callings: Finding and Following an Authentic Life*, "callings keep surfacing until we deal with them." He notes that in the Bible, God often needed to call to the prophets by saying their names twice. "Abraham, Abraham." "Jacob, Jacob." "Moses, Moses." Once, it seems, was not enough to get their attention.

One of my dear friends got my attention through a note she added to the card she sent me later that fall after finding out about my hospitalization:

"Dear Ed, Dear Friend,

> I've been thinking of you since you called last week. I'd also had you on my mind for at least two weeks before we talked on the phone. No accident, I see now. I have some thoughts to share with you. My primary message, though, is on the front of the card (*"I have an appointment with spring"*). All the time I've known you, you have, I think, tried to live in a way you believed to be responsible. It's been a long time you have been reaching for change with one hand while holding on to what's been important to you with the other. Now, in a way you could never have imagined, parts of you long denied are saying they will wait no longer. To me, no matter how and when and where this happens, this is a *break-through*, not a *breakdown*.
>
> I believe you will earn your way through this turbulent time, and with accruing wisdom slowly shape the life that has been waiting for you. It's a surging up of spirit, something sacred in us, something calling for expression and acknowledgement that has to do with why we are on this earth. I think this is so for you – a holy mandate. May you be gentle and caring of yourself now."

I so appreciated this message when it arrived. I read it over and over until I had a thought about altering a few of the words. I don't believe I had a *break*-through. I feel I'm *breaking*-through. It's a never-ending process, a journey. The destination is and should be unknown. I also feel a breakdown is a process as well. I was in the process of *breaking*-down for a long, long time. And the process may repeat itself in my life. I just don't know.

My friend was so perceptive in her thoughts. I did not know until I began this writing that I had denied parts of me, and those parts of me were taking me into the hospital as a patient because they had been "patient" long enough. I'm hopeful that the wisdom coming to me as I write is finally recognizing that the life I'm meant to live has been a part of me since the day I was born. This writing is helping me find some of those missing parts of my life. This journey toward wholeness, as you will read later, is a never-ending process; however, the telling of my story is a necessary beginning.

While attending to my depression, I received additional encouragement from others. One couple sent me an encouraging card, in which they said, "I heard somewhere we should always remember if God had meant for today to be perfect, He would not have invented tomorrow. Each day will be better."

My son Eric sent me a note after I began my outpatient treatment and was allowed to come home at night: "Welcome home, Dad. I'm really happy that you are home! I hope your progress continues to get more and more positive. I'm really glad you're my dad, and I can't wait to see you in a couple of weeks. I gotta run, but remember to 'shine your life like a light.'"

During my time of hospitalization and recovery, my mom sent me four cards, which I treasure. She added a note with each card, and I would like to include two of those four notes. In one she wrote, "I was glad Bonnie called me, but sorry to hear that you are in the hospital. I hope things are going all right and you will soon be all right again. I am remembering you in my prayers." In another she said, "Hope you are still continuing to feel better. I love you and pray for you."

Finally, a friend sent me a card with a picture of Winnie the Pooh and Piglet on the front, the two walking into the sunset and Piglet saying, "It is hard to be brave when you're only a very small animal, but sometimes it's easier to be brave with two." My friend added this note, "When I talked with Bill, he mentioned life had given you a bag of 'lemons.' I just wanted to let you know you are in our prayers. I pray each day you can turn one lemon at a time into 'lemonade,' that the sweetness of life will return." These special thoughts from friends and family did get my attention during this difficult time in my life – a time when the familiar became unfamiliar and the comfortable became uncomfortable.

Gregg Levoy said we must be willing to be shaken up, "to submit ourselves to the dark blossomings of chaos." In doing so, Levoy said we gain the blessings of growth. He described the paradoxes of stress bringing breakthroughs, crises creating opportunities, and chaos contributing to the creative process. Levoy said, "We introduce a little bit of chaos in order to prevent a lot of chaos" when we immunize society against disease. The immunization carries a bit of the chaos of the disease, in order to avoid the greater chaos of actually contracting the disease.

The stay in the hospital introduced me to a little chaos in order to prevent a lot of chaos that I would have experienced if my depression had continued undetected. Although I didn't see it at the time, my hospitalization, and all the time since, has truly been the beginning of the…***beginning***, not the beginning of the end. I did, for one of the few times in my life, have to turn and face head-on my demons. My mom, my family, my friends – no one – could do the work I had to do. But I was so afraid. I felt like a description of himself the writer Robert Raines gave during a difficult time in his life. In his book *Going Home*, he wondered where he was being taken and if he would be safe. He wondered what would happen to those he loved. He was scared. He asked to be treated gently and to leave him a place to sit or kneel or just lie down. He felt the waters surging over his head. Finally he said, "I can't see the way ahead. Be gentle with me; let your wind die down a little. Let your fire warm me, but don't burn all my house down." Like Raines, I hoped to be treated gently because I was gasping for air as the waters surged over my head. I knew I needed help. I was so frightened and didn't know anything about what was ahead for me in the hospital. I hoped I would be safe. I knew I had to take this part of my journey by myself. I could no longer "take the sun for granted." I could no longer stay on my porch in suspended animation.

In my role as a high school principal, I had offered lofty thoughts to graduates about taking risks, about "going out not knowing," seeing life as full of wonderful challenges and opportunities. It was time to "walk the walk" and not just "talk the talk."

One who in my mind has always walked the walk is my son Eric. He has always placed his family foremost in his life, and my hospitalization was no exception. Eric is a caring, warm human being for whom I am very grateful, and he loves his family. If you can picture a map of the United States in your mind, you will see a fairly straight line – cut on a diagonal – between Moab, Utah and Savannah, Georgia. Eric had been leading a series of bike tours in and around the Moab area. At the end of that series of tours, he was to drive a van, with an attached trailer filled with over twenty bikes, from Moab to Savannah. A leader who was going to begin a series of tours around the South Georgia countryside needed the bikes for her work there. Shortly after I entered the hospital, one of the nurses came to me one day as I was sitting alone in a chair in the hallway outside my room. We were between group sessions, and I was just staring out the window, enjoying the beauty of the fall colors in the trees just outside. The nurse said, "Your son is here to see you."

"That can't be possible," I replied. "Eric's somewhere between Moab and Savannah right now."

"Nonetheless, Eric is here to see you."

If you have ever spent time as a patient in a mental health facility, you know the staff members there have to be very, very cautious of who knows you are there and how and when people get to see you. In fact, before I could take incoming calls from family or friends, each of them needed to know the code word I had given both to them and the nurses; otherwise, their calls would not come to me. When I entered the hospital, I had to remove my shoelaces, give up my toiletries, and use only an electric razor to shave. A staff member was always present even as patients were in the bathroom shaving and preparing to meet the new day. An important part of the job of the medical professionals was to make sure I did not do anything to harm myself while I was there and to keep me safe from unwanted intruders. I remember entering the third floor inpatient wing and hearing the huge, steel double doors close and lock behind me. I had left some personal items in my car that I needed, but once in the wing with the doors locked I could not leave. A member of the hospital security staff had to go to my car and retrieve the forgotten items. At the same time, I felt both trapped and relieved. The hospital became my oasis at a time in my life when I was lost in the desert.

Because of the need to maintain privacy and to insure security for the patients, it was very appropriate for the nurse to tell me about Eric's visit and to make sure it was okay with me if he came onto the floor. I assured her it was fine; however, I still could not believe he was there. In a few minutes this redheaded young man came bouncing down the hall and into my arms. Having him there was one of my best gifts ever. We hugged for such a long time. I asked what he was doing there, and he said he had taken a "detour" on his way from Moab to Savannah to see me. If you are still imagining that map of the United States in your mind, you will realize it is more than just a slight "detour" to go through Chicago on the way from Moab to Savannah.

During Eric's three-day visit, we talked about all that had happened during the past several months. He learned so many interpersonal skills during his work with Backroads and he used them with me as we talked. He asked good, probing questions. Eric is a good listener. Unlike my earlier years, Eric doesn't rush into a conversation to tell the other person all the wonderful things he is doing in his life. He listens. I was always so full of myself and couldn't wait to tell others just how important I was. I began to listen while in the hospital.

I could tell Eric was concerned about me and interested in what was happening to me in the hospital. Sometimes Eric and I talked alone and other times my whole family was there. I felt a great sense of comfort in seeing my family all together. I marveled at Eric's sense of caring and concern for me, and his willingness to take so much time from his work to visit me in the hospital. I couldn't help but think that when I was his age I did not show that same sense of caring and concern by what I did. I talked a good game, but I didn't live it.

I was so happy to have him there. He stayed three days and then headed south to Savannah. What a joy it was to see him. The waters were receding from over my head and I felt the warmth of Eric's visit.

One of the lessons I learned from Eric's visit is appreciating, valuing, and understanding often follow adversity. If you can imagine a train wreck with all the cars off the tracks in many patterns of disarray, that is how I felt when I first entered the hospital. I was beginning to realize the understanding that comes from chaos. For the first time in my life, I had to consider the fact that I was a human being, not a human "doing." I had been "doing" for so long in my life, carefully keeping myself busy, so I wouldn't have time to consider who I was and how I was leading my life. It was time to sit quietly and listen. In his book, *The Deeper Wound*, Deepak Chopra says, "If you take the time to listen to the voice of silence, you will be astonished at the power you have at your command, however long this power has been overlooked."

I had taken a time out in my life; the solitude of my oasis allowed my silent voice to be heard. I had power at my command throughout my adult life; however, it was power that was externally motivated. It came from outside of me, not from within. I had not been silent long enough to find my inner voice, and I could not find my soul.

While in the hospital, I began to find both my voice and my soul – although at the time I did not know I was making these discoveries. Through my new friends and fellow patients, and with the help of my family, the therapists, and counselors in the program, I began to realize I didn't know who Ed Poole really was, outside of my profession. I had become so identified by my work, that outside of those identities there was no definition. There was no transparency at all that could help me find myself. I lived in a shell of fear.

I would not allow myself to become transparent, to let the real me show because I didn't know how. Harold Kushner, in his book, *When Bad Things Happen to Good People*, said when we choose to become transparent to those pulls of our own likes and dislikes, we are letting go. "To be transparent requires that we allow fears and insecurities to play themselves out in the field of full awareness." I was full of fears and insecurities. I did not know anything about being fully aware of my life and myself; however, I was being led to find some new level of understanding. I was looking for my angels, my saints – those inner guides who could help me find myself.

In the words of theologian Paul Tillich, "Saints are saints not because they are good, but because they are transparent for something that is larger than they are." To be a saint means to take a focus beyond one's self. It takes a faithful search for the reality or substance of life below the surface, above the clatter, and within the complexity. As Lesbia Scott's hymn reminds us, "The saints of God are just folks like [you and] me, and [we all can] be one too." Richard Bode, in his book *Beachcombing at Miramar*, said, "Not all men are born to be saints, but I believe we are all born with a voice within that we tend to ignore until it becomes so indistinct we barely know it's there. The voice doesn't come from an almighty God in the sky; it comes from an in-dwelling God in the soul." I did not even know I had a voice within. As you will read later, I had spent my entire life up to this point listening to and being affirmed by the voices outside of Ed Poole. I did not know about an "indwelling God," and I had not discovered my soul.

To become transparent is to become vulnerable, and to become vulnerable is to suffer loss and learn how to grieve. As we become vulnerable, we become accessible to others. Being vulnerable goes with being human, but vulnerability also requires a time out, a time for sanctuary, oasis, and shelter. In Jungian terms, the masculine God is calling us out of our *safety* to <u>leave</u> home; the feminine God is calling us out of our *vulnerability* to <u>come</u> home. How wonderful it is to have ears to hear both callings. When we become transparent and vulnerable, we learn how to trust – both others and ourselves. The words of Jung gave me my first clue that safety and vulnerability allow us to realize that we can leave <u>and</u> return home.

Lessons from the Porch is about leaving home and coming home. Most of my adult life I have been trying to define home with a feeling that I had to leave, to get out into the world to make a difference. Growing into a realization that we all have both masculine and feminine sides, I have been better able to understand this balance of being called both out of my safety and out of my vulnerability to leave and return home, to the porch.

During my four months as a patient, I experienced for the very first time in my life the meaning of total trust. Like many of you, I had been sitting in meetings for much of my professional life. Unfortunately, during most of those meetings, the <u>real</u> agendas were not those printed and distributed prior to the meetings. The real agendas were played out either before or after the meetings, sometimes in the parking lots. These "parking lot agendas" contained the real and honest feelings of the participants. The parking-lot agendas never found their way into the meetings because people didn't trust each other with that information. In the hospital, we carried our own pain and despair. Yet, somehow from our very souls we were able to, and wanted to, reach deep down and find ways to help each other and ourselves during that process.

We had a safe environment, and we were beginning to trust a process. There were no parking-lot agendas during our group sessions. The friends I made while in the hospital represented a variety of illnesses. Those with whom I began developing a trusting relationship included paranoid schizophrenics, those with multiple personalities, friends who were bi-polar – experiencing both the manic and depressive states of their lives, and those dependent on alcohol and drugs. They had become my friends through the common bond we held as a group – the need to begin the process of healing.

While in the hospital we had to get up very early, which was difficult because depression had drained us both physically and emotionally. Feeling an emotional emptiness was more difficult for me than enduring a physical fatigue. Breakfast always came first on the day's agenda. We ate all our meals together, and at breakfast each morning we pre-selected our meals for the next day. We spent most of each day together in our group. In some group sessions we discussed a short reading we were given, while in others we talked about our own problems and issues. Those who were open during these sessions received the most help because others provided a support system. Many of my new friends were much more open than I in talking about their lives. At first, I was reeling from the thought of being depressed. I didn't want to talk to anyone. I didn't care about my physical appearance. I was in a foggy haze. At first I didn't even want my family to visit. However, in time visits from my family and friends helped me to begin talking. I had been a closed person for so long, I didn't know how to be open. We had weekly physical and art therapy sessions. During our free time, we could watch television, talk, relax, sleep, etc. Lights were out for all of us fairly early each night.

In the hospital we patients had an opportunity each day to read a thought or an idea about which we then had dialogue. Much of this material was from various Twelve-Step Programs. I have become a passionate believer in Twelve-Step Programs, whether they are focused on alcohol and drug abuse, gambling, over-eating, sex, etc. Each of us enters these programs for his or her own reasons.

The stay in the hospital was the very first time in my entire life where I was forced to call a "time out" to my frenetic pace and deal only with me. I had no choice. I was captive, but also captivated.

During this time, I had the opportunity to begin the reflecting process, not realizing at the time that I had returned to "the porch." Often I thought of my parents. Dad died in 1989, and Mom in 2001. Mom always said people would say Dad was a hard worker. I never doubted that for a second. When my mother died, I finally realized I don't want my own children to look back on my life with anger and frustration and say, "Well, Dad surely was a hard worker, but he always had time for..." and not be able to complete the sentence. One pattern I had inherited too well from my parents was their work ethic. I worked so hard I had conveniently scheduled no time for me. Until recently I had both a full-time and a part-time job. Together these jobs accounted for about 70 hours per week. Again, how convenient. I worked to get more "things" and to avoid working on discovering me.

Contemplating my own death and my kids' memories of me had an impact on my need to achieve better balance between work and play in my life. It is hard, and I'm still trying.

I worked and worked to avoid understanding myself. Because of this lack of understanding, I had been sitting on the porch for much of my life, afraid to leave. A great line in an Eagles song says, "Why don't you come to your senses? You've been out riding fences for so long now." I had been so busy "riding fences." Could I "come to [my] senses"? I had been riding my fences from two different perspectives: the work involved in building the fences and the straddling I'd done in sitting on a fence and not being able to decide which direction I wanted to jump. Fences, if we sit astride them long enough, can have their own way of holding us in suspended animation.

I began to realize the importance of living with the questions in my life. In parts of my life I am able to tolerate a fair amount of ambiguity. Why did I need to answer the questions right then? Just knowing some of the questions was an important step along the journey. I was able to relax and quit looking for answers that weren't ready to be revealed. If the answers came too soon, they would be either incomplete, or I wouldn't be able to live them.

Slowly, as I began to understand the process I was experiencing through help from the Twelve Step Program and my friends in the hospital, I realized that each of us has our own personal relationship with our Higher Power – what a relief, what freedom. I want to recognize, value, understand, and celebrate the richness of many religions in our world, some of which do not recognize God as a supreme being. Throughout the book, I will use the words God and Higher Power interchangeably. Even these references will not identify with all your religious beliefs and preferences. Please substitute your own words.

When I returned to the question of why, with all these trappings surrounding me, I wasn't happy and felt unfulfilled, I had no answer. A voice in me said,

"I need... need...need," or "I want...want...want." My needs and wants were resting only in my eyes and my head, not in my soul and my heart. I had no idea what I wanted or needed or how to find out about my needs. My needs were hard to identify because I hadn't spent any time trying to gain this understanding. I couldn't take that long, deep, relaxing, cleansing breath and feel all is well in my world. All my life I thought if I could just acquire this or if could just get that job or if I could just read this book, I'd be fine and stumble into some answers along the way.

As I moved from job to job and community to community, thinking these actions would fill that void within me, very quickly I discovered all the same fears, concerns, unanswered questions, and pain were still with me. Imagine that! Until recently the porch never became a connection between what has been and what can be. It was a place I thought I needed to leave. What I needed was to get better acquainted with myself. I had been trying to get acquainted with Ed Poole; I just did not realize what I was doing. In fact, I didn't realize it because I *was* doing, and not being.

Something else I realized I needed, in addition to discovering Ed Poole, was to redefine the term "spirituality" and determine its meaning for me. I had carried around a lot of anger concerning "religion," "spirituality," "God," and I needed help in coming to terms with these concepts in ways that made sense to me.

The Twelve Step program allowed me the opportunity and the time to begin focusing my attention on my spiritual needs. As I thought about needing "things" in my life, I never considered that my own spirituality was a major need missing from my life. I had followed all the outward trappings of a spiritual life – professing a belief in God, attending church regularly, making sure our two children experienced a religious setting – I had simply ignored the very important inner need I had for a spiritual meaning in my life. My hospitalization prodded my soul toward a spiritual search. Whenever a crisis interrupts our lives, causing us to lose control, our unresolved emotional pain will come to us, often demanding an understanding of our spiritual life.

Along with finding out about myself and revisiting the importance of spirituality in my life, I needed to <u>remember</u> what I had just experienced while in the hospital. Perhaps like you, after emerging from a tough period of time, I conveniently forget what I was thinking and learning during that down time. In fact, until this point in my life, I really didn't want to remember. I was afraid this time would be like all the others, but the difference this time is I wanted to remember, so I began reflecting on lessons from the porch.

When I left the hospital, I moved into therapy on a weekly basis with a therapist who worked in the same group as did my psychiatrist. He goes by the initials of his first and middle names – "J.R." I began to use "J.R." as not only a way to communicate with my therapist by name but also as a prompt to mean "**J**ust <u>R</u>emember." Because I still want to remember this experience after I was in the middle of it, perhaps "J.R." is working for me. I talked with J.R. about the reflecting I was doing, and I told him I thought a "new" Ed Poole would emerge from my introspecting. He said he didn't think I would find a new Ed Poole, but a "different" Ed Poole. I was satisfied with J.R.'s observation. He is the only therapist I've ever had who could kick me in the butt when I needed it but do so in a way that allowed me to leave the session respecting him and learning something important about me. The remembering is helping me do the reflecting and the writing. Remembering my past has enabled me to go back in time and write this book. I believe that God gives us memory so that if we didn't play the roles of enriching and ennobling others and ourselves at earlier points in our lives, we can have another go at it. As I make this journey with God there are three <u>intertwined</u> lives I will discuss: my work, my relationships, and my self.

So, I invite you to join me in viewing a work in progress – my journey. I still need to spend much time on the porch (and off) — <u>R</u>esting, <u>R</u>efreshing, and <u>R</u>eflecting. If I wait any longer to write my story, it will never be written because I will always need my "3 R time" on and off my porch.

The twenty-two lessons you are about to experience are <u>my</u> lessons. Your lessons may be different. Still my journey may help you make applications to your own life lessons and journey. **J**ust <u>R</u>emember that the "products," the lessons, are not going to turn out to be as important as the journey we take to find them and to develop and apply them to our lives. The process is the important element here. The book, *A Course in Miracles*, describes our quest as "a journey without distance to a goal that has no end."

Everyone is on a journey in life. However, two distinct groups comprise "everyone": those who already know they are on a life's journey and those who are on the journey but do not recognize it yet. *Lessons from the Porch* is written for both groups – for those of you who already recognize the journey you are making, as well as those who have yet to discover their journey. Your reactions to what you read will differ, depending upon which group you identify with at this time.

"Eddie, don't get too close to the
edge of the porch because if you
do you might fall off."

Ruth Poole

"Stay on the porch!"
"Don't go near the edge!"
you heard your mother say.
"Don't risk!"
"Don't chance!"
"Don't wander too far!"
And obeying her
you've wondered far too long
who you are,
where you're headed,
and why the attic in your head
is filled with boxes of regrets.
Did your mother know
when she told you not to chance
that you'd never learn to dance
with all those opportunities for growth
all dressed for the prom?
Damn! She didn't.

And neither did you!
But, I've got a clue
you're back in the attic
searching for your dancing shoes
and a place to waltz
a 'fer piece' from the porch!
Greg Asimakoupoulos

I invite you to join me on my journey toward self-awareness and self-understanding. As you read, you will discover, if you don't already know, each of our stories contains thoughts and ideas from all of our stories. Part of my journey is yours, and part of your journey is mine. The story of my journey includes some ups and downs in my life. If you can leave the book at its ending, agreeing with me that the journey I'm on is more than worth the price of admission, and can see the story as one of hope, challenges, and growth, I will be satisfied.

How I wish my mom had helped me see each day of my life was full of anticipation, mystery, growth, and excitement by saying, "Get out there, Eddie, and see who wants to play. It's a beautiful day, and I know Max, or Jim, or Larry, or Richard is out there somewhere ready to explore the day with you. If you get thirsty, come on home and get something to drink. When you get hungry, we'll have a nice lunch, and if you get tired, come in and rest awhile and then get back out there." Rather, Mom would always say, on those mornings full of anticipation, mystery, growth, and excitement, "Eddie, don't get too close to the edge of the porch because if you do you might fall off."

The Journey I've Been on All Along

In the first few years of my life, my mom issued this cautioning statement whenever she saw me playing too close to the edge of the big porch that surrounded two sides of our home — a cautioning not unlike that of other parents in efforts to protect their children from harm.

This cautioning from Mom, however, stayed with me for many, too many, years, and the words stayed with me because I allowed them to be there, deep within me. I didn't understand her words or the reason they still played such a prominent role in my life's decisions. Why did Mom's caution stay with me until well into my adult life?

The answer to this question is the purpose for this book. *Lessons from the Porch: A Gathering Place for Telling Our Stories* is my story as I begin to understand myself, remembering my past and accepting and dealing with changes in my life – personally, professionally, and spiritually. I am not telling my story as much as I am talking with you about my life's journey. Parts of my life story have been omitted. I have included those parts that relate to my twenty-two lessons. The lessons evolved from my own reflecting and reading the thoughts of others. Those places in my life where I was feeling the most pain got my attention.

The pain in parts of my life had become so severe and I needed to find its cause. As I thought and read over a long period of time, the lessons I was learning began to emerge. Eventually I wrote them down on paper, looked at them and continued reflecting. Later, in a somewhat random manner, I began writing about each of the lessons. As I wrote I found my own thoughts were affirmed by the thinking of authors who were addressing ideas similar to those in my twenty-two lessons. Over time, I was able to talk about those parts of my journey related to each of the lessons. As it turns out, there were twenty-two lessons inside me as I began this process. When I finish writing about these lessons, I hope to continue reflecting and reading. I'm sure other lessons are inside me, waiting to be brought into the light of day. I say this because I am certain I will continue to experience both the joy and the pain of being human as I continue to find my place in the world. As I learn new lessons I will tell those parts of my story.

The journey is far from over, but now that I've discovered that I'm actually on a journey, I hope to "stay the course" and see how and where my journey unfolds. Journeys are very important in our lives, and we cannot avoid them. I did not recognize the journey I was on until a few years ago.

A friend, when I left a job, wrote the following titled "Journey,"

In the mazes of my soul, a myriad of twisting and turning paths are connected only by doors.
Impossible to know which doors will open to happiness.
Impossible to know if all doors lead there too.
Impossible to know if closing a door means it can never be reopened.
I journey…somewhere I've never traveled.

In the mazes of my soul, I am guided by my heart following the richness of the love that I feel.

Impossible to know if my heart can see what's right.
Impossible to judge if love will lead to light.
Impossible to know if love's obsession can be tamed.
I journey…somewhere I've never traveled.

In the mazes of my soul, I journey by my faith, letting angels open doors for me.
Impossible to know if my angel hears my prayers.
Impossible to know how much strength I have to fly.
Impossible to know if my faith will find what's true.
I journey…somewhere I've never traveled.

In the mazes of my soul, my guides are family, friends, and colleagues invited on my journey.
Impossible to know if the path is wide enough for more.
Impossible to know where paths will cross or separate.
Impossible to see through tears of happiness and pain.
I journey…somewhere I've never traveled.

In the mazes of my soul, my heart, my faith, my family, friends, and colleagues open one door and close another.
Sometimes finding sorrow, sometimes finding joy.
Sometimes finding paradoxes, sometimes finding truth.
Impossible to know – I trust, close one door and always open another.
And I journey…to somewhere I'd gladly travel.

Janice DiVincenzo

In order to journey to somewhere I'd gladly travel, I have to embrace my past and the memories reaching out to me. Doing so requires going back through my life to fill in some of the gaps that were unnoticed at the time.

Some don't try to remember, and I didn't for a long time in my life. But the desire and ability to remember have become an essential part of my journey.

Remembering the Past

With no discernment whatsoever, I had been struggling to unload my past – to begin anew. Until I began this writing, I didn't realize that I must remember my past and frame those remembrances in ways that allow me to grow, learn, and mature as an adult.

Isn't it funny what we remember from childhood? In the book *The Soul's Code: In Search of Character and Calling*, James Hillman said, "Our lives may be determined less by our childhood than by the way we have learned to imagine our childhoods. We are less damaged by the traumas of childhood than by the traumatic way we remember childhood..." My childhood memories caused only anger and frustration; I had just one thought: "How can I get rid of all these unhappy memories?" I now realize that remembering my childhood is critical to understanding who I am today and where I am going on my journey.

In one of his books titled *A Room Called Remember*, author Frederick Buechner devoted this entire writing to "remembering." Understanding the importance of remembering his past came to Buechner through a dream. In the dream he was staying in a hotel, and he was given a room that he loved and in which he felt very comfortable. He was happy and at peace in this room. As his dream continued, he described the wanderings he made from this room to a variety of other destinations. When he returned to the same hotel, he was given a different room – one he didn't like and in which he felt uncomfortable. Buechner described his new room as being dark and cramped. He wanted to return to his first room where he was happy and at peace. The desk clerk told Buechner he could have that room any time he wanted; he just needed to ask for it. The room was called Remember.

Buechner realized the dream had been a good dream, but he wasn't exactly sure why. He saw the dream as both blessing and healing in his life, and he took great security from the fact that he could return to the room whenever he wanted and needed to. Knowing this allowed the healing and blessing to emerge for him. The still unanswered question for Buechner was "What are we to remember – all of us? To what end and purpose are we to remember?" Our memories often come and go in some disorganized fashion and much of the time from no conscious choice we've made.

Buechner's room called Remember allowed him to realize that he could enter and leave the room through his own choice, and therefore, remembering became <u>his</u> power to exercise by <u>his</u> choice. And, with this freedom, he chose to remember. He wrote, "But there is a deeper need...and that is the need – not all the time, surely, but from time to time – to enter that still room within us all where the past lives on as part of the present...where we are most alive ourselves to the long journeys of our lives...and to where our journeys have brought us."

I had always wanted to forget, not remember, my past because I did not realize the importance of my past living on in my present. I didn't know that remembering past memories was the only way I was going to understand where I was at any given time in my life's journey. I feel a sense of relief knowing I can choose to remember and I have the freedom to make those choices where and as I desire. Remembering my past helps me to bless it, not feel cursed by the events in my life. As I blessed those past memories through my writing, I began the healing process. Forgiving God, others, and myself is possible for me only as I remember.

Richard Bode spoke of the importance of remembering our past in his book *First You Have to Learn to Row a Little Boat*. He talked about moving to California from New York as an adult. He arranged a luncheon meeting with a boyhood friend from Long Island, someone he hadn't seen in years. At this luncheon Bode and his friend talked about their years growing up on Long Island. Bode talked about what he remembered and what he missed and how, as a man, he had to come to terms with what losses he had suffered as a boy. His friend was surprised that Bode was "still struggling" with events that had happened so long ago. In answering his friend, Bode said he wasn't struggling but "savoring" what he was remembering about his childhood. He said, "The desire to forget the past is a form of suicide...What should truly frighten us is the possibility that we might lose the power to recall the life we have lived, which gives us our connection to ourselves." Until I fell off the porch and entered the hospital, I had no clue about the value of remembering past experiences in my life. I was trying to forget many of them. I knew I was struggling in my life, and I did not know that I was beginning to savor those past experiences. I also didn't know that savoring my past brought with it the need to address a lot of emotional and spiritual pain. My porch became the place I savored my memories and learned to understand the pain I experienced as a boy and now an adult.

THE IMPORTANCE OF PORCHES IN OUR LIVES

Late in life the porch Mom cautioned me about has become a metaphor allowing me to honor my past while at the same time representing change in my life. The use of metaphor is a helpful tool to aid in our understanding of life, and it is the most ancient of teachings. Native Americans have always used wonderful metaphors in their stories. Metaphors address the subconscious, which is where our beliefs are stored. Because metaphors address this subconscious, the holder of our belief systems, these metaphors are very important and powerful in our lives. They work on the cerebral level, and they use both sides of the brain in a balanced way. As I got older and began to see the porch as a metaphor for change in my life, I always felt my mom's cautions about getting too close to the edge had been the reason for my not being able to get off the porch and accept change in my life. Now I realize getting off the porch has always been my responsibility. Remember what my friend said in her card to me after I left the hospital? "It's been a long time you have been reaching for change with one hand while holding on to what's been important to you with the other." The porch became my safety zone where I observed life going on around me. When I actually had to get out in it, life became very, very scary. I'm not certain how I will finally experience the full cycle of leaving home and then returning home. I sought change in my life, but once I found it, I retreated to my familiar world. I used my mom's cautioning statement for many years to withdraw from changes in my life. I was in conflict and I was afraid. A part of me wanted to change and a part of me wanted to stay on the porch. About fifteen years ago, I ran out of excuses and began to take control of my life and my decisions.

We all have a "porch" in our lives – that place to which we return and from which we reflect about our lives. For me it is my porch. For you it may be that stream meandering lazily through the countryside close to where you were raised. For others it may be the lapping of the waves along the seashore, as you walk the beach with your feet in the water. Your "porch" may be that easy chair at home that gives you the opportunity to get away from the pace of life and just "be" and reflect for a while. Wherever and whatever that place is for you, you have come to value and honor its presence in your life, just as I have come to do with my porch.

Over the years porches have been an important part of the American landscape. In the days of quiet strolls and slow rides in our carriages and cars, porches held a place of honor. By diminishing the distinctions between indoors and out, porches invited families and friends to gather, sip glasses of tea and lemonade, exchange generations of advice, tell stories listened to with bright eyes, and beckon passersby to share a weathered swing or rocker. Somehow we've lost the porch and its function in today's world. The *front* porch has been replaced by the *back* patio or deck, thus insuring a more private existence – where friends can't see us as readily and therefore can't be invited to join us in telling their stories as well as listening to our own stories.

Porches can still offer a friendly window to the world, as well as to the house on the other side of the porch. Porches are regaining the favor of American architects, thus capturing once again that rare blend of comfort – half indoors and half out. The porch attached to the house in which I was raised has assumed a special meaning to me.

My wooden porch was painted gray. Over the years the paint would chip, and Dad would have to sand down the porch and repaint it, but it was always gray. Rain and snow had warped the ends of the boards and made them uneven. The edges of those warped boards curled up, and my hands and bare feet could feel their wooden texture. The unevenness of the warped boards added a certain quality to my porch. The porch looked huge to my childlike eyes. It doesn't seem so big now as I drive past it when back in my hometown.

The ceiling of the porch was made of smaller wooden slats, also painted gray. A big swing hung from chains, and I used to love to sit in the swing and rock back and forth. The swing was positioned so I could see right out onto the street in front of the porch. On a hot, sunny summer afternoon, the swing was a place to relax and observe life going on around me. A big maple tree was just to the left of the porch, offering much-welcomed shade in the summer. Across the street was a city playground managed by the parks department. I used to love leaving the porch to go there to play – basketball, tetherball – and to talk with the counselors. A firehouse stood next to the playground, and I would often get an ice-cold Coke out of the vending machine – a Coke that cost a nickel, I might add.

Many authors have written about porches from a variety of perspectives; however, within these perspectives is a recurring theme: porches are havens of rest, places of refuge, corners of the world on which wonderful conversations can occur, and one of those places that gives meaning to our lives. I include some thoughts from these authors because they set a wonderful context for the many ways we have of viewing porches in our lives, as well as the many ways we utilize those porches. See if you can visualize yourself on the porches described hear the sounds, smell the smells, see the people as they interact, and picture in your mind and heart the vivid descriptions of the environs around the porch:

> But somewhere along the journey, a picture began to develop in my consciousness...There's a screened back porch lined with rockers, and

a laughing crowd of siblings and cousins flows constantly between that porch and the kitchen, where the family is anchored by a sturdy round oak table set dead in the center.

James Morgan, ***If These Walls Had Ears***

Best of all I loved to go to Josie's, and sit on the porch, eating peaches, while the mothers bustled and talked: how Josie had bought the sewing machine; how Josie worked at service in winter, but that four dollars a month was "mighty little" wages; how Josie longed to go away to school.

W.E.B. DuBois, ***The Souls of Black Folk***

Once Jess had settled on the porch swing and Ty on the top step, his spot, I felt a rare rush of luxuriant delight. The evening lay before me, and all I had to do was receive it. Jess took two or three deep breaths. The swing chains rattled and twisted against one another. The lilacs were over with, but I'd cut the grass around the house that morning, and the sweet fragrance of chamomile floated on top of the sharper scent of the wet tomato vines I'd watered before dinner..."This is nice," said Jess. "This is exactly what I was looking for."

Jane Smiley, ***A Thousand Acres***

It was early November. There was heaviness to all movements, to all sights. It was impossible to look at the sky, at the trees, at the cattle in the fields even, and not know that it was November...He stood on the porch, and the air, when he breathed deeply, went all the way down into his chest; he felt good. He felt like wrestling an alligator.

Rick Bass, ***The Watch***

The Early Years

One would think I had "the world on a string." I grew up in the forties and fifties in modest but sufficient surroundings in Columbus, Indiana. Columbus had about 25,000 residents at the time, and it still had that "small town" feel to it. Located in south central Indiana, about forty miles directly south of Indianapolis, it is a town noted today for its wonderfully diverse architecture.

Columbus has been named "the Athens of the Prairie" because of its beautiful buildings.

Four major manufacturing industries in town provided jobs for many of the town's population as well as commuters from surrounding communities. When I was a youngster growing up in Columbus, there were two decidedly different sections of town: Columbus and "East" Columbus, divided along socioeconomic levels. East Columbus was home to the working-class families, and the professionals – those with more money and prestigious jobs – inhabited Columbus proper. I grew up in East Columbus. I never knew about the "other side of town" until I was in eighth grade when my family moved to a modest home in a very nice part of Columbus.

My parents worked hard all their lives, having barely survived The Great Depression. Because Dad's early years with Grandpa and Grandma Poole were tough financially, he never had a chance to be a boy. He was always working to help support his family. Having dropped out of school at the end of sixth grade, he went to work full-time with his father, a carpenter and builder. At one point in Dad's young adult life, he and Grandpa Poole lived in a tent along a riverbank, and the only food they had was the fish they could catch.

Mom's early life was equally difficult. She was raised on a farm in southern Indiana. Her dad died when she was six. Mom, her two brothers and two sisters all had to work very hard on their family farm. Because Mom's family didn't have a car, a neighbor came by the farmhouse on Saturday mornings to pick them up to go to town. When they got to town, Mom and her brothers and sisters bartered the farm produce they had brought with them for the essentials they needed the next week. Like Dad's family, they had very little money.

Likewise, our family did not have much money when I was a young boy. The house into which I was born was remodeled when I was five years old Until that remodeling our family had no indoor restroom facilities. We had an "out house" at the back of our lot. I can still see that old building standing there, except for one Halloween when someone tipped it over.

The two primary roles Mom and Dad learned growing up were those of provider and protector. Certainly Mom performed her protector role well, perhaps too well. Through my parents' hard work, my sister and I always had what we needed materially growing up. My parents even saved enough to send me to college, and I then went on to earn, on my own, a master's degree and a doctorate. I've been very fortunate throughout my professional career to have had excellent experiences, ones from which I've grown immensely, even making several presentations at international conventions of organizations to which I belong. I share this part of my story with you, because I want to make a point: Even though my parents struggled mightily during their own early years, as a couple they realized the value of creating a better life for my sister and me. They could have ignored this realization, but they didn't.

You might ask: "Why is this guy struggling so much with his life? It seems he has all the trappings for the good life." Even though I seemed outwardly to have had the trappings of a good life, I continued to have great difficulty getting "off the porch," and out into life. I could not begin my own journey, because I didn't know how.

I didn't know how to "leave home" at that time, not realizing I could return to it at any time – the home that is in my heart. Robert Raines wrote a book titled *Going Home*. He discussed his struggles with leaving home but soon discovered that his journey was very important, often painful, but life affirming. For Raines, leaving home meant moving out into a transitional period. It was simultaneously frightening, scary, risky, promising, and energizing. To physically leave our home is painful and involves grieving. I certainly found this to be the case. Leaving home meant letting go of the family I had known for eighteen years. Jon Kabat-Zinn said, "It's akin to letting your palm open to unhand something you have been holding on to." For me, leaving my family home meant leaving my family, never to return as the same person I was before I left. Raines talked about leaving home as "going out not knowing."

When we leave some place without knowing the future, we have to rely on faith. For me, leaving home meant having to learn how to say good-bye, and having to hear others say good-bye to me. That was very hard for me. As we prepare for and actually begin our faith journey, we discover that faith is not knowledge. It is not having answers, but being driven and drawn by questions. Raines said, "Faith is not managing our destiny, but losing control of our destiny. Faith requires us to learn to trust the process." I learned very late in life the importance of trusting the process. I was afraid of falling off the porch and not having anyone to break the fall.

When I was growing up I was never very close to Mom or Dad. The paradox, then, is the difficulty I had in leaving a place where there was little communication, no outward expression of affection, and no affirmation of my life by either parent. Why was it hard for me to leave home? I was afraid of life off the porch. My mother protected me and I was very dependent on her. In my early years my needs for protection and security overshadowed the support, love, and affirmation I did not feel. I was trapped. A part of me knew I needed to break free but the porch became an insurmountable barrier. I "settled" for the life I knew and was fearful of a life I didn't know. The dynamics of my childhood family set the parameters around which my personality and my images of maleness developed, and which shaped my adult relationships. Saying this does not mean I cannot change as I move through adulthood. It does mean that the particular struggles I face as an adult were dealt to me as a boy, and mostly by my family. Writing this book has allowed me to reflect on these struggles and to better understand what I have to overcome if I do not want to repeat the adulthood I saw in my parents.

Above I said my sister and I had the *material* things we needed growing up: food was always on the table, and clothes were always on our backs. What I found out much later in life was that, like my dad, I had missed my childhood. The little boy still inside of me was never encouraged to "get off the porch," to play, and to be a little boy. And when I could have encouraged myself off the porch, I didn't. In many parts of my life emotionally I have remained a child all these years. The child in me got squashed very early in my life by: Mom and Dad, me, and my early religious training. That child never had a chance to grow and mature, so childish behavior was the result. Now I'm looking for the other child in me – the wondering child and the one who opens his arms to the possibilities of the world. By reflecting and writing this book, I have concluded that I do have a tremendous ambivalence toward new events in my life.

For my entire professional life I have talked with others about the importance of anticipating and accepting changes, both personally and professionally. When many of the opportunities for change were presented to me I jumped back on the porch, not fully understanding my behavior. It is as if I went looking for something new, and once I got it I didn't want it. As we change, as we get off the porch, the newness is often worse than before we changed. As human beings, we have a tendency to want to retreat back to the known and the comfortable – for me the porch and its swing. I've often been unwilling to stay in the DIScomfort zone long enough for the unknown to become known. Lack of patience and fear of the unknown led to a very small comfort zone for me. I could intellectualize about change with the best of 'em. I could not walk the walk in my personal life. I will describe in Chapter 3 the reasons why I did not get off the porch when those opportunities were presented to me.

Our house was filled with workers who didn't have much time for each other – Mom and Dad worked very hard; my sister worked; and as soon as I became old enough, I worked as well. In Indiana, the minimum age one had to be to get a work permit was fourteen. On my fourteenth birthday, Mom took me to an office in downtown Columbus to get the permit. I can remember how excited I was finally to get that permit so I could work like everyone else in the family. I never even thought of questioning it. I saw my parents working, my sister working, and I just knew it was now time for me to work. I've been working ever since. From the time I was born until I was nine my dad was gone much of the time due to his work. Among other jobs, he worked for a moving company and for the railroad. He made long trips with the moving company and he spent all week at the railroad work site, coming home Friday night and returning to the work site Sunday evening.

In addition to a household of workers, our house was also filled with a family who showed very few outward signs of affection. I never saw Mom and Dad show any affection toward each other in public. I do not remember a single time seeing them hug or kiss in front of my sister or me. They also never spoke the words "I love you" either to themselves, that I could hear, or to my sister or me while we were growing up. My parents didn't see affection and love shown outwardly in their younger years, and they also never heard anyone say, "I love you" to them.

Neither Mom nor Dad had good modeling of how to be a parent when they were growing up; yet they modeled parenting as well as they could to both Mary Belle and me. As well as they knew how, they loved us, protected us, and provided for us. But they were busy, and they were bone tired much of the time. After Dad died, Mom would say "I love you" to me but only after I said it first to her. I never heard the words from my dad, and that missing part of growing up left a tremendous impression on me.

Harold Kuschner, in his book, *How Good Do We Have To Be?* offered some insights. "His father never said 'I love you' because the father was an emotionally constricted man, not because the son wasn't lovable...But none of that is enough to fill the emptiness represented by the words he never heard from his father." As my dad was nearing death from a progressively debilitating illness, I wrote him a letter, thanking him for being my dad. I ended the letter with the words "I love you, Dad." Shortly before he died, I received a letter back from Dad, and at the end, he said, "And I love you too." The words were written and not spoken, but that was the first time those words had ever come from Dad to me. I have that letter in a bank lock box.

The Deafening Silence

Another characteristic of my home environment is that it was barely communicative. In a home of minimum communication, the silence became deafening at times. None of us is very good at silence. It says too much. We get uneasy, self-conscious, and uncomfortable – like when we are riding in an elevator with a stranger. We want to fill the yawning chasm of silence with words or music or whatever sounds comfort us because silence can be deafening. Have you ever listened to the silence – I mean really listened? It can be loud. It can be heavy, throbbing, like the rhythms of our own body. Silence can be a friend, but sometimes it isn't welcome. We long for any sound, no matter how discordant, for any word no matter how trite. When the silence lasts too long, we can feel abandoned, alone, without resources, afraid. The silence in my household was always present, deafening, and lasted much too long.

As I grew older, I realized that what I perceived through the silence as my parents' pulling away from me was actually my pulling away from them. My parents were as close to me as an adult as they had been when I was a child at home. As a friend told me recently, "You were as close to your parents as they would allow you to be."

The Wrath of God/The Love of God

A large part of my environment as a boy was the church I attended. I was raised on guilt in a very fundamental Christian church – a church that promoted a very strict interpretation of the Bible. Guilt is said to be "the gift that keeps on giving." For me, that was certainly the case. I have told many people that I left for college knowing much more about a vengeful, angry God than I did a loving and forgiving God. I never knew this loving God while attending my parents' church. I knew an angry, punishing God, and everything was in terms of "going to hell" if I misbehaved and "sinned." God would get even; He would bring his wrath down around me, and most certainly was "keeping track" of every "wrong" I ever did. Having this notion pounded into my head throughout my early years created great fear deep inside of me. In his book, *When Bad Things Happen to Good People*, Harold Kushner said it this way:

"When we claim that God is the answer to the question, 'Is somebody up there watching me, keeping a book on all my sins and preparing a moral report card on me?' we help fashion a religion grounded in fear and unrealistic expectations." I used to leave those Sunday services scared to death. It's hard not to be afraid of such a God. I imagine many other parishioners felt the same. What I learned growing up has been in me at the very cell level – that deepest part of me. This early religious training is now bumping up against me. Even with the education I received I stayed for a long time in the same mudholes I thought engulfed my parents. I'm supposed to feel sin and guilt and I don't deserve pleasure in my life. Part of my struggle in my every day dealings with people is not wanting to see them as naturally bad and sinful, but as positive, responsible human beings.

There is no word for "religion" in the Bible. The closest phrase is "fear of God." Early religion was based on the fear of punishment. God commands and I obey. A life of obedience based on fear, however, was not what Ecclesiastes was searching for, so even when, on his quest for happiness he finally turned to religion, he still could not find the satisfaction and happiness he was seeking. What he found was a God of fear. Like me, he found a religion that gave answers and did not en<u>courage</u> Ecclesiastes or me to find our own ways in the world.

Being encouraged is a positive feeling. Fear makes me want to run away from my Higher Power, not draw closer. As I began to examine my own beliefs I found a God who does not expect unquestioning obedience. This kind of obedience in God's eyes is a failure to act as an adult and to take responsibility for my own life. Because my spiritual quest came very late in my life, I've remained a child in viewing my religion and I translated that childlike, cornerstone of understanding into the rest of my life, my work, and my family. I read all the books I could find about <u>how</u> to live, only to find that the meaning of life isn't found in the reading – it's found in the living as well. Having all the information about how to drive a car does us no good if we've never been behind the wheel in a driver-training course, to live what we've been reading.

I now know that my Higher Power <u>expects</u> me to go into uncharted parts of my life – to explore and to learn. He wants me to find my own path in the world and in so doing to know He is always with me, sharing my journey. If God created us in His own image, which the Bible proclaims to be true, and we as humans struggle, God surely is struggling. I wonder what "porches" God has in His life? Does God continue to develop? The answer is "yes" if we assume human beings continue to grow and develop. The journey I'm on is the exact journey every Biblical character ventured out on. I'm trying to come to myself – breaking away from who I'm not and trying to become who I am. God is capable of loving even the most flawed among us. And Ed Poole, you are loved and forgiven by God and by those on this earth who matter to you.

As a young boy I wanted to be obedient, to the God I knew then and to my parents. As I have reflected from the porch I now realize, like Ecclesiastes, that I needed encouragement not fear. As a boy when I found something or did something that made me disobedient, the guilt came because I was going against something that had been such a part of my life. I was questioning my parents and the child in me that wanted to be obedient made it difficult to have those questions. I was struggling with wanting to break out, and at the same time – in order not to disappoint my parents and the child within – I was trying to be obedient, do as I was told, and not question.

I've told many people that the church in which I was raised gave me a very "black and white" perspective about religion, and that perspective was transferred into how I was raised in general, as well as my home environment. The devil was actually more real for me than was God. I saw pictures of this red creature with horns, a tail, and a pitchfork. His image was always surrounded by fire, smoke, people "weeping and wailing and gnashing their teeth," working hard carrying out coal, crying loudly, and generally being a very unhappy lot. I knew exactly what I would look like and what kind of "furnace" I would be living in if I were unfortunate enough to be damned to eternal hell upon my death. When the pluses and minuses were totaled in the "big black book in the sky," if I were in a deficit, that's where I was going. Everything was pretty simple, very clear cut, very black and white, and extremely scary to me.

I was telling a friend about this recently, suggesting that I only found the shade of "gray" between the black and white later in life. My friend then told me, "Ed, don't you know that between black and white is not gray, but rather all the colors of the rainbow, in perfect sequence." I didn't understand this at all. So she went on to say that if black is completely devoid of color and white contains all the colors, between these two extremes must be, in perfect sequence, the colors of the rainbow: violet, indigo, dark blue, green, yellow, orange, and red. What a new perspective for me about the "in-betweens" of black and white. My friend went on to suggest to me that when we give up the extremes of black and white, we are not settling for mediocrity but rather are surrendering to all the beautiful colors of life and all the wonderful details of loving who we are in the here and now.

This early perspective of right and wrong created a sense of fear of the God I found in my church and was an effective way of getting folks to return the next Sunday. But why go back the next Sunday just to become even more fearful? I think the fear of not returning the next week must have been greater than whatever new fears people would learn to feel once they were there. I didn't gain a concept of God that I could use to help me. Enough was never good enough, and anything bad that happened was because I wasn't good enough. So my life wavered between perfectionism (unattainable) and fear (unending).

I was afraid to make a mistake because I remembered all too well the aching feeling I had every time I disappointed my parents. I tried to maintain this pretense of perfection. Because I feared mistakes, I exposed only those things that I knew would not disappoint my parents, and I kept secret all my other adventures. My cautious behavior on the one hand, coupled with my secrets on the other, prevented learning and growth.

If I lied, I was going to hell. If I stole, I was going to hell. If I did *anything* wrong, I was going to hell. Perhaps some of you can identify with my feelings. Whether my crime was lying or stealing was a non-issue. Regardless of my specific "sin," I had shaken hands with the devil. My parents and my church spoke to me, convincing me I was going to hell, and I was afraid. Because I was young I didn't understand my own religious beliefs. I had not had time to allow them to develop. The beliefs were imposed upon me and as with most young people, my beliefs had been given to me before I could even ask for them. I did not seek my own path, even after I was old enough to do so. I did not know myself well enough, even through college, to find my own way in the world – to make any spiritual connections with how I was leading my life – so I followed the paths of others, and I got lost.

I can remember having to attend both Sunday morning and Sunday night church services at a time when most of my high school friends were going only on Sunday mornings – if they went at all. During adolescence my church did not unite me with my friends but kept us separated. Not only was Sunday night a time for regular church services, but also an hour before that service began, I was expected to attend the youth meeting. One Sunday night I just had to see my girlfriend, Donna. I planned to skip the youth meeting from 6:30 to 7:30, dash out to the ice skating rink in town, where I knew Donna would be skating, spend some quality time with her, returning to church before Mom and Dad arrived for the 7:30 service. It worked like a well-oiled machine. And I was home free, until I walked out of church with Mom and Dad after the service ended. As we got halfway down the front steps of the church, David Alka, at the top of the stairs, yelled in his loudest voice possible, "Hey, Eddie, we missed you at youth group meeting tonight." Well, as you can imagine, I had "been had." There are those secrets again! I had some explaining to do, and, of course, in the process of the conversation, I was going to hell for lying.

Only after beginning my college career did I learn about a loving, forgiving God. I sang in the college choir at my little Presbyterian liberal arts college. Because the village next to the college was so small, the Presbyterian Church there didn't have a church choir. The college choir became the church choir on Sunday mornings. I spent four years in that choir loft realizing it was acceptable to leave Sunday services with questions in my head. This acceptability came as a result of the sermons I heard, interactions I had with my colleagues in the choir, and courses on religion I took as part of my undergraduate program. I learned about this loving and forgiving God. Some, but not all, of my fears subsided. I felt there just might be hope for me.

I certainly didn't feel that hope while I was at home, but I now realize much of that hope was my responsibility to find. For reasons I still do not completely understand, whenever I moved to the dark side and began to feel threatened, I retreated to the comfort of my mother. I felt threatened while visiting my shadow side because I didn't want to get caught. I didn't want to go through another guilt trip with my father and I did not want to make Mom cry. I retreated to the light side of Mom in the hopes I would not get caught or would decide not to have an experience on my shadow side that would cause her to cry. When I came back to my light, Christian side I had many masks I could wear at any given time – masks behind which I could hide what I knew at that time as the real me. Putting on my masks kept me from being hurt, but it also kept me from growing. I believed that in order for life to be good, I had to avoid pain. Avoiding pain became a problem because I did not learn to feel <u>anything</u> – joy, hope, awe, inspiration, and encouragement. Because of this fear of pain I mastered the art of detachment. You will read more about my masks in Chapter 6. For now, I will just say that my early masks kept people from learning who I was. I had the reputation at church, at school, and among my relatives as being this "good little boy." I would often think: if those people knew I did this or did that, what would they think of me? A constant tension existed between a shadow side I was growing to enjoy on the one hand and the ever-present fear of "being found out" on the other. The experiences I had with cheating, stealing, lying, having sex, and drinking were enjoyable, as long as I didn't get caught. My parents lived in a house that did not encourage communication, not only among family members, but also with anyone else. No one knew of my "sins" because my parents never shared those parts of me with anyone. Mom and Dad helped keep my secrets.

The Secrets We Keep

The secrets that were kept and the half-truths that were spoken caused me to lose trust in my parents and caused others to lose trust in me. I didn't know that word at the time, but not trusting and not believing have been part of my life for a long time. I believe my parents kept their secrets because they were secretive people. I also believe, although they didn't recognize it as such, keeping secrets allowed Mom and Dad to maintain control over my sister and me.

The secrets began early in my life. In first grade we got our inoculations against childhood diseases, and I was deathly afraid of getting a shot. Mom sent a note to school with me on the day shots were to be given. She said the note told the teacher I didn't have to get the shots. What she ***didn't*** tell me was the note to my teacher also said Mom would take me to our family doctor that night to get the shots. So, I was pretty happy at school that day. No shots! When I got home from school that afternoon, Mom said we were going to the doctor so I could get a check-up. When we got there and went into the examination room, I discovered my mother's secret. The shot was waiting for me. I felt scared and betrayed. I thought I was home free with no shot, until I saw Dr. Davis coming at me with that needle. It was what Mom ***didn't*** tell me that has stayed with me. Why do I remember this incident from the time I was six? This secret became the first time I can remember not trusting Mom. Once that lack of trust was set in place, it never left.

One of the best-kept secrets in my home was of Dad's adoption. Dad was placed in an orphanage when he was four. Because we didn't talk at all about his experiences in the orphanage, I do not know why his biological parents placed him there. A family who lived in Indianapolis adopted him along with his brother, but Dad was returned to the same orphanage sometime later when the family realized they couldn't afford to raise two sons. Another family later readopted Dad, and he stayed with them during his years of growing from a boy to a man.

After Dad died, I went back home and spent a day talking with Mom. We talked into a tape recorder. I was trying to capture some of the missing pieces about Dad that I didn't get from him. I do not know why my parents didn't talk to my sister and me about Dad's adoption. We didn't talk about my father with each other, and we didn't talk about him outside the family either. There were times when it seemed Dad was a secret we were trying to keep from each other. Over the years, I have made some assumptions about why we never talked as a family about Dad's early life. The thought that has continued to be with me all these years is the pain Dad must have felt during that time in his life. Dad was adopted not once but twice before he was four. Not talking about these experiences with his family may have been Dad's way of trying to forget a painful part of his past. My father was not comfortable talking about his personal life – <u>any</u> part of his personal life. He was always a very private person.

Would anything have been different in my life had I known about Dad's early years as a boy, including his adoptions? I have thought about this question many times and I don't know the answer. The feeling I continue to revisit is trust. I am convinced that my inability to trust others is connected to the secrets my family kept and the lack of communication of any kind in my home. If Dad (or Mom) had been more open with me, I might have learned to trust others more than I have in my life. I also recognize that the ability to trust others and to be trustworthy myself primarily has been my responsibility. I do not know if I would have behaved differently as an adult if there had been no secrets when I was growing up. Would I be a different person today if my family had been more open and less secretive? As I've grown older, I have realized that keeping secrets greatly damages our ability to trust and to be trusted. Often I did not know if my parents were being honest and open, or if they were speaking a half-truth and keeping secrets from me. Don't talk, don't trust, and don't feel became the unwritten law of our family.

A question I asked Mom that day we were talking after Dad died had to do with some specifics surrounding Dad's adoption. I remember her having a lot of "I don't knows" and finally saying: "I just figured he didn't want to talk about it, so I never asked. But he was so young, I doubt if it made much of an impression on him." I have clarified two thoughts as a result of those comments: (1) Mom and Dad must have had pretty poor communication between them, and (2) Mom didn't know much about child development. I immediately thought the opposite: <u>*because*</u> Dad was young, his adoption must have made a <u>*very big*</u> impression on him.

The day after Mom died, I was on the road to my hometown to help my sister with the funeral preparations. Mom had been living with my sister and brother-in-law following Dad's death. When I arrived, Mary Belle said she had found an old metal box under Mom's bed. She was so surprised when she opened it and found all the information about dad's two adoptions. The information she found included the fact that on the same day Dad was adopted the second time, Grandma and Grandpa Poole also adopted a girl. Dad never spoke of her. My sister and I were left with yet more questions.

At first I was angry with Mom. She had to have known about these papers when I asked her for specifics about Dad, not only immediately following his death but also during the many times I had asked her that same question over several years. But how could I be angry at my mother two days before her funeral? I was. My only consolation came while talking with my sister, and we concluded Mom must have made an agreement with Dad that she would not talk about his adoption after he died. She kept that agreement. I still find it unbelievably difficult to understand the environment in which my dad was raised. My Grandpa Poole drank a lot and had to move from job to job in order to apply his skills as a carpenter and builder. We were a household of secrets.

The secrets my family kept spilled over into my high school years. I grew up in southern Indiana where most babies have a basketball placed in their cribs while they are still in the hospital. The summer between my sophomore and junior years in high school I was working until 10:00 each night at a root beer stand in town. My job prevented me from participating in an evening basketball program the high school basketball coach supervised at a park close to where I lived. Unable to participate, I didn't improve my skills during the off-season.

Years after leaving high school, I found out that the coach came by my house one day when I was not at home. He explained to Dad how important it was for me to keep improving during the summer months by participating with others in the summer league. My father said I could not do this because I had to work. A starter and regular on the junior varsity my sophomore year, I didn't even make the team my junior year. The coach did not explain to me why I didn't make the team and he did not tell me about his conversation with Dad. My Dad never told me about the visit from the coach. I didn't put it all together until years later when Mom told me about Dad's conversation with the coach. The coach had his secrets and so did my parents.

My secrets extended into my adult life. One of my secrets was my drinking. As an adult, I still enjoy an occasional alcoholic beverage; however, when

Mom and Dad felt well enough to visit, I always hid the liquor bottles. Another secret. Mom said one time that Dad drank before they were married. She told him she didn't want him to do that anymore and he stopped. When my parents visited, I once again became the child I was at home. I did not know myself well enough to behave any differently. I still thought I needed to keep my secrets and not disappoint Mom and Dad.

Secrets come in all sizes and shapes. I kept secrets because much of my behavior would not have been approved by my parents had they known what I was doing. My parents had very strict expectations for my behavior. I wanted to hide behind my secrets – hiding from public view. Initially I kept my secrets to avoid punishment from Mom and Dad. Later on the secrets were kept because I didn't want anyone to see the real me, and my inadequate sense of self which began developing at a very early age. My self-concept will be discussed later in the book. In my early years I doubted my ability to venture off the porch. Mom's cautioning left me afraid. My parents did not reinforce my thinking with their own confidence in me. I didn't want to keep secrets, but I did.

At first, I felt guilty keeping secrets from Mom or Dad. It didn't take long, however, for me to embrace the keeping of secrets as just a natural part of my life, and there were parts of my life even at this early age that I didn't want my parents to know about. After a while, I grew to like my secrets.

Many families have secrets from other family members. Why do I remember some of the specific secrets in my family? Late in life I concluded that keeping secrets prevent the formation of trust. Until I began writing I did not make this connection. How can I be trusted if I keep secrets? How can I trust others if I think they are keeping secrets from me? The secrets themselves are not the critical point here. The lack of trust that results from the secrets is a monumental problem.

Celebrating Our Shadow Side

With our lack of communication at home, "closeness" became a very relative term, so I learned to keep my secrets and to open my own channels of communication. One of those channels was my dark side, my shadow side, and I made frequent returns to the dark side of my life from about age eight right on through high school, college, and into the present. Our shadow side contains those parts of us we keep hidden from others. For many, the shadow side emerges at midlife, and midlife has very little to do with our chronological age. As Connie Zweig states in her book, *Meeting the Shadow: The Hidden Power of the Dark Side of Human Nature*, "At midlife I met my devils. Much of what I had counted as blessing became curse. The wide road narrowed; the light grew dark. And in the darkness, the saint in me, so well nurtured and well coiffed, met the sinner." At a later point in the same book, Zweig and Jeremiah Abrams compare our light and shadow sides to a "Dr. Jekyll and a Mr. Hyde"-type existence. "Each of us contains both a Dr. Jekyll and a Mr. Hyde, a more pleasant persona for everyday wear and a hiding, nighttime self that remains hushed up much of the time."

Journeys into our dark side are essential if we are to find the light. These journeys allow us more clearly to define who we are. In *The Common Table* John Cowan wrote: "Demons must be ridden. They are the horses that move us forward. Demons must be bridled and controlled, for the sake of others and perhaps for the sake of oneself." When I was young, I knew I should not travel in darkness because my parents would not have approved. Mom and Dad would not have approved of my secrets because my journeys to find my shadow side were always outside the parameters of what defined a good, Christian young boy – the boy my parents very much wanted me to become. Thus my travels and travails left me with guilt and a sense of failure for not living up to my parents' expectations – that I walked this very narrow line of Christian ideals in a black and white world. In this world, all behavior was easily classified as acceptable or unacceptable. I became more interested in those unacceptable behaviors and I kept those secret from Mom and Dad.

Although I didn't realize it at the time, this movement to my shadow side was very normal and natural. We all have that shadow side of us as part of the yin and yang of our being – that Chinese masculine and feminine balance in our lives that offers a complete explanation for all that comes to be. In *Calling the Circle* Christina Baldwin said: "In every path that leads to maturity, there is some form of dark night, a readiness to enter into shadow, to explore what we have kept hidden. We enter into darkness by dealing with the wounding we have endured and the wounding we have caused...and the place we are aiming toward...is sacred center."

Some of us are more reluctant than others to recognize our shadow side, but doing so adds greater understanding, completeness, and meaning for our lives. To me, however, during my early, more formative years, I saw this shadow side as something inviting and something bad all at the same time and I felt guilty. There was always the guilt, and there were the secrets I had learned to keep so well.

During the second half of our lives, we can better get in touch with our shadow sides, which we all have – that side we've kept hidden to varying degrees all during our lives. Facing the dark side and exploring its peaks and valleys are activities that draw us like a magnet into reflection. I don't want to die without a better understanding of the yin and yang of my life – the relative balance or imbalance – so I am trying to welcome my shadow side to know myself better.

The choice of the dark side was perhaps a rebellion on my part for lots of reasons. I was my parents' child. I had my secrets, and I could keep them. I felt uncomfortable with my church even at an early age, which I will talk more about later. I didn't feel close to my parents, and it seemed if they were "for" something, I was "against" it – not uncommon for boys and girls growing up. Whichever direction I turned, I saw the other world. I saw it through drinking, stealing, sex (yes, by this time, I had discovered girls), smoking, and lying. I did it all, feeling both excitement and guilt at the same time. Some may feel my explorations with my shadow side are insignificant compared to your own experiences growing up. The concept of a shadow side to our lives is a relative one, and comparisons here are not helpful. If you remember the environment in which I was growing up, these "transgressions" seemed significant to me at the time. Now I'm able to view them as normal events in the process of transitioning from childhood to adulthood.

When I was in high school, some of my friends and I would buy beer and find somewhere to drink it. I can remember working on my senior thesis paper. Two friends and I went to a town nearby on several occasions so we could use the college library for some of our research. We would get a six-pack of beer to drink on the way home.

I would keep a pack of cigarettes hidden in the garage, and when Mom and Dad were gone, I'd venture out and enjoy a smoke. I often wondered if Mom and Dad knew about my smoking and drinking and just didn't say anything. I do believe they were wiser and more aware than I ever gave them credit for being.

Even at a young age, I needed to compete with others for "things." When I was about ten or eleven, my dad was superintendent of the Sunday school program at church – the classes that met each week right after the Sunday morning worship. One of his jobs was to collect and count the offerings that came from each of the classes. I volunteered to go to each class and gather the collection plates with the offerings in them. On the way back to where dad was working on other Sunday school matters, I would slip some change out of the plates and into my pockets. Over a period of weeks, I could collect a lot of change. Being the "clever little guy" I was, I put that pile of change on top of the dresser in my bedroom. One day Mom was in there and saw the money. She talked with Dad, and the two of them pieced the whole thing together. My father was usually the one who came to me when one of my dark side trips had been discovered and his message was always the same: "Eddie, don't you know you made your mother cry?" Once again, I was going to hell for stealing. I had to return that money and reimburse the other money I had taken over the past few weeks. Needless to say, I didn't collect the Sunday school money after that incident. I do not believe Mom and Dad had any idea how much guilt Dad's admonition caused me to feel. And I do not know why making my mother cry left me feeling such guilt but it did. That message from Dad invoked in me greater feelings of guilt than anything else my parents did or said to me.

In those days, "Eight Pagers" were books full of explicit pictures of naked women and men engaged in various sex acts. Each book was eight pages long, hence the name "Eight Pagers." These books sufficed because there were no others from which to choose: *Playboy*, *Penthouse*, and *Hustler* were not even visions in someone's eyes at this time. I had accumulated several of these books that were so wonderful to a junior high boy whose only sex education from my father was fifteen words: "Son, if you ever get a girl in trouble, just don't bother to come home." Dad probably had the same sex education from Grandpa Poole.

These books were kept in a wooden case Dad made for me. My father was an excellent carpenter. He built a beautiful wooden case to hold my Lionel train set. One day, for reasons unknown, Mom was examining the wooden case that held my train set, and she found my treasures. Again, she told Dad, and again he was sent in with the bad news: "Son, don't you know you made your mother cry?" The guilt was tremendous and I was surely going to hell for looking at such books. In order to escape the guilt of my father's admonitions about making Mom cry, I kept all my visits to my shadow side as secrets from Mom and Dad, and most other people as well. I had my secrets, and I kept most of them well.

When I was in high school, I ran with the elite of my class. The friends I had made in my church – way out in East Columbus – were unfortunately quickly discarded so I could be part of the "in crowd" when I got to high school. I was so into being popular and having the right friends. Believe me,

I was way out of my league. However, in order to "keep up with the Joneses" I had to have all those external signs of having it all together when on the inside I had nothing together. I did not know who I was. I was always full of guilt because of my many secrets.

One of those indicators of success to many high school students then and now is the clothes we wear. I had to have nice clothes. Mom and Dad were not in a position to buy me nice, expensive clothes. Thoughts I had of being with the "right" social group of friends are still typical for some high school students when peer pressure is a big part of their lives. However, knowing that now still doesn't excuse the way I got my nice clothes. I worked in a very fashionable clothing store my junior and senior years in high school. I don't remember what my hourly pay rate was, but in those days, it wasn't much – not enough to buy the nice clothes one could find in the store. So, what did I do? From time to time, I would steal some nice shirts, sweaters, etc. just so I could look like my peers who came from families with money. If folks had only known what this "nice little boy" was doing...

Some of my stealing was petty in nature, but it was stealing nonetheless. There is a delightful soda shop in my hometown that has been there for years. When I was in school, this shop was a wonderful place to meet a friend and have a soda, or sundae, or other homemade ice-cream treats. When I was twelve or thirteen, I went into the shop one day just to look around. In those days the hard candy in wrappers was displayed in huge quantities in open bins. On one "looking around" visit, I stood in front of those candy bins, and the temptation was just too much. I grabbed a handful of candy, stuffed it into my pocket, and scooted out the door as fast as I could. I hid in the entryway to another store just down the street. Much to my chagrin, one of the owners was following right after me, came up to me, and said he had seen me steal the candy. The only thing I could do was pull the candy out of my pockets and give it back. The owner told me I was never to step foot in that store again. Lucky for me, he forgot this incident. Two years later, I was hired there as a "soda jerk" and enjoyed my experience very much.

I traveled to my shadow side to discover sex. Many people born more or less when I was learned not to talk about sex. I believe that sex is a topic that, to one degree or another, most of us keep as a secret from each other. When my high school sweetheart and I wanted to "make out" and engage in what I have come to view as pretty normal teenage sexual activities, we always pulled into the dark alley right behind my house. Each time we went there, I couldn't help but think how ironic: we're parked right behind my house, doing things that, if my parents found out about, would result in another of those "You're going straight to hell" speeches from Dad. The car was always parked about fifty yards from the house and about three feet from the garbage can. I'm glad my parents didn't have any garbage to put out while my car was parked there. Another secret kept.

I lived in both worlds, my dark world and the illuminated one. When I was living in my dark world, I often felt a stranger to it, suffering from panic and bad conscience. At times, however, I preferred living in this dark world. When I returned to my world of light, as necessary and good as it may have been, I often felt I was returning to something less beautiful and more boring. I learned a lot about "the devil" as I grew. The devil, sin, and my shadow world were all the same in my early view of the world. I always encountered the devil when I got off the porch. He was never at home with us. Off the porch, I was followed by a darkness foreign to the world inside my house. Moving to the dark side resulted in more secrets. Looking back on those early years the only time I got off the porch was to experience my shadow side. Always while on the porch I lived in the world approved by my parents.

I've grown to realize we all have our dark sides, or hidden parts of our lives. Unless we choose to share our dark sides with others, only we know those important parts of who we are. Shadow sides should be brought forth and celebrated as part of the yin and yang of our total beings. I know some of your belief structures will not allow you to agree with or to condone some of the things I did growing up. My belief structure today doesn't allow me to feel good about some of those experiences I had growing up. Perhaps you have your own itineraries to your shadow side. I have made my peace by asking forgiveness for what have turned out, for me, to be perfectly normal parts of the growth process. Your growth process has its own sense of normalcy.

The Loving Hold of Mom

Because my permanent home was my light side, I replaced dependence on others with dependence on Mom. I could not find my path alone. Even though I relished many parts of the darkness, I always chose the old, familiar "Mom's world of light."

If I would have asked my mother if she felt she had a hold on me during my life, I'm certain she would have said "no." My sense of reality, however, answers a big "yes." And the reality was mine, not my mother's. As I retreated to my shadow side over the years, Mom always came screaming across my mind. While I was growing up, my dad's words – "Don't you know you made your mother cry?" – got etched permanently in my brain, and perhaps even my soul. What son would knowingly want to make his mother cry?

After Dad died, and Mom and I spent that day talking into my tape recorder, I noted that during all my years growing up at home, I could never remember Mom and Dad openly (publicly) arguing or disagreeing about anything. I then asked Mom, "How did you two do that?"

Without a moment's hesitation, Mom said, "Well, I guess because I always got my own way." And I guess she did.

I perceived my mother was the dominant figure in the household. She managed all the money and paid all the bills. I can remember Dad faithfully bringing home his check from the factory each Friday and dutifully turning it over to Mom. Mom had a series of small, brown envelopes in a metal box on the floor of their bedroom closet – one envelope for each bill due at the end of the month. As she cashed the weekly paychecks, she put one quarter of the monthly payment into each envelope, so that at the end of the month Mom could pay the bills.

On many occasions, Dad said to me, "If it wasn't for your mother, we wouldn't have anything." Dad respected my mom's financial acumen. I do not know how much Mom and Dad paid for the first house they owned after they were married. I know they bought it in 1937 and paid off the loan in 1944. During that time Mom told me she and Dad paid the interest themselves. Mom said, "We didn't count that in on our principle because I figured if we did we'd be paying interest on interest. 'Course that made our house payments less." As a family we moved into a new house in 1956 and the loan on that house was paid off in 1962. That new house cost my parents $15,000. Based on their income at the time, that cost was enormous. Dad was probably wise in having Mom handle all the finances. I wasn't that smart. Because I viewed Dad as the weaker parent and Mom as the dominant, controlling figure, I was committed <u>not</u> to allowing my marriage to be the same. I controlled the money, sometimes with disastrous results. I hate to make budgets so I never had any long-range plan for our family's finances. The bills came in and they were paid. I did not think about saving or forgoing instant pleasures for longer-range financial security.

I also controlled many other parts of my family. I was silent and noncommunicative much of the time just as I had experienced in my home growing up. By keeping many things inside me I controlled many of the family decisions. This control may not always have been evident to the observer, but it was there. I had my hold on my family.

I felt this "motherly hold" – her control – over me to the extent that, after she died, I had a "freeing up" feeling. My initial reaction to that feeling, as one might imagine, was guilt. My mother had just died. How could I feel freed up? I came to realize that this "hold" I *perceived* that Mom had over me was lifted. To this day, I don't believe her control was consciously designed. It was there because I allowed it to exist within me, a presence that didn't leave until after she died. I think of the words Phil Jackson wrote in his book, *Sacred Hoops*: "It struck me…that I had inherited my mother's mind and my father's heart, and those two sides of my character were still in conflict. The part of me that was like my mother, always searching for logical answers, always trying to exert control, usually won out over the part that, like my father, was moved by compassion, trusting the song in my heart." I tried to exert control over my family just as my mom did over her family. I did not experience the emotions of living with my family – those emotions were never allowed to surface. I believe Dad must have had an emotional, loving side to him that I never saw.

I had not realized until late in life that both "home" and "porch" aren't physical places, but places in our hearts. Early in our years at home, we begin to define our personhood, to value ourselves, to feel worth as an individual, a member of a family and other groups as well. Only later in my life have I begun the process of finding value in myself and feeling my worth as an individual; I was so dependent on Mom, the control I allowed her to impose, and her opinion of me. As we age, our journey includes becoming less reliant on perceptions others hold of us and more reliant on our self-perceptions. I haven't made that transition well at all. Even today I will "hang" on the feedback of others concerning a project or activity in which I'm engaged or an event at home. For example I still seek from others affirmation for class activities at the university where I teach. I smile when my doctoral students give me positive feedback on a class session. I always feel better when my wife or children encourage me by their comments. To some degree all of us want and need affirmation from others. I have always felt I needed others to assure me and reinforce what I'm doing to a greater degree than other adults my age.

The Loving Hold of Dad

Since Dad worked hard all day, my sister and I knew to be quiet when he got home – no talking, no "roughhousing," and no "anything else" that would upset him. Home wasn't a happy, growing place for me. It was not a place that was welcoming to children. I do not remember many times in my life – after I started school – that friends came over to my house for any reason. The neighborhood kids were around when I was young, but never would a friend from some other place in town come for a visit. I never invited them because I assumed, without bothering to validate this assumption, Dad would be tired and would not want to put up with kids running and playing either in or around the house. Because this was my perception of reality, it was my reality. Should I have checked it out at some point – yes, I should have, but I think I preferred to keep the image I had of Dad intact. And that image involved no extra kids around to make noise.

As I got into high school and entered that phase in life where I wanted only the best for Ed, including clothes, car, and the best friends from the more affluent side of town, I actually became embarrassed to take those friends to my dinky little house with small rooms and paper-thin walls.

Late in life I have become convinced that my father had his own controlling ways with his family. Dad, through Mom's instructions to my sister and me, controlled the level of noise and lack of communication in our home. I don't know how Dad must have felt physically in the later stages of his battle with emphysema; however, I do know that physical condition contributed once again to a very quiet household. When my family visited with Mom and Dad, Eric and Tracie could play but quietly. I just do not have memories of doing many fun things with Dad. As an adult, I can understand wanting the house to be quiet after a day of hard work. As a child, I didn't understand this need to be quiet.

Perhaps some parts of my early years were not unlike many of your own. However, I've not been able to say, "That's the way it was" and let it go. I've been haunted these later adult years with a desire to try to understand better this environment in which I was raised and the impact all this has had on my life.

Our Journey Through Storytelling

The point of the life story is to give people the opportunity to tell their story the way they choose to tell it. Life stories serve as excellent means for understanding how people see their own experiences, their own lives, and their interactions with others.

Robert Atkinson, ***The Life Story Interview***

Unfortunately, unlike one of my favorite writers, Robert Fulghum, I didn't learn "everything I needed to know in kindergarten." I have added to my "kindergarten learnings" by embarking on my journey and by learning the skill of storytelling.

Storytelling is immensely interesting and important. It matters enormously because it is a story that stands at the heart of our faith and, more than any other form of discourse, speaks to our hearts and illumines our own stories. The story of any one of us is in some measure the story of us all. As we talk about our lives, we provide form and substance to those events we have experienced. By telling our story, we realize new patterns and dimensions of meaning to our lives. Talking about our lives allows us to have feelings now that we may not have had, or we didn't know we had, at the time the event occurred. As we tell our stories, we continue the healing process. Old scars begin to heal, and events that were painful may become humorous as we talk about them.

In his book *The Power of Purpose*, Richard Leider suggests that every one of us will eventually face his or her own story, "the time when we are challenged to define our life on this planet, our reason for being here. Our story often surfaces with a crisis or a transition in life." Whatever we have experienced in life, we find our life easier if we can tell someone our story. As we tell our stories, the growth is both in the telling and in the listening being done by the person with whom we're sharing our story. Having someone hear our story is healing because, when we are telling our story, we are in relationship with those who hear it. As you read my story, I hope you feel a relationship is beginning to form between us, and I will be the better for that formation. I do not know the form this relationship will take, but I know it's there.

The telling of my story isn't the end in itself; rather, it's merely one step in a long process – it's a vehicle allowing me to begin the process of turning myself inside out and sharing thoughts and feelings that are way down deep and have never before surfaced. It's a way of communicating where I am at this particular time and why and how I got here. I hope you will see the connections between my story and your own journey through life.

We all have recurrent stories, messages, and motifs as we sit on the porch. We need to pay attention to those stories that are repeated over and over. What are the messages? What do we want to remember? What are we trying to release? Generationally speaking, it is a part of oral tradition, the storytelling that is so powerful – one to another, as human beings. Print, movies, or DVD's will never replace the love and joy for hearing stories told aloud, and the porch is a gathering place for those stories of our lives.

Transmitting our oral traditions was an important part of our culture until the mid-twentieth century. For over 300 years, beginning with the first pilgrims to America, our culture was shaped by storytelling. We had no other way to insure that younger generations would learn about and carry on the traditions of our families and our country. We did not have the technological luxuries we have had since the middle part of the last century. If you are old enough, you can remember friends and relatives gathering on your porch or in your home and talking about their lives. There was no television to watch, and newspapers were not very current in their stories. We laughed, cried, played, and worked. Being together with our families was important.

I've gained the courage to feel that maybe I <u>do</u> have a story to tell. I never viewed myself as a writer. Instead of writing, I've always felt there is just one more book or article I need to read, surely some other point of view I need to consider. I now realize that this quest for more, newer material has been a convenient excuse not to write. After all, if I fill my time doing research, I won't have time to write. I was filling myself with useless information. I opened myself up, but only long enough to let the words I was reading flow inside. I never stayed open long enough to see how the words I was reading applied to me. Much of my reading still left me knowing little about myself. I convinced myself that I surely haven't had the experiences I would need to tell my story to others. Can I actually become that transparent with myself as well as with others I don't know?

What finally gave me the courage to start writing is a statement Nikos Kazantzakis made in his book *The Saviors of God*, in which he writes:

> The cry is not yours. It is not you talking, but innumerable ancestors talking with your mouth. It is not you who desires, but innumerable generations of descendants longing with your heart... They have

> become ideas and passions, they determine your will and your actions…It is not you who calls. It is not your voice calling from within your ephemeral breast. It is not only the white, yellow, and black generations of mankind calling in your heart. The entire Earth, with her trees and her waters, with her animals, with her people and her gods, calls from within your breast. Earth rises up in your brains and sees her entire body for the first time.

After reading this, I became alive with the thought that all my relatives and friends who preceded me have been waiting for me to sit on the porch and write. I firmly believe that my "tribe" who have gone before me will now be able to help me in ways they could not help when they were alive. I wouldn't let them help me. I wasn't open to their thoughts. Even though my extended family did not talk a lot, I'm certain signs and signals were there that would have made me realize they could help. I was just too closed down. After all, how could my parents possibly help me? How wrong I was. Now they are able to give meaning to my thoughts, affirmations, and lessons that they couldn't give me on this side. I think I am finally getting the message. I am not writing alone; I am not coming to these lessons alone.

I feel as if I'm "standing on the shoulders" of my tribe as I write, honoring the energy that is there and gaining a new viewing point. I'm the transcriber of all of their thoughts, and not just my hand is guiding this work but the hands of others as well. The legacy from Mom to me is now having her permission to tell my story. I am writing this and then getting out of the way to see what I'm supposed to do next. My goal is to get my story out of me and onto paper. I have no control over what happens to the story after that, so I am removing from the equation how this is all going to end. It's very easy, however, to allow my ego to stay involved in the writing process. My intent is to tell my story, not sell my story.

I'm working hard, throughout the process, to let go of my ego. You will read more about my huge ego later in the book. I can very easily focus on a destination – the finished product – and miss some beautiful scenery along the way – the writing process itself.

I need to be able to remember where I've been and what I've learned while there. I am looking for a balance: the opportunities to remember the past and yet stay focused on the present task. Although I need to remember, I'm hopeful I can do so and avoid those "traps" of arrogance and a heavy ego that were big parts of my past. Even today I still find them hanging around, just waiting for opportunities to surface again in my life.

Recognizing Changes in Our Lives

Along with the theme of remembering is the theme of change. As with many others, change in my personal life has always been more difficult than in my professional life. Real change is real hard. I'm reminded of an interview Scott Peck gave some years ago concerning his best-selling book, *The Road Less Traveled.* Peck said the success of his book, he was convinced, stemmed from the very first sentence of the book, in which he said, "Life is difficult." And because life is difficult, change is difficult. I want to talk about change at both a personal level as well as describing a more global perspective. These two aspects of change cannot be separated.

On a personal level, I didn't even see any need to change "me." Things were going well in my life. I had always secured excellent jobs. I was married and my wife Bonnie and I had raised our son and daughter. Our two children went to college, got married, and are living happy lives of their own. I agreed wholeheartedly with Wayne Dyer who, in his book titled *You'll See It When You Believe It*, wrote, "I never imagined myself needing to change. I did not have a plan to change my old ways, or a set of goals to improve anything in my life. I felt confident that I had my life running the way I wanted it to. I was extremely successful professionally, and nothing seemed to me to be missing."

Change affects us personally and this personal relationship with change impacts how we view change on a more global level. When change occurs in our lives, we need to fill the void in ways that take care of us.[1] The pace of change is frenetic. We are a culture that moves too fast. And even though we know it, and at times decide to change our pattern, we rarely do. Amidst all of life's hustle and bustle, we need to find an oasis, a place of peace, right smack dab in the middle of our chaotic, hectic, fast-paced lives. My oasis has become the porch.

Continuing to relate personal change with a more global perspective, we are a people in a hurry. We value faster more than deeper and getting there more than growing. We miss the tiger lily on the way to the arboretum and the bird's song on the way to the concert. We miss the child on the way to the adult. We hurry to do things ourselves because we find the steady, deliberate slowness of our Higher Power irritating and scary. I have been in such a hurry to get to places and goals in my life and thus have missed a lot of beautiful scenery along the way. The beauty of life is the journey itself, not arriving at a

1 The writer is grateful to Robert T. Baggott, III, Senior Pastor of the Wayzata Community Church, Wayzata, Minnesota, for ideas contained in this section.

destination. In the book *When Things Fall Apart*, the author Pema Chodron wrote, "Life is a good teacher and a good friend. Things are always in transition, if we could only realize it. Nothing ever sums itself up in the way that we like to dream about. The off-center, in-between state is an ideal situation, a situation in which we don't get caught, and in which we can open our hearts and minds beyond limit."

We experience both personal and global change almost every day – in fact we are living in a world of change, a world of transition. The old world into which we were born has ceased to exist, and, as Peter Drucker says, "The new world which our children and our grandchildren will inherit is not yet here." At some point we crossed over the divide into the new century. We passed the creeds, commitments, and alignments that shaped our world, leaving us few landmarks to guide us on our journey.

The rules for the game of life, however, seem to change every time we turn on the television, pick up a newspaper, or read a periodical. And the change has taken place not only in our world and our society but also in our personal lives. We have children who were twelve and are now eighteen, and parents who were eighty and now seem to be twelve. Where we could once define ourselves by where we worked and what we did, we now retire and have to do it all over again – defining who we are.

We're caught in this roaring current of change – currents so powerful that they overturn countries, overturn institutions, shift values, and sever roots. We have had to learn to live in the whitewater of change in our lives.

Change is the process by which the future invades our lives. Even though change happens around us at a fast pace, some would suggest that today's fast-paced change is being balanced by a slower, more gradual, often unnoticed type of change. As a society, we have become aware of this more gradual change only in the last fifteen years of the 20th Century. We now have this paradox of change: on the one hand we see the frenetic changes that occur every day all around us, while at the same time we are asked to understand changes that have been evolving over a long period of time, unnoticed. In the mid-1980s several Fortune 500 companies began waking up to the fact that their businesses were in grave difficulty. From all outward signs, the businesses were doing well. As the economy began to decline these companies realized their businesses had been declining for a period of time – a decline that had gone unnoticed.

I'm reminded of the "Parable of the Boiled Frog." Do you know it? If you put a frog into a pan of water, set at room temperature, and very gradually increase the heat under that pan of water, the frog will not notice the change in water temperature. Finally the water boils, and the frog dies. If, however, you drop a frog into a pan of already-boiling water, the frog immediately jumps out of the water and is saved. At times in our world, change is happening to us, and we don't recognize it. We *don't* wake up one day to see that things are not the way they were.

Change is inevitable; growth is optional. How we anticipate or respond to the changes in our lives is the key. Some events, such as the disaster of September 11, 2001, happen as fast as the clapping of our hands. Other changes are gradual, and we only hope we are still awake when they happen. If we are that poor frog in a pan of water with the temperature gradually increasing, we don't see the change.

Walk, Talk (and Learn) with the Animals

The animal kingdom accepts change as a normal process of survival. They shed a coat; they change colors; they move from one watering hole to the next. Animals see change as the normal process of living their lives. My golden retriever knows this better than me.

Bonnie and I have a porch where we now live that allows us to go from the garage into the family room and not be bothered by the elements. This past spring, a mother robin built her nest under the protection of the roof on that porch. She built it right on top of our mailbox, so we had to leave a note for the person delivering our mail, asking that the mail be put in the box on the bench below the mailbox. In order to try not to bother the mother robin as she sat on her nest, we even used another door to go into and out of the house because every time we used the door to the family room, the mother robin became startled and flew away. When we forgot to use the other door, she screeched as she flew away; her screeches became louder, and her look angrier after her baby robins were hatched.

We watched the four eggs in the nest, and after the appropriate amount of time, we saw, one by one, three of the eggs each hatch a baby robin, scraggly and wet from the birthing process. In time the babies developed their fluffy down. Each time I passed the nest, the babies had their little mouths wide open, waiting for food. I was fortunate to be passing by the nest when two of the three babies took flight from the nest, landing first on the porch, but then flying off to their new life "off the porch."

As I watched the mother robin and her babies on our porch, I began to see a parallel with my own life, my porch, and my journey. The mother robin worked hard to build her nest. My parents worked hard to provide a shelter for my sister and me as we were growing up. The mother robin found food for her babies; she brought it back to the nest; and she nurtured and fed those baby robins many times each day. Instinctively, she knew that was part of her role as a mother, and she performed her role well.

As I walked past those babies with their little mouths wide open, hoping for food, I wanted so badly to make them understand that their mother was out searching for food and would soon return to the porch and their nest, and their tummies would be filled once again. My own parents were always out there searching for work and buying food, and I knew they would return to my porch and home to fill my tummy. When the baby robins, one-by-one, determined it was time to risk getting off of their porch, they tried to take flight. They failed at first but eventually took that first flight off of the porch, never to be seen again. It's interesting to me that when the babies did leave the nest, the mother robin was nowhere to be seen. Did she know, when she returned to the porch, that one or more of her babies would be gone? Likewise, my parents were nowhere to be seen when I finally realized I needed to get off my porch, take flight and leave. When I got serious about reflecting on my journey, both my parents were alive, but they didn't know I was leaving the porch. I observed the baby robins got all their early nurturing from their mother. Like my own early life, the baby robins had an absent father.

I was in awe of this process of giving life and taking flight that I observed with the robins. Where did the mother robin learn how to build a nest? How did she know where to find food for her babies? How did the babies know when to take flight and leave the security of their home on the porch? Animals see change as the normal process of living their lives. In his book, *Callings*, Gregg Levoy observed that we take chances by going "out there" into the world. Certainly both the mother robin and her new baby robins knew this. How frightened and excited must the babies have been as they first took flight, going out not knowing. We build our nests and our dreams in the face of a blowing wind. Levoy said: "We hope they're secure, but we don't know, and we need, always to hold on, but not tightly."

When did I first connect with the porch in my life and feeling this need to "get off it"? I had these points driven home to me one evening when I was walking my golden retriever Katie. I put her on a leash, and we set out on our walk. When we got to the park, I turned her loose. She ran and sniffed, ran and sniffed, cocking her head every once in a while and looking back, just to see if I was still there. Seeing that I was, she was content to continue to run and sniff, run and sniff. Periodically, she returned to where I was standing, sat down in front of me with her tongue hanging out, panting loudly. All she wanted at those times was a pat on the head and a sweep of my hand with a "get back out there, Katie!" She took off again, running and sniffing and cocking her head and looking, just to be sure I was there.

Finally, Katie returned to me, sat down and again panted loudly! When I told her to "get back out there," she just sat, and then I knew she was ready to go on with the walk. So, from Katie, I learned what it might have felt like to have been encouraged to get off the porch as a young boy, and I also learned about unconditional love. I did not know about this kind of love during my childhood.

When we're on our porches as children, it's nice to have a parent or other adult give us encouragement as I gave Katie. I now know I would have wished that encouragement from Mom: "Eddie, it's a beautiful day. Get out there and see who you can find. When you get thirsty, come on back home and we'll get something cool to drink. When you get hungry, we'll have some lunch, and if you get tired, you can come home, sit on the porch, and rest."

As adults, we need to be giving this same encouragement to our children and ourselves. We can create a safe place – the porch – from which we venture forth to make new discoveries, learn, make mistakes, learn some more, and come back to the porch at times for the "3 R's" of life: **R**esting, **R**efreshing, and **R**eflecting.

Somewhere along the line, we human beings were taught to see change not as affirming but as unsettling, as disruptive, as life taking, not life giving. We've been conditioned to view change as something that takes away, not something that gives. And we dance with it.

Change is part of the fabric of life. There is nothing we can do about it. But it's not life-taking; it's life-giving. Our mind is our predicament because it wants us to be free of change, free of pain, and free of other obligations.

I'LL SEE IT WHEN I BELIEVE IT

The next point is not so elementary as the point that change is not life-taking but life-giving. It requires much more of us than just accepting that change is part of the fabric of life. There is a difference between accepting and believing. As I've said earlier, I grew up with the saying, "I'll believe it when I see it." You know that I've reversed that statement to "I'll see it when I believe it." Knowing and believing are different than accepting. I'll accept it <u>only</u> when I've "seen" it. This second point requires us to believe that nothing *essential* has changed as part of something new coming into our lives. The things we perceive as important to us may change, but the essentials to us do not change. There is a difference between what we see as important and what is essential to us. Our home and our job are important; we place importance on our community and our life-style, but these are not the essentials of life. What is essential is not our home; it's the sense of acceptance, belonging, connection, and place that we receive there. What is essential is not our profession, our job. Rather, it's the sense of involvement, of achievement, of that part of defining who we are by what we do. What is essential is not our life-style; it's the spontaneity, the choice, the playful pleasures we have.

What is essential to us remains the same: goodness, love, justice, acceptance – these things cannot be destroyed by a change in our lives. When we experience change in our lives, in most cases it affects what is important to us, not what is essential to us. We may lose some of what we have in life, but we can never lose who we are.

As I began to understand and use the porch as a metaphor for change in my life, that "portable porch" has become my oasis to which I can retreat and from which I can leave again at will and as needed – just as Buechner did with his room called "Remember."

But too often the fast pace of change is all around us, and at times our priorities get tested. I'm reminded of the story of the contented fisherman. A rich industrialist was horrified to find the fisherman lying lazily beside his boat, smoking a pipe. "Why aren't you out fishing?" asked the industrialist.

"Because I have caught enough fish for the day," said the fisherman.

"Why don't you catch more than you need?" queried the industrialist.

"What would I do then?" asked the fisherman.

"If you caught more than you needed, you could earn a lot of money. With that you could have a motor fixed to your boat. Then you could go into deeper waters and catch more fish. Then you would make enough to buy nylon nets. These would bring you more fish and more money. Soon you would have enough money to own two boats…maybe even a fleet of boats. Then you would be a rich man like me."

"What would I do then?" asked the fisherman.

"Then you could sit down and enjoy life," said the industrialist.

"What do you think I am doing right now?" asked the contented fisherman. Change is not linear but cyclical, and the essentials remain the same.

THE PHASES OF CHANGE

As we venture off the porch, we experience three distinct phases of change: (1) <u>letting go of whatever it is we had</u> (deciding it's time to change something); (2) <u>living in a neutral zone</u> – anticipating something different (still on the porch but anticipating a change); and (3) <u>welcoming new beginnings</u> (walking off the porch and going into a house down the street that looks inviting to us). We cannot short-circuit any of these phases. And the phases won't always be followed in linear fashion but rather a cyclical, never-ending process.

Sometimes we have trouble with the ending/beginning connections of change. They are linked, and one causes the other. In life, we often cannot separate these two phases. When we let go of something, we have to let it go with our hands, our minds, and our hearts. For me letting go with my hands has been much easier than letting go with my mind and heart.

The neutral zone stands alone. T.S. Eliot said, "What we call the beginning is often the end, and to make an end is to make a beginning. The end is where we start from…"

I've often remained in the neutral zone of the porch and unable to let go, so it has always taken me a long time to get to the new beginnings in my life because I could not let go of the endings. Over the years I've found myself both afraid of and, for some reason, comfortable in this neutral or transitional image of the porch. For example, I didn't know how to grieve the letting go of either the male image I never found on the porch or the female image I had become attached to. I was in that suspended animation of the neutral zone for so long in my life.

Some of the phrases I learned growing up gave me the wrong impression about endings and beginnings. How many remember hearing as a child phrases like "A stitch in time saves nine"; "Haste makes waste"; "Every cloud has a silver lining"? Which ones did you learn that were about endings, without the word ending appearing in the statement? Others are: "Out of sight, out of mind"; "Don't cry over spilt milk"; "Let bygones be bygones." There are two cautions when living through beginnings and endings: (1) focus on the ending, without letting it suck you down; and (2) figure out what has ended.

We've also internalized some wrong ideas about our neutral zones. We often go through our neutral zones much like kids learning to cross the street for the first time. They go to the edge, plant their feet right at the edge of the curb, move their heads quickly back and forth several times, and then dash across. This is how many of us go through the neutral zones. It's okay to sit in the middle of the road once in a while. It's essential to give ourselves permission to stay there and not speed up the change process. The purpose of the neutral zone is to find out about ourselves from ourselves. The time I spent in the hospital became a neutral zone for me. I began to find out about myself. Throughout my life I have not run with breathtaking speed through my neutral zones. I hung in them. Unfortunately, until I was hospitalized with clinical depression, I didn't take advantage of the time there to find me. I was just there, not knowing why.

During much of my life, I have kept others in <u>my</u> neutral zones. Doing so allowed me to exercise over them the same controlling behaviors I allowed my mother to hold over me. Sometimes I felt I was controlling others because I'm deathly afraid of being controlled again in my life. The porch froze me in time – not in real time, but in terms of emotional growth, maturity, and growth of the soul. So, just as Mom said, "Because I always got my own way," I have been fairly insistent in getting my own way. As I grew and controlled, I often got what I wanted, just like Mom.

In the new beginning phases, everything is not perfect. In our new beginnings, we face the problem of integrating the new with the already existing, realizing doing so changes both the new beginning and the existing parts of our lives.

In addition to the three phases just mentioned, two uncertainties occur within us when change happens. Our equilibrium gets upset because we're not sure what the future holds – we have to go out not knowing. And if we don't know what the future holds, we don't know if we can handle it when it gets here. Secondly, when change occurs within us, it changes our discernment of what we ought to live for, what we should consider important. Our commitment changes because we're not really sure if what we commit to will be here in the future. For example, people will say, "I'm not sure what the future is going to look like; it's scary." Another will say, "It's very unsettling." And yet another might suggest, "I'm afraid now to make friends because they may be gone soon to a new job assignment." "I don't know whom to believe any more," says another; "We don't control our destiny; someone else does." With change all of our answers now turn into questions.

One of my favorite movies of all time dealt with change in our lives. It was nominated for four academy awards – *Driving Miss Daisy*. It's a story of a strong-willed southern lady who is having a very difficult time dealing with change. And her guide through her discovery, through her acceptance of what is going on, is her black chauffeur, ever patient, ever kind. In one scene the chauffeur is driving down the road, Miss Daisy sitting where she always sits – in the back seat of the old, 1958 Cadillac. She says, "There's no such thing as change. Things only look different." The chauffeur looks out the window and then looks in the rearview mirror and says, "Miss Daisy, I'm sorry but you is wrong. Everything that was nailed down is now comin' loose." And so it is at times with our lives.

"If Ya Can't Run with the Big Dogs, Ya Better Stay on the Porch"

Many of you have seen the above statement on t-shirts and plaques. It was adapted from the Big Dog manufacturing company and appears on all sorts of shirts, mugs, etc. For much of my life, I felt I could not run with the big dogs, so I stayed on the porch. I was afraid of the big dogs I found off the porch – the job offers, the expectations of others, the visits to my shadow side. I had no confidence in myself or knowledge of myself that would suggest I could actually get out there and survive with the big dogs of the world. It was not until later in life that I gained any helpful understanding of my porch.

Now the porch is a connection, a transition, between home and life off the porch. To stay on the porch, we're in transition between the known and the unknown – the home on one side, and "life," change, and newness off the porch. We need to encourage others, as well as ourselves, to experience new adventures, which allow us to create new meanings in our lives. The porch can become the connection between what has been, what is, and what can be. It is not a place for suspended animation. Porches need to be places we feel comfortable and safe in leaving, knowing we can return when we want and need to.

Twenty-two lessons learned from my time on and off the porch are helping me to feel I can "run with the big dogs" of my life, and with myself:

My New Realizations

- The porch provides a site for camping, as well as a moor for launching; therefore the porch is the place to which we can return – a place to convert anger and frustration into growth and understanding.
- The trick is knowing when and how to get off the porch and back on again – the porch and the home are both portable.
- The sailing course we chart from the porch needs to be flexible.
- The porch is the place for understanding our past, anticipating our future, and wondering before wandering. We are searching for wholeness in our lives.

Doing the Work of Going Out Not Knowing

- The porch is a transition between the known and the unknown.
- The porch helps us see the second half of life in terms of "soul-time" not "chronological time."
- To trust getting off the porch, we have to be trustworthy and trusting.
- The porch is the perfect place for working from the inside out, as well as from the outside in.

Standing Quietly in the Silence

- We can't be anyplace other than where we are right now. Sometimes we have to stand still and let it hurt; sometimes we have to stand still and let it feel good; and sometimes we have to just stand still.
- Porches make great "viewing points."
- The porch gives us a chance to stand quietly in front of the full-length mirror and learn how to "see" something only after we "believe" it. It's a place to learn about "being" in relation to "doing."
- A fall from the porch is not always bad: I hit the ground, and I'm getting grounded.

Learning to Be Me

- The porch helps me see I'm my own white knight.
- What we do on the porch shouts so loudly people can't hear what we say. How do we connect our actions in life with the beliefs we espouse?
- I designed some beautiful masks while on the porch.
- Ed, you have got to **learn** and **live** humility.

What We Leave for Others as We Say Good-bye

- Legacies can be left from both off and on the porch, but we can't learn to fly a kite from the porch. We gift each other as we leave legacies.
- I didn't learn how to say good-bye to Dad.

Skills for Our Journey

- We need toolkits when we venture off the porch.
- "May I help you with your bags?"

The Past x The Future = The Present

- As we learn to get off the porch, we also learn how to get out of the box.
- The porch, the beach, and *Carpe Diem*: Learning to Live Each Day to the Fullest.

What follows is a snapshot, a Polaroid, of my lessons at the time of this writing. I will never fully understand the lessons – at least I hope I won't. Without complete understanding, I will still grow in my understanding of them. I will no doubt add new lessons as my journey progresses, and then I will need to try to understand and apply those lessons to my life as well. I also want to caution you that the twenty-two lessons are not mutually exclusive. They are integrated although they have been categorized into the clusters listed above. You will, at times, read some similar thoughts in more than one cluster. To allow for my own growth, it could not be otherwise – life is cyclical, not linear. Your contact with similar thoughts in different sections of the book is a point I want to emphasize. As you read the book, you will likely say to yourself, "Hey, I just read a similar thought in an earlier chapter." It is impossible for me to understand my lessons without seeing the connections among them. Life does not follow along in one neat, straight path. I have had to double back and apply my lessons to many aspects of my life. My lessons from the past teach me about the questions I need to be asking today.

Life begins with questions. The questions we ask shape our lives, and these days I keep returning to three: "Who am I?" "What am I meant to do here?" and "What am I trying to do with my life?" I have often asked my graduate students what I call the "impossibility question." This question can be asked of any topic: our work, our family, our community. If I were to ask this question of myself, it would look like this: "What in my growing up years was impossible to do, that, if it could have been done, would have fundamentally changed my view of that critical period in my life?" I recognize that I cannot change past events. Answering this question for myself allows me to bring more clarity to the present. The opportunity to talk about my story is my way of beginning to be sensitive to answering my own impossibility question.

I hope you can discover the path that has chosen you and that you become familiar with the signs and symbols along your path. Finally, hopefully you will choose to pass along to the rest of us the wisdom you acquire. We all need to share in your journey and your wisdom.

We turn now to the twenty-two *Lessons from the Porch*. I hope, through the lessons, I am getting better acquainted with myself, and I also hope my soul work is allowing me to redefine spirituality and its meaning to me. My writing is one way for me to remember what I have experienced in my life that has allowed me to arrive at my current stop along my journey. You will gift yourself if, by reading about my lessons, you can continue your own soul work and possibly create your own lessons. That work is taking place whether or not you recognize and acknowledge it. For me, the work I am doing involves shifting life's pain to lessons and growth, from judging myself to accepting who I am now and who I am becoming.

We tell you this: we are doing the impossible. We are
teaching ourselves to understand ourselves and
our journeys together. When we are finished,
the strands which connect us will be unbreakable;
already we are stronger than we have ever been.
The fibers which we weave on our insides will be so tight
nothing will be able to pass through them.
We tell you this: when we are finished, we will
be a proud people.
We are making ready. We are making ready.

Adapted from ***Tribe***, Martha Courtot

The porch provides a site for camping as well as a moor for launching.

The course we chart from the porch needs to be flexible.

The trick is knowing when and how to get off the porch and back on again.

The porch is the place for understanding our past, anticipating our future, and wondering before wandering.

Sailing Life's Journey

Throughout my life, I have needed to see relationships among the experiences and the thoughts I have. How does one thought, idea or experience connect to others? How does this action affect other actions? I cannot talk about my porch without finding a way to leave and return to the porch, connecting what I'm doing with how I'm doing it. I have found it helpful to think about sailing as a way to make my transitions in life – leaving and returning to the porch.

Sailing a boat is not unlike negotiating a life or an organization. The winds of change that impact both lives and organizations might blow from any direction at any given time. The winds may gust, they might diminish to almost nothing, or they may be seemingly still.

We don't *pick* the wind, but we can *sail* the wind – against it, sideways to it, with it. Sometimes we have to wait it out with extreme patience if we want to move ourselves from where we are to where we want to be – either away from or back to our porch.

Day to day life is like the wind with all its variations and moods. The wind is shifting, blowing north-northeast, northeast, then north – just as we in our lives are constantly shifting directions. As the sailor sails the winds, so we must sail the shifting moods and challenges in our lives, both on and off our porches.

To change directions is a difficult task at best, whether sailing the winds of our boat or sailing the winds in our lives. We're doomed to failure in both, destined to becoming a prisoner of the wind, if we attempt to change courses in ineffectual ways – to get off the porch or back on it in ways that have no meaning for us. The best way to come about in a boat, as well as our lives, is to understand where we are and where we want to go – to wonder before we wander off the porch.

Changing, then, requires slow, careful maneuvering of our lives. We must honor the winds that have brought us to this point and then determine how to capture the wind by adjusting the sails for our next course – for our next opportunity to get off the porch and become a participant in life. The best example of honoring what I have done and making ready for sailing my next course has been in my role as a parent. As Tracie and Eric grew, I realized that my role as a parent was changing. They no longer needed the father they knew at age six or ten or twenty. As Tracie and Eric went to college and then married, my role changed – still a parent, but a different parent. This example makes two points: (1) I am honoring my role as a parent, and (2) I am always making ready for sailing the next parental role.

When our life's sails are properly adjusted, our life skims over the water as if running on smooth glass. If, however, the sails are not properly adjusted, our life may go in the wrong direction. The boat might slow down or come to a complete stop in the water. We may end up in suspended animation on our porch once again.

As you read in the previous chapter, the speed with which we lead our lives is accelerating at phenomenal rates. Due to this speed, adjusting the sails as we leave the porch or want to return to it has become an increasingly difficult, and sometimes impossible, task. We may feel as if we're floundering, with no direction in our lives. As I mentioned earlier, this shift we are to make in our lives as we mature – moving from an external to an internal locus of control – is all about personal autonomy. It's about being able to empower ourselves so that we can choose the courses of change, when we should leave the porch, and when we should return to the porch - the porch is a site for camping as well as a moor for launching. If we don't or can't make these discernments for ourselves, others may make them for us. And, surely, if we're caught without wind in our sails, we'll be captive to the bidding of others because we become stagnant.

The importance of capturing the wind in our life's sails became evident to me several years ago when I was introduced to the writings of Edgar Lee Masters. One of his famous works, *Spoon River Anthology*, is a fictional account of a small Midwestern town. Those buried in the Spoon River cemetery have the uncanny ability to look back from their graves and see what epitaphs had been etched on their tombstones. In his writings, Masters had a constant struggle with the task of reconciling conflicting impulses. He was very aware of the contrasts between what people say they want to do and what they actually do. He also knew that, as human beings, we have weaknesses. Of the 244 characters in the book, the one who got my attention twenty years ago was George Gray. As Gray looked back from his grave to read his tombstone, here is what he saw:

I have studied many times
the marble which was chiseled for me.
A boat with a furled sail at rest in the harbor.
In truth it pictures not my destination
but my life.
For love was offered me and I shrank
from its disillusionment;
Sorrow knocked at my door, but I was afraid.
Ambition called to me, but I dreaded the chances.
Yet all the while I hungered for meaning in my life.
And now I know that we must lift the sail
and catch the winds of destiny
wherever they drive the boat.
To put meaning in one's life may end in madness,
but life without meaning is the torture
of restlessness and vague desire –
It is a boat longing for the sea and yet afraid.

After reading George Gray's epitaph, I became convinced that, if I didn't get off my porch and put some wind in my sails, someone could surely etch these same words on my gravestone. I didn't want that to happen. My inability to take that long, deep, cleansing breath was getting stronger for me. I kept trying to catch that breath and blow wind in my sails, but it wasn't there. I didn't know how to unfurl my life's sail, and I wasn't aware that by not understanding the role my porch has played in my life – a safe harbor for my sailboat, as well as a place to launch my life off the porch – I didn't know how to get started. I didn't know how to make ready, as the words of Courtot describe at the beginning of this chapter.

Building a Sense of Community through Relationships

"He who plays alone never loses. And, of course, never wins."
Anonymous

Making ready is part of the process leading toward heightened self-understanding. Part of making ready for our journey involves building a sense of community, not only understanding ourselves as individuals but also as members of a group. We can only understand ourselves when we are in relationship with others. The qualities that make us human emerge in the ways we relate to other people.

Creating a sense of community became important during the last two decades of the twentieth century and up to the present time. My journey includes building a sense of community – within myself and with others. If I don't have those relationships, whether they are with one person or lots of people, I cannot understand who I am. As I began this journey, I aimed to discover Ed Poole stripped of his job titles. To do so I had to learn how to be open with others in order to begin this process. Author Sam Keen has said, "The new community is the community of those who are not afraid to ask the questions." Learning to live with life's possibilities, encouraged by the questions we ask, helps to build community because considering possibilities is best done in relationship with others.

*The relation**ship** of life, work, and change,*
*and the companion**ship** of love requires*
*the steward**ship** of grace for the friend**ship***
to last forever. This fleet of four ships,
*along with the flag**ship**, spirituality, allow us to*
successfully navigate through the storms of

life, and guarantee safe passage to
wonderful ports of call.
Adapted from Greg Asimakoupoulos

The Relationship Journey

The relationship journey, as with all our journeys, never ends. I can never say, "I have arrived," for the moment we reach the conclusion we're there, we'll find ourselves no longer on the journey.

I had no idea what having a relationship with others was all about while growing up. Very few of us do, I suggest. As I sat on my porch during my early years, I was usually alone. My parents were busy working, and my sister didn't usually join me on the porch. I did not learn about relationships while sitting on the porch. I learned how to be alone with my thoughts and myself. Looking back, I wish someone had joined me there to talk about the day. Since I did not learn about relationships while on the porch, I had to leave the porch to learn about them, and I got a lot of inappropriate messages about relationships off the porch.

Anger sometimes took the place of my understanding of these relationships. Once I realized the value to me of my porch metaphor, I spent a lot of time feeling angry about not being able to get off the porch and into life. I didn't realize – both early in life and as an adult – porches are for questing, just as I didn't realize that "blindness is for fishing."

One day a blind fisherman asked a friend to run an electric wire down to the end of his dock. At the end of the wire the friend attached an electric bell which rang every thirty-nine seconds. The blind fisherman always rowed upwind to begin his fishing for the day. If he couldn't hear the bell, he knew he could still stop and fish, knowing he would drift downwind and get back to his base with the bell. I needed a base from which to quest and to know that however far I strayed on my quest, I could listen to my inner bell and return to my haven, my porch. But I was still blind to the possibilities of relationships in my life, and I could not get off the porch to row upwind. Rowing a boat is often a solitary activity that can be a time for reflecting. The blind man was alone with his thoughts and his fish but he had a relationship with the friend who provided the bell. Sometimes my relationship is with myself. Understanding that relationship helps me to more meaningfully interact with others.

As I came to realize this idea of both getting off the porch and back on it again – just as the blind fisherman was able to leave the dock and return – I gained understanding and confidence, which has begun to allow me to get past those fearful feelings of the unknown and unfamiliar. Once I realized the porch was a gift, as well as a curse, I began to feel more comfortable about leaving it from time to time. But I was as blind as the fisherman, <u>with</u> my sight, and not nearly as wise. He had much more "sight" than I. I fell victim to that line in an Eagles song: "You can stare up at the stars, and still not see the light." As I stared up into the black night, I could not see the stars, and I couldn't hear the bell.

Until recently I could not identify the causes of my uneasiness. I would apply a quick, temporary solution and move on, much as did the inhabitants of a small town in the Bavarian Alps. The town had a problem and did not have a solution. The only way to get to the town from the valley was to follow a winding, treacherous road. Along this road was one very difficult curve. In fact, many automobiles had run into danger there. The town council decided that something needed to be done about that curve; people were not visiting the small town because of this one curve. The people of the town agreed; so they had a fund-raising effort.

In about ten months, they had raised enough money to do something about that dangerous curve on the winding road from the valley up to the little town. Perhaps they could put up a guardrail around the curve, so if a car lost control, it would hit the guardrail instead of plunging over the embankment and dropping 900 feet into the valley. They decided not to do that. Maybe they could erect a sign before people arrived at the curve, warning the drivers of the danger in the road ahead. They decided not to do that. Perhaps they could do what they did with the Eisenhower tunnel in Colorado. They could just shave off part of the mountain and take the curve away. They decided not to do that either.

Instead, they decided that at the bottom of that 900-foot cliff, they would simply build a hospital. I think a lot of us from time to time are like the town with our relationships in life. We address the symptoms instead of dealing with the real issues. For much of my life I felt the enemy was out there somewhere – never inside me. I did not know the importance of looking within, or doing some introspecting to understand myself better. When a problem came along, I applied a quick fix, never trying to get to the real issues that were impacting me.

Harold Kushner, in his wonderful book, *When Bad Things Happen to Good People*, talks about relationships by describing an occasion when he was walking on the beach. He came upon a group of children building a sand castle. He watched them working so hard and helping each other build that sand castle. As you might expect, the children did not take the incoming tide into account during the building phase, so a big wave eventually came along and wiped away that beautiful sand castle. The children who built the castle just laughed and laughed at what they saw. Kushner suggested that everything in our lives, including all those complicated life structures that engulf us, is built on sand: "Only our relationships to other people endure. Sooner or later, the wave will come along and knock down what we have worked so hard to build up. When that happens, only the person who has somebody's hand to hold onto will be able to laugh," Kushner wrote. I was not in a relationship with anyone as I sat on my porch during those early years. I didn't have a hand to hold onto, and I was afraid.

In January 1991 I wrote a note to Bonnie. At this time I was struggling with having left a job as high school principal that meant so much to me, and having taken a job as superintendent of schools in the summer of 1990. I told Bonnie what I have just told you about Kushner's walk on the beach and observing the children building the sand castle. I then said, "The wave came along and knocked down all the hard work, effort, and commitment I had at Naperville Central. I made the decision to leave that paved the way for the wave to come – I just didn't realize what it was and how destructive that wave was going to be. If I hadn't had your hand to hold I would have surely been swept away by the water, which has come in the form of tears shed. I also know the work, effort, and commitment at Central haven't really been 'knocked down' but I feel that way, and I haven't gotten to the point where I can run up the beach laughing at it. What a year this has been. I know my growth would not have been so rapid, or even at all, if we'd stayed in Naperville, but it's happening now. I'm grateful for that and I have to know that growth causes pain sometimes, or maybe pain causes growth. I know all the reasons for this year are there and are valid reasons. I just wanted you to know I'm struggling, not feeling good about me right now, but feeling that out of the struggles will come some good and some peace, comfort, direction, and priorities for me and my life. Thanks for being you, Bonnie."

As we begin developing relationships, we realize others sharpen our perceptions; they help shape our lives and our personality; they challenge our ingenuity; they enlarge our sympathies. We are relational creatures.

Truths About Relationships[2]

Many have learned two truths about relationships: (1) A relationship can create some of the most beautiful moments of wholeness, beauty, warmth, grace, and joy that we will ever know in our lives. (2) A relationship can become a street of fire, burning us with some of the most intense pain we have ever felt. Relationships have power both in their potential for life and in their potential for pain.

Because of the possibility of pain, I often shied away from relationships and missed many of life's joys. Because I did not learn how to be in a loving relationship with my parents, I didn't know how to be a part of a meaningful, loving relationship. I talked earlier about not being able to take that long, deep, cleansing breath and feel all is right with the world. My inability to take that breath was, in part, because I was not aware of my soul and the spirituality that allowed me to get in touch with my soul and enter into relationships with others.

Long-term relationships occur in two stages. The first stage in our relationship with others is spirit time. The second period is soul time, and to move from the spirit time to the soul time of a relationship is a difficult task. But the soul time of a relationship is where the wine is; it's the place where, amidst the winter, there is the endless summer. For me the ability to reach the soul time in relationships has come from the creating and then the writing about my twenty-two lessons. Without going through this process, I could not have known how to reach the soul time of a relationship. I have learned that as I have a relationship with another we have to accept each other in that relationship just as we are. When we begin to judge others and hold up their weaknesses, we don't get to soul time. Judging and comparing prevent our journey toward humility.

Because I didn't know I could also have a relationship with myself, I always thought I had to leave the porch and get out in life to enter into relationships; I didn't see the porch as portable. I have started seeing the porch as a haven for rest, thought, and safety, and not something always to be leaving to find relationships – it's a site for camping, as well as a moor for launching.

In my early years I had no positive view of my porch. I did not know I could leave and return; therefore, I was angry over my admonitions from Mom

2 Thoughts from Bob Baggott contributed to this section.

about falling off the porch. During the summer between my third and fourth grades in school, I fell off my bike and fractured my skull. In Mom's eyes, that accident was a fall from the porch, and she was even more convinced of the need to be my protector.

More recently I have realized that surely I wanted Mom to caution me as a youngster. Had I not had those cautions, I may well have fallen off the porch. In the second half of life, I've realized that I will now consider myself lucky to make a fall from the porch. Mom didn't always know when to stop with her cautions and her protection of me. When I was quite small my mother was always fearful that I would kick my covers off at night and catch cold. To help prevent the covers ending up in a heap at the foot of my bed, Mom would always take two very large safety pins and literally pin the covers on either side of me, quite tightly, every night as I went to bed. The tightness of those covers on me every night, there out of love by Mom, became suffocating as I entered my adult life. The cautions and protections extended long into my early years. And, I assume full responsibility for keeping them as a part of my life for as long as I have.

Once I began to realize the portability of my porch, the next task (still in progress) has been to discern when and how to get off the porch and when and how to return. I now realize that this skill doesn't come naturally to me. It's one I have to learn. I have further realized that one of the best ways to learn this skill is to practice it.

My porch became portable as I began to understand it as a metaphor for change and growth in my life. Until I began looking inwardly to find the root cause of many of my problems, the porch was a physical representation only – it was that actual porch attached to the house I grew up in. The only thought I had was the porch was the problem and I just could not get off it and feel freed up to get out into life. The porch, for me, is now a state of mind. I can always carry the metaphor with me wherever I go, and I can metaphorically leave and return to my porch whenever and wherever I want.

Having Options on Our Journey

Carl Rogers, a noted psychologist, has said, "The good life is a process, not a state of being. It is a direction, not a destination." Seeing life and living as a process has helped me see the necessity of charting a sailing course that is flexible. Make your plans, but hold them loosely. In *Conversations With God*, I found these words: "There is no such thing as an incorrect path – for on this journey you cannot 'not get' where you are going. It is simply a matter of speed – merely a question of when you will get there." Author Wayne Dyer has said, "Each place along the way is somewhere you had to be, to be here."

The above thoughts indicate to me that, while on our journey, we will reach temporary stops along the way, but they're only temporary as we wait to resume the journey. For much of my life because I have been so focused on my destinations, I haven't paid any significant attention to the journey. The flexibility was just not there. I have missed some beautiful scenery along the way, missing the beauty of nature all around me as I'm trying to get to the arboretum. The destination, the place toward which I think I'm going, is the journey itself, not a final stopping place.

The flexibility of our journey has to do with how we move through it. The sailor will seldom move from point A to point B by going in a straight line. Rather, in most cases, he follows a zigzag line, accommodating the wind and the relative calmness of the water at any particular time. Sailors, as I've suggested, constantly adapt to change and need to anticipate a changing wind by adjusting the sails before the actual change in the wind's direction becomes a reality. Sailors need to be proactive, not passive, observers. If we sail our boats correctly, we will precipitate a change of direction before we hit a crisis – a crisis in our lives or a crisis of having our boat run aground in shallow water.

We cannot change the winds of our journey, but we can adjust our sails, anticipate, and harness the wind to help us move along. Doing so is the mark of a seasoned sailor. Sailors understand the need for flexibility. Non-sailors, steering a course through the journey, must be equally flexible. At times, the sails of our journey are too taut, too rigid, which forces us over onto our side. Our sails need to create a vacuum, a certain flexibility, for our journey. Without this flexibility we run our lives, as our boats, with little sense of the wind. As James Autry said in *Love and Profit*, "It is not where you are that counts, but whether you are moving forward."

In her book, *Plain and Simple*, Sue Bender describes growing up in New York and going into Latham's Men's Store in Sag Harbor. It was there she noticed quilts hanging on the wall and she asked who had made them. She was told the Amish made them. She returned to that store every day that summer, just to look at the quilts. Later Bender moved to California. She never lost her curiosity about quilts, so she spent some time, on more than one occasion, living with the Amish in Ohio, learning about making quilts. As she learned about quilts, she came to realize that "the relationship of the individual parts to the whole, the proportion, the way the inner and outer borders reacted with each other was a balancing act between tension and harmony." Bender learned that the results weren't important, because when focusing on results, a person doesn't realize his or her potential. The joy comes in every step in the process of doing. And if each step is pleasant along the way, the product has that much more meaning because it is nourished by what is going on. Bender came to a wonderful awareness as she worked with the Amish on the nine-patch quilts – nothing is fixed, and there is no right way for the patches to be arranged on the quilt. They can be moved around, the quilter taking advantage of both their strength and their fragility. "Life's all about moving your patches around," noted Bender.

Flowing with life's movements, experiencing the transitions, moving our patches around, and freeing ourselves up of others' expectations for us are critical steps in being able to enjoy the journey and design our own set of flexible charts for the trip. We don't know what really matters in our life until we're into the journey. And as these important understandings become a part of us, we realize we must take those zigzag lines from where our journey has led us to where the next stop may be. When we get wrapped up in expectations others have for us, we're not free to be who we are becoming in life as we make our journey. Our journey into adulthood begins when we ignore, or disobey, the expectations of those who have control over us. Freedom from my parents came late in my adult life, and happened only when I began to understand I am not the child my parents wanted me to be. Coming to this understanding is just fine, and the way it should be.

I became convinced that Mom's concerns for my getting too close to the edge of the porch meant I really needed to make this effort to get off that porch. Being more at ease with myself and appreciating the fact that creating options for my journey is my responsibility and was never Mom's have contributed to this flexibility. Finally, much later in my life, I've come to realize that all these expectations, requests, and in some instances, demands got real old, and it was time for me to yell "uncle." I am finally getting the sense of movement in my life, and if I trip, I trip; if I fall, I'll get up again, or others will help me up. Joseph Campbell, in *The Power of Myth*, says, "Where you stumble, there your treasure lies." Letting go of expectations so that I am free to be me is so important in charting my journey. I'm not there yet because I still haven't completely turned that corner that allows me to rely on myself for affirmation of my journey. I am still trapped by others' expectations. Maybe they will never go away completely. But this reliance on external voices in my life is not as smothering as it was before I discovered the porch, sailing, and their lessons.

Knowing I am an unfinished experiment gives me permission to be flexible. I can tolerate a fair amount of ambiguity in my life, so coming to terms with the need to be flexible wasn't as difficult as it otherwise might have been. The difficulty for me is remembering it.

Our journey is not about "mastery" because we will never get there. Hopefully we will be learners until we die. One of the characteristics of being flexible in charting our journey is that lesson I am learning about the porch being a place to which I can return for <u>R</u>esting, <u>R</u>efreshing, and <u>R</u>eflecting.

Getting off the Porch and Not Knowing Why

Who am I when I am not working?
A lack of energy loosens me this morning.
I am waiting for my life to catch up with me.
A fallow time.
The injunction to get busy and produce
still pokes me,
But I am smiling at it today.
Being out of harness
and losing my grip on routine
threatens
but also
intrigues me.
Who am I when I am not working?
I don't know.
But it's time I found out.

Robert Raines, ***Living the Questions***

Earlier in my life, when I didn't know the importance of those "3 R's," I most often "wandered" before I "wondered." Those times I did venture off the porch without taking time for the "3 R's" often found me wandering aimlessly. I had no purpose for my wanderings. I was off the porch, but I didn't know why. I would head down the street, go into the first house I saw, and if I didn't like what I saw in that house, I would leave and head on down the street to find another house, still not knowing the purpose of the trip.

This behavior of reversing my wandering and wondering became especially apparent to me as I searched for jobs. In my professional life, I have darted from job to job primarily because I didn't reflect about why I was looking for a new job – I didn't wonder before I wandered. Oliver Wendell Holmes said, "Most people go to their graves with their music still inside them." Many people live their entire work lives and go to their graves never finding out what they wanted to be when they grew up. By finding our calling, through wondering before wandering, we can find ourselves and make our contribution, however large or small, to our society. If we remain open to the possibilities life presents, we believe we will eventually hear our calling.

I have had eleven different job offers over the last seventeen years – offers I had actively pursued and then turned down. Two of these eleven job offers I actually accepted and later (within a matter of days) resigned. For one of those two, my wife and I put earnest money down on a house we had selected in the community where I would work. When I got back to where we had been living, I panicked. I called the realtor, and we got out of the deal, losing our earnest money, of course. Then I called the potential employer and told her I was not taking the job.

I was offered a job in another state, an advancement into a position in a nationally recognized school district in Colorado. I resigned my job as principal in a Naperville, Illinois, high school in order to accept this job offer. Because my position as principal was significant in the community, my resignation made the front page of the local paper. I went to Colorado and worked in my new job for a <u>week</u>. During those nights in Littleton, I did not sleep. I was in a constant state of panic. "What have I done?" I constantly asked myself. In retrospect I so needed my porch but did not know it at the time. As the superintendent was taking me to the airport at the end of that week so that I could fly home to see my family, tears welled up in my eyes. My friend asked, "Ed, what's wrong?" I told her I just didn't see how I could do that job – it wasn't what I thought it was going to be. She understood and told me I didn't have to stay. I returned home and tried to regain the position I had just resigned. Fortunately, the Board of Education had not acted on my resignation letter, so the superintendent withdrew it from the agenda of the next board meeting. Of course, my return was also news for the local paper, so on the front page of the next issue was a story about my returning to my principalship.

The first headlines of *The Naperville Sun* read:

> "Ed Poole accepts job in Colorado district." Portions of the article said the following: "Naperville Central High School Principal Edward A. Poole was expected to be officially named Assistant Superintendent of High School Education by the Littleton, Colorado, public school system last night, **The Sun** has learned… 'Dr. Poole surfaced from the beginning as someone who displayed rigor in carrying out his duties. He is obviously a very effective communicator,' said Cile Chavez… 'We sent a team of administrators to Naperville, and there was no doubt about their enthusiasm with Dr. Poole's strong human relations skills, characteristics that came across to everyone from our district who has met him,' Ms. Chavez continued."

One week later to the day, *The Naperville Sun* carried this article on the front page:

> "Change of mind keeps Poole in familiar role. Despite favorable first impressions, three days on the new job were enough to convince Ed Poole that being the Assistant Superintendent of High School Education in Littleton, Colorado, was not everything he had hoped. Poole, the principal at Naperville Central High School, had planned on submitting his resignation to District 203 officials and had been ceremoniously accepted by the Littleton public school system at a July 19 board meeting. But after last week's trip to the Rocky Mountain city of 28,600, located 12 miles south of Denver, the southern Indiana native returned to Naperville for good this weekend. 'Sometimes, situations which appear one way at first glance, take on a different meaning with additional examination…This past week, I had an opportunity to spend more time in Littleton and find out some things about the position there…Being in Colorado for those three days allowed me to determine that, although the opportunity there was challenging and the district is certainly an excellent one, there are more important and valuable things for me to do personally and professionally as principal here at Central…I have declined the offer in Littleton and look forward to putting my total efforts into the principalship at Naperville Central…I just enjoy working with people in the building…I like to help make things work on-site rather than to do so from a central office position, apart from the situation. There is no better principalship than at Naperville Central…This is the place I want to be, and I hope to be here for a long time.'"

I wasn't sure how I would be welcomed back into my community. "What's wrong with this guy?" I expected to hear a lot. I was embarrassed by the whole situation. The morning after my return I met my dear friend Joe Cassano for coffee – as we did most mornings. Joe said, "Ed, some people will do *anything* to make the front page of the paper two weeks in a row." We both laughed, but then Joe went on to say how much he admired me for making the decision I did. "It took guts to do that, Ed. I'm glad you're back." Joe had no idea how much his reaction meant to me. Fortunately for me, Joe's comment became the prevalent one I encountered upon my return. But the question still haunted me: How could I have done all that? It's one thing to buy a house, then back out of a job and the house deal. It's quite another thing to take a job, hold it for a few days, and then return to what I had been doing.

I didn't understand it all, but I also didn't spend any time trying to understand it all. In fact, I spent so little time trying to understand that two years later – *two years* – I accepted a position as superintendent of schools, conveniently forgetting what I had said in that second newspaper article when I returned to be a principal, "This is the place I want to be, and I hope to be here for a long time."

I was simply running around looking, and looking around as I ran — determining what I thought was best for me, with little regard for the lives of anyone else involved in the decision, and no regard whatsoever for how I should be living my life through my work. I had no grounding. I had done no inner work. My heart had not been consulted as my head was making all of these decisions. It was as if I were disconnected at the neck, and the head and heart had no opportunity for conversations.

Because I understood Ed Poole only from the outside in, I did not know my true nature. A scorpion, being a very poor swimmer, asked a turtle to carry him on its back across the river. "Are you mad?" asked the turtle. "You'll sting me while I'm swimming and I'll drown."

"My dear turtle," laughed the scorpion, "If I were to sting you, you would drown and I'd go down with you. Now where is the logic in that?"

"You're right," cried the turtle. "Hop on." The scorpion climbed aboard and halfway across the river gave the turtle a mighty sting. As they both sank to the bottom, the turtle, resigned, said, "Do you mind if I ask you something? You said there is no logic in your stinging me. Why did you do it?"

"It has nothing to do with logic," the drowning scorpion replied. "It's just my nature."

When we work on change only from the outside in, our nature is not affected. For growth to be real, it must begin on the inside – by wondering before wandering. Until recent years my nature has been shallow, superficial, and very much identified by others, not by me. I had no idea about my own nature. I did not know me. As I've created and then reflected upon my lessons,

I'm beginning to discover my nature.

I can remember my son Eric asking me a significant question as I was considering that move to the superintendency. Eric, twenty-two years old at the time, asked, "Dad, don't you think it would be better if you were an assistant superintendent for a while, before becoming a superintendent?"

"Of course not, Eric," I replied. "This new school district has only a few more students in it from kindergarten through twelfth grade as I now have in my high school. I can handle this." "Out of the mouths of babes" – Here is this twenty-two-year-old young man, who had never been in the education profession, asking me what turned out to be a very significant question.

Had I analyzed Eric's question, I might have prevented another emotional crisis. I remember being on a family vacation in Carlsbad, California. My wife Bonnie's brother Bob and his family joined us. We had put our home on the market before leaving for vacation, and I had been at my new job as superintendent for about a month. We gave our real estate agent our phone number in California so he could call us with news about interested buyers for our home. During one of our vacation days, our realtor called to say he had received an offer on our house. Through our realtor we did some long-distance negotiating on the price and finally reached an agreement with the buyer.

After hanging up the phone, I just sat in the middle of one of the beds in our hotel room and sobbed. I was so very sad, but I wasn't sure why I was sad. I had held onto the hope that our house wouldn't sell because if it did, I would actually have to move physically to the community where I was in my new job. Now I would have to get off my porch and find a new porch in some other place. I was crying; my children and wife were with me, and all four of us were trying to understand. Why was I crying on such a happy occasion as the sale of our house, thus freeing us up to look for a new home in our new community? There was so much grief in leaving my town of eleven years and so much fear in venturing off the porch into a new wilderness.

Now I wish I would have wondered a bit about Eric's question rather than simply dismissing it out of hand and wandering off to yet another new job. His question didn't have so much to do with whether or not I should "leapfrog" over an assistant's job to become a superintendent. It had to do with my lack of wondering about what I should be doing in my life, my lack of reflecting from the porch. Remember the insightful words of my friend as I left the hospital? "It's been a long time you have been reaching for change with one hand while holding on to what's been important to you with the other."

Because my porch is a site for camping as well as a moor for launching, this metaphor is a paradox in my life. I refer to the porch in positive as well as negative terms. For too many years I saw the porch as a prison, restricting and limiting. I saw it as a trap from which I could not escape. The porch has taken on new meanings in my life, as a direct result of "camping out" – Resting, Refreshing, and Reflecting. When I felt trapped I wasn't camping with any feeling of comfort. Feeling trapped meant I needed to escape. Now the porch is a haven and a place to reflect and discover.

When I would get an opportunity to apply for a new job that I thought I wanted, I would engage in all sorts of activities I thought would help insure that I got that job. I would call a "friend of a friend" who knew someone in the organization I wanted to join, asking him or her to make a phone call on my behalf. I was so into the "good old boy" network, and I used it to get those jobs. Because I had not wondered before wandering, I had no idea that, if I were supposed to get that job, there was nothing I or anyone else could have done, that would have prevented me from landing that job. At the same time, however, if I were not supposed to get that job, there was absolutely nothing I or anyone else could have done to make that job happen for me. I was so into trying to control outcomes. I had no idea at all that I was supposed to let go of the results because I had no control whatsoever over those outcomes. I did not know that. I thought if there were hoops to be jumped through and games to be played, I would gladly be a participant. At that time in my life, I was not good at connecting what was happening to me with how I was supposed to be living my life.

My wanderings led me to accept this nomadic life-style of frequent moves to new places, where I hoped to find the answers that were always inside me. I never stayed one place long enough to look at myself – I was afraid. I wasn't grounded. The experience of discovering my porch, a place I once feared and didn't understand but have now grown to love, has allowed me to reconnect with and gain a better understanding of my past.

Beginning the Long-Avoided Inner Work

I kept some notes taken during sessions with my therapist a few years ago, prior to my hospitalization – notes that pertained to our discussions at the time: "How did I want to live myself out through my work?" I already wanted to leave the superintendent's job after less than a year. My therapist was fearful of my leaving that job and community, taking a new job, and not thinking differently about myself than I did before leaving. In my case looking for jobs conveniently took me away from the inner work I should have been doing. I was afraid to face myself. I'm not sure if I was afraid of failure in the jobs I didn't take or if I was, in reality, afraid of being successful in those jobs. My notes said I actually looked forward to the inner work, and it needed to continue. As I was re-reading those notes a few years later, I made a side comment to myself: "Ed, it was all bullshit. You took the new job and promptly let the inner work go – just like always, the 'master avoider.'"

I was working strictly from the neck up, and I felt this work moved me to a higher level. The deeper work, which I didn't know how to do, was afraid to do, and therefore not ready to do would have gotten me closer to how I wanted to live my life through my work. I was definitely not ready for soul time. As I re-read my thoughts from those sessions, I made another note to myself: "Ed, are you finally going to stick with this long enough to <u>do</u> the inner work?" My notes said that my hope for leaving the one job of less than a year and moving to a new job was to gain a clearer understanding of my life/work path. Later as I reviewed those notes, I said to myself: "You know, you didn't gain that clearer understanding! You went to that newer job for the wrong reasons."

Each of those job moves thrust me out into the wilderness of my life. On the one hand, I wanted to see if I could meet the challenges of a more demanding and prestigious job but on the other hand, I did fear success because I didn't believe I was worthy of it. I can remember as a very small boy, whenever I was with Mom and someone came up to her and shared some positive comment about me or my achievements, Mom constantly responded "Pretty good, *for a little boy.*" It was never quite good enough. In all fairness, I think Mom didn't want me to get a big head. Still, that little kicker Mom added to compliments about me has been burned into my being. I gave all the outward appearances of self-assuredness but had none on the inside. I didn't feel good about me.

Even though Mom tried her best to keep me from feeling <u>too</u> good about myself, my job searches were "ego related," not "self-related." Using my ego is what I've done all along. I have continued to tempt myself with job-hunting, in part so I can keep the needed inner work on temporary hold. The headhunters became my ego talking. My self-worth increased by being selected for an interview and, in some cases, being offered a job.

Again, in notes I made referring to my earlier sessions with my therapist, I noted a new respect for what my father did when he asked to be removed as a supervisor/foreman and returned to an hourly position in the wood shop of the factory in which he worked. Achieving a foreman's level was quite an accomplishment for a man who quit school after sixth grade. But since it was all about "me," I was angry with my dad. I thought my father was a failure, unable to handle the tough stuff at work. I was getting ready to go to college, and I needed "things." I couldn't get as many things because Dad was getting less money at work. How selfish could he be? As I looked over those notes, I again said to myself, "Hell, he was a lot smarter than me in recognizing his own limitations and what he was willing to do and not do in his work." My dad wanted a lower-level job because he did not want the pressures of being a supervisor. He was on call most of the time. I surely didn't see it thirty-six years earlier. I have never given my father the credit he deserved.

I have worked with therapists for over twenty years. It wasn't until I began my job as a superintendent that I began some introspecting. I asked myself some significant questions: Why am I unhappy? Why can't I turn this corner and see the glass as half full? Did I have my mind made up about this job even before I ever took it – that I didn't want it and wouldn't like it? Maybe, just maybe, some self-reflecting was beginning, but I surely didn't recognize it as such. I was not a fun person to be around in those days. At one point my wife said, "I seem to do pretty well and am reasonably happy until I get around you, and then you pull me down. Maybe <u>I</u> make <u>you</u> unhappy. I can't see spending the rest of my life like this. Maybe <u>you</u> make <u>me</u> unhappy." At that point in my life, she was right on both counts. But I didn't recognize or accept that I was the major problem in our marriage. After all, it had to be others; it couldn't be me.

My wife, like my therapist, was fearful of my making another move so soon and falling back into an old pattern. She wondered if I would want to move again in another year? I can remember asking myself a question: "Is the Ed Poole I say people haven't seen in my job this year lost forever? Why can't I lighten up?" Who I <u>thought</u> was Ed Poole – this outgoing, seemingly self-assured, successful professional – didn't show up in the superintendent's job. But the Ed Poole then isn't the same as the Ed Poole today. I did not know until later why I could not lighten up.

I think I have begun to know some of the answers to this question of "why." And the tentative answers I have come to realize, by taking some "3 R" time on the porch, all center on this desire I had to wander before I wondered.

Listening to Others, but Not to Ourselves

Over these years of job offers and declines, I had no internal locus of control. I was not guided by feelings that were inside me and that were grounded deep within my heart and soul. I was flattered by all these offers. They expanded my already over-sized ego. I just didn't know what was important to me in my life. I spent too much time living out the expectations of others and listening to the advice of others, with no internal frame of reference through which to filter what I was thinking and hearing. Even with a large ego I still sought advice from others. My ego was big but it camouflaged a very confused, superficial me. I compensated for a lack of understanding of Ed Poole by creating this public persona of self-assuredness. Because on the inside I felt afraid and insecure I constantly turned to others for advice, just as did the young nomadic leader in the story below.

Thousands of years ago a small nomadic tribe lived in the desert. The tribe's elder, its leader, died quite unexpectedly. The heir to the throne was the elder's young son. He was young and unprepared; he had no idea what he should do as the new leader of his tribe. The poem by Martha Courtot at the beginning of this chapter said, "We are making ready." In this instance, the young leader had not made ready.

He went to talk with his grandfather to see what advice he might obtain. After talking with his grandfather for days, carefully exploring many options, the young boy decided to go forth across the desert, accompanied by his grandfather, to find a new location for the tribe.

Off went the two, with the young boy riding on the donkey and his grandfather walking along in front, holding a rope tied to the donkey's bridle. They decided to travel this way because the grandfather knew his way across the desert. He could be the guide by walking ahead of the young boy who was atop the donkey. After a few days, another nomadic tribe came upon the young boy and his grandfather. The tribesmen vigorously berated the young boy for the arrangement they saw. "Your grandfather is old and feeble. Why are you riding and making him walk through this hot desert?" The young boy listened to them, and he and his grandfather switched their positions of walking and riding.

A few more days went by, and along came yet another nomadic tribe. They inquired about what the two were doing with a donkey out in the middle of the desert. "We are looking for a new location for my tribe," said the young leader, "and my grandfather is older so he is riding and resting, and I am walking."

"How foolish," responded one member of the tribe. "Don't you realize how much more knowledge of the desert your grandfather has than you? You may be allowing him to rest, but as you lead the donkey, if you don't know the way through the desert, resting will do your grandfather no good because you both will be dead, along with your donkey."

The young leader had not thought of this. So he and his grandfather once again switched their positions of walking and riding. After many days of traveling on through the desert, they began to reach some mountainous terrain. They came to a great precipice, and they didn't know what to do. As luck would have it, just at that time another nomadic tribe came along. The young leader asked for advice. "What should we do now? How can we go on from here?"

A tribesman suggested, "Take this long pole and this rope. Tie your donkey upside down, strapping his feet together around the pole. Put the pole over both your shoulders and then, choosing your steps very carefully, you and your grandfather can make your way down this side of the precipice and then carefully walk up the other side and proceed with your journey."

The young leader thanked the tribe, and he and his grandfather followed the tribesman's advice. After positioning the donkey securely on their shoulders, the young leader and his grandfather began their descent. After a few steps, the grandfather lost his footing, causing him to lose his balance and let go of the pole holding the donkey. The donkey went crashing down the mountain and died. The moral to this story is: If you listen to too much advice, you'll lose your "ass." When we turn too much to others for answers, we really <u>don't</u> want to hear the answer that is <u>within</u> us, and it's possible in the process to lose our "ass" – and I did.

I didn't know why I was doing all this searching for jobs and still not permanently getting off the porch, so I listened to the advice of others. I listened to anyone who would talk with me about what I should be doing next. The problem is, I never talked with myself about these questions. I did come to realize that at those times in my life, I was afraid to wander too far off the porch, and if I did, I certainly didn't stay very long before returning to the safety and security of the porch. I was in such inner turmoil: I <u>thought</u> these changes were activities I <u>should</u> be doing, but a part of me was so afraid of making a mistake, a bad decision and never finding my way back to my porch.

I also know I was listening to the words in that Ann Murray song, running away from the storms and trying to find the sun. What was important to me – the dollars, the lifestyle, the recognition, just the hunt itself and the job offers, the desire to feel needed by someone? I just didn't know, and didn't spend much time trying to understand. I do know, like my parents, I was driven by my role as a provider. I did learn that lesson. More was better for me. My kids and wife needed the good life, I thought – in reality my ego told me ***I* needed** the good life. I wasn't listening to anything inside me. I was pursuing my career ladder as one with a doctorate is supposed to do, whether the jobs were things I wanted or not. I was just supposed to be making these moves. As the old saying goes, and it certainly applied to me, "I climbed the career ladder of success, only to find when I got to the top it was leaning against the wrong wall." I, perhaps like you at times, was looking for the wrong walls, recognizing signs to reinforce my unending, somewhat myopic, climb up the ladder. I now know that every single brick used to build that wall that held my ladder was a brick that contained others' expectations for me. There was not even one brick in that wall that I put there with my own expectations for myself. Little wonder when I got to the top of the ladder I realized it was leaning against the wrong wall.

Becoming Centered

If the whole of me is about a sense of self, there has to be an integration of inner and outer environments. I convinced myself that, although making a job move might siphon off some of my energy in the short term while getting acquainted with my new position, in the long term a better outer environment might facilitate the inner work. Later I noted it didn't work out that way. I gave lip service to the notion of inner work for over six years. The real motivation to begin understanding myself from the inside out occurred while I was in the hospital and has continued to this day. I was not close to being centered into myself in those days of job searching. Leaving one job with the thought of being in a better place to begin understanding Ed Poole continued to leave me off center.

The importance of being centered within became apparent to me as I thought about how a potter works with her clay. Have you ever watched a potter at work at her potter's wheel? She works the large mass of clay until she has it just right. She places it in the center of her wheel and begins moving the wheel around and around. Her feet and legs work hard and fly out in different directions as she makes her wheel move around. She adds some water here and there and continues to shape the pot until she has it just as she wants it. Do you know what happens if the clay isn't centered on the wheel at the beginning? If it's not centered, the moving wheel will create a centrifugal force strong enough to cause the clay to go flying off the wheel and into the distance or up against a wall. Since I wasn't centered in my personal or professional life, I was like the potter's clay that wasn't centered on the wheel. The whirl of activity centered on the job searches caused me to go flying off into the distance or sometimes up against a wall.

So, looking back on what I've just written, what is different about me today? What have I learned as a result of all these "job hopping" experiences? I am a more centered person today. Am I totally centered within myself? No. Will I ever be? I don't know yet. My sense of knowing what is important to me, compared to what others think <u>should</u> be important to me, has increased. As I continue to do the inner work, I can be more assured than I used to be that the clay on my potter's wheel will not fly off and end up splattered against the wall. These days, as I reflect on changes in my professional and personal lives, I seem to be able to return to the porch and do some wondering before I begin to wander. I've learned that porches are comfortable, safe places, as well as transitional spaces in our lives. There is life beyond my porch, and I can return to the porch anytime I want. There are two points in my life where I believe the move toward being more centered occurred. The first was my time as a superintendent and the second was my time as a patient with clinical depression. On both occasions I felt a bottoming out in my life – things could not get much worse.

Recognizing Our Calling through Soul Time[3]

Each of us has a calling in life. I'm coming to believe that a calling is more than an occupation. And answering our calling in life is so different than working at a job. It's all about that soul time we search for in the second half of life, and the second half of life does not refer to our chronological age. Rather it refers to that deep understanding of ourselves that results from standing in front of the full-length mirror and defining who we are.

I've never doubted or questioned my occupation and my identity within that occupation; however, until recently, I had never questioned who I was

3 Some of the information in this section comes from the thoughts of Mark Gerzon, as reflected in his book *Coming Into Our Own*.

within my calling. I knew myself within my jobs, and I allowed them to define me. Because the jobs did not satisfy me, neither did the definition.

While an occupation refers to our job,, the word vocation comes from spiritual traditions. Having a vocation means having a "calling." We do not decide what our vocation is; rather it comes to us, and we have no choice. The calling does not come from outside us but rather from within – from that inner work we need to do in order to enhance our sense of who we are. Answering our calling gives us purpose and meaning in life. Because I had no idea whatsoever about a calling and had no definition of my spiritual being, I could not find my purpose in life. I was allowing many others to define my purpose, not knowing that only I can do that.

Author Joseph Campbell has told us to "follow your bliss" – the life that makes us happy and joyful. As I follow my bliss, I am in search of my calling in life. Not only did I not know what my "bliss" was about, but also I did not know that the journey is more about "following" than it is about "bliss" – more about the journey than the destination.

When we consider our calling in life, we raise questions such as, Is doing my thing doing the right thing? Is denying my thing doing the right thing? Who knows ahead of time? How can I gain a sense of purpose beyond myself? Why do I like myself better when my heart is open to others and I don't like myself as much when I am angry or afraid of others? What if obeying our calling means to respond to the new energies churning out of our deepest soul? Obeying our calling might mean having the courage to obey that inner yearning that calls us to leave home and go out on a wilderness journey. To have no choice about our calling means we are apprehended to go on a wilderness journey. We find out that no external power has pulled a string but that the inner trap door has been released; the gate of change inside us can only be opened by us because we are the holders of the key.

When we embark on our journey to discover our calling, we find ourselves falling out of yesterday's securities and constraints and toward tomorrow's movements, meanings, and uncertainties. Calling is falling, and being apprehended means we are leaving home – going out not knowing. Realizing that each of us has a calling in life, we spend time in the second half of life going out in search of that calling. The journey toward our calling happens whether we want it to or not.

One of the important parts of adult life is our occupation – our work. We spend a lot of time in that work, and the work becomes a way by which we can define who we are and how we relate to the world. In my case, I was so identified by what I was doing that I did not allow myself time to discover my calling and my identity within that calling. I thought I liked who I knew in my work – that person who controlled others, who was driven by the perceptions of others and who gave an outward appearance of assuredness. However if I had truly liked who I was in my work, I would not have continued my search for other opportunities.

Fortunately, I received regular recognition for what I was doing. My ego kept growing, and my personhood kept being more and more identified by what I did. I didn't fully realize that what I did shouted so loudly people couldn't hear what I said. I definitely took my self-identification from what I did. I didn't know then what I am coming to understand now in the second half of my life: when we are on the journey toward our calling, a part of that journey is being able to discern our path between two important questions: "What is right for me?" and "Where am I willing to be led?"

This need to work is a basic human need. We get the job and we venture out with reckless abandon. After a while and, in my case not fully understanding why, we reach the point where we tend to need more than a paycheck, more than just the financial resources that come with work. We reach the point where we need to find meaning in what we do, and we need the meaning more than we need the paycheck.

Psychologist Carl Jung has a theory that suggests the adult journey is broken into two periods: the first is the ascent period, the time that we desire to position ourselves in society. All of our focus is on starting a career, finding a mate, crystallizing our personality – a time when much energy is spent on moving up life's ladder. But Jung also says that around the age of thirty-five or forty, our lives begin to change. At that moment we start the descent period – a time when finding position in society is no longer as important to us as finding meaning and purpose, finding our calling – when working on our career is not as important as working on ourselves and finding out what our career means.

We hear a voice bubbling up from within us, calling, telling us to stand up for our dreams and face our honesty — the voice asking, "Is this all you are – just what you do?" An adult metamorphosis, like a caterpillar, dissolves, dies, and is reconstituted into a butterfly. The transformation of the adult is less obvious than the caterpillar because the adult metamorphosis happens on the inside, rather than the outside, and it continues for a lifetime.

What Happens to Our Dreams?

If we don't keep our dreams alive, we won't
have our dreams any longer. But
if we can take a chance now and then, seek and
search, discover and dream, grow and go
through each day with the knowledge that
we can only take as much as we give, and
we can only get as much out of life as we
allow ourselves to live,
then we can truly be happy. We can
realize a dream or two along the way,
and we can make a habit of reaching
out for rainbows and coloring our lives
with wonderful days.

Collin McCarty

As we move into soul time during the second half of life and discover our calling, the dreams we had during the first half of life get revisited. Our dreams are connected to the very fabric of life, connected to who we are and who we want to become. Dreams tap into that very important part of us, the subconscious, and allow it to come forward in our thinking and planning. In my case, since I didn't know who I was or "what I wanted to be when I grew up," the dreams I dreamed found me, at times, in the kind of life that did not make me happy. Until I moved into my current job as a university professor, I did not fully realize how important all my previous jobs were in preparing me to integrate my occupation and my vocation.

I felt a lot like Willy Loman in *Death of a Salesman*. Willy just wanted one more door to open. He had such dreams. Finally he realized he had to make peace with where he was in his life, with the reality of where his life had gone. Tragically, Arthur Miller writes that Willy just couldn't do that. And if you know the story, you know he died on a dusty road with his son standing over his grave, saying, "Poor Dad; he never knew who he was."

Maybe this is why audiences sometimes cry when they leave *Death of a Salesman* because they know that some of their dreams may never be realized. Not all of our dreams can always come true. Many of us struggle with insurmountable obstacles in our lives because the dreams, the goals we've set for ourselves, are simply unattainable. Our lives have gone another way with dreams that are never going to be reached, yet we keep grinding and pushing and chastising ourselves because we can't reach some of them. I kept climbing up an occupational ladder only to find my calling ladder was leaning up against an entirely different wall. I still pitched my tent by the dry streambed because I was waiting for that dream to come true. I refused to leave my porch to answer my calling.

In the play titled *Duet for One* Tom Kapinsky wrote about a woman named Stephanie who was forced to dream some new dreams. Stephanie was a noted violinist, who contracted multiple sclerosis and was confined to a wheelchair. The entire play takes place in a psychiatrist's office, and at first Stephanie is very blasé about what has happened to her. She says, "I'm very tough. I can handle it. I can make the best of this situation." But eventually, over time, she begins to break and finally admits it's hell to live with broken dreams, with impossible ambitions. Finally she verbally attacks the psychiatrist for not helping her, for not giving her the words she needs.

The good doctor, who has sat for so many hours and listened to Stephanie talk, finally reaches the point where she has to say something, and she says these powerful words, "What a coward you are, Stephanie. Don't you know how beautiful life is? So what if you've been traveling down a beautiful road and now realize you can't continue on it. Don't quit. Don't quit because you're at the end of the beautiful road. You can go back to the last fork in the road, and take another way. Maybe you won't like it as much as the first, but it's a good road too. All roads in life are good roads, and one day you may find the new road is more beautiful than the road you were on to begin with."

That is the good news for those of us who can't realize all of our dreams. Other roads can be as beautiful as the one we wanted to travel in the beginning. Life can be as good, or better, after we change direction. It takes courage to admit that the road we first chose to travel will never lead to where we wanted to go. And this courage is a quality in all of us. There are other roads to follow. And all we have to do is have the courage to go back to the fork and start the journey all over again. Doing so gives us the opportunity to continue on the quest for our calling.

The inevitable detours allow us to return to our dreams and revisit them with new light – a much-needed return to the porch for Resting, Refreshing, and Reflecting. The detour can be the fork in the road we've been seeking. This second half of life is allowing me to see that I can be proactive and assume personal responsibility for my own dreams. I no longer want to aspire to the dreams others have for me, personally or occupationally. I no longer want to wander through life before I wonder about it. I no longer want to define my own calling to be what others think it should be. I no longer want to view my porch as a prison, but as a place that can free me up to be the person I want to be. No one can dream my dreans for me, and I shouldn't allow that possibility to happen.

Bruce Hornsby, in a beautiful song titled "There's Nobody There but Me," says it so well:

Oh, I wish I could laugh when I look way back,
to find out who stole all my dreams. Oh, I wish
it was easy to face the fact – there's nobody there
but me. 'Cause when the sun comes up and my
dreams die down, there's nobody there but me.
Well, it feels so good to be back on dry ground,
after drifting so long at sea. 'Cause when the rain
says run, when it's all said and done, there's
nobody there but me.

Stages In Our Work

Douglas Hall, a professor at Boston University, has given us five stages we experience in our work life: (1) the exploration stage when we become acquainted with what we do; (2) the trial stage when we develop our skills; (3) the establishment stage during which we earn our trust and we've been given authority; (4) the maintenance stage where we begin to sense the need for adjusting what we've built; and (5) the disengagement stage when we learn to do without the power and authority, and we relish retirement. Hall says it's the fourth stage, the maintenance stage, when we desire more than a paycheck. It's at this time that we need more than just work, and it can happen at any one of our chronological stages. Remember, we're not talking about chronological time here, but about soul time – the time we begin to listen to our heart. The demand to pay attention to what our heart, our soul, is saying happens when it happens – in terms of psychological and spiritual demands.

When this stage happens, we have a desire to rediscover our calling. Mark Levinson, a psychotherapist in San Diego, defines this stage as the dark night of the soul. It's the time we realize we are successful in one area of our lives but there is another dimension that's still waiting to be born. When we survey all we have and we realize we've reached certain dreams, it's then in this second half of life that we realize we haven't reached much of anything, and we find ourselves wondering, "What am I going to do with the rest of my life?" Those earlier dreams for my life were pretty typical – marriage, children, and a job. As I moved into the soul time of my life, those earlier dreams seemed shallow. I did not know myself. I moved from job to job, carrying unhappiness with me. I felt unfulfilled as a person.

Have you ever been there? Have you been at that stage where you have bottomed out, when what you do for a living becomes mechanical? We ride the same train; we make the same drive; we sit at the same desk. The spark is gone; it's snuffed out. What we were "supposed to do" seems gone forever. Like Don Quixote we chase the windmills early on, and then the chasing stops and we level off. We can sense it.

When we follow our calling, we're not just following a career path. We're following our soul, our spirit, our heart, and if we don't listen to it and allow it to come forth, we finally end up surveying all there is and then asking, "Is this all there is?"

The next question is: If we reach this point, this plateau, does that mean we have missed our calling? If we begin to experience the dark night of the soul, does that mean that we've missed it? The answer is "no." It simply means we need to revisit our calling, not our job.

At this time in our lives, the challenge is for another kind of job interview. It's not to dress up. It's not to rehearse our lines. It's not to sell ourselves to a potential employer. The challenge, if we want to listen to the voice of calling, is to take off our makeup, take off our ties, forget our lines, and dare to enter into ourselves. The calling belongs to the soul.

As I'm now realizing the opportunity I have to journey toward my calling, toward a greater understanding of my soul, it helps me to remember a plaque that hangs above a bar in a tiny western town. The plaque reads, "I ain't what I oughta be, and I ain't what I'm gonna be, but I ain't what I was." Entering into my soul time of life allows me to see that I'm definitely not "what I was." But it's also helping me to redefine the "oughta be's" and the "gonna be's" of my life, not in chronological time but in terms of the meaning in my heart and soul.

I'm hoping this "backward journey," as I move forward, will help you begin or continue your own backward journey in life – moving both backward and forward at the same time. Søren Kierkegarrd said, "Life can only be understood backwards, but it must be lived forwards."

Everything is on its way
to somewhere.

From the movie ***Phenomenon***

Not I, not anyone else, can travel that
road for you. You must travel
it for yourself.

Walt Whitman

I went to the woods because I
wished to live deliberately…
and see if I could not learn
what it had to teach, and not, when I came
to die, discover that I had not lived.

Thoreau

The porch is a transition between the known and the unknown.

The porch helps us see the second half of life in terms of "soul-time" not "chronological time."

To trust getting off the porch, we have to be trustworthy.

The porch is the perfect place for working from the inside out as well as from the outside in.

Before I began wondering about my life, I was totally unprepared to understand and address the four lessons in this chapter: (1) I did not see the porch as a transition point in my life. I just wanted to get off it, didn't know how, and was terrified to find out. (2) I knew nothing about the soul time of my life, much less how to get to it. (3) I was untrusting of others because I myself was not trustworthy. Knowing I should not be trusted, how could I trust others? (4) I could talk a good game about the importance of knowing Ed Poole but I was so very afraid of getting acquainted and had no clue about how to get to know myself. I was lost, so very lost, and did not know how to help myself. I wanted others to help me – my family, my friends, my colleagues at work. They did help, sometimes so much that I was relieved of the responsibility of helping myself. During and since my hospitalization I concluded that enough is enough. I had to step up to the plate and bat for myself. For too long I used designated hitters in my life.

I came to view the porch as a transition point, a place between the known and the unknown. My porch can grab hold and can let go. Figuratively, I felt my porch was holding onto me, not letting me get off. However this feeling was accompanied by a sense of relief since I was afraid to leave my porch.

Once I understood that my porch is <u>supposed</u> to let me go <u>and</u> call me back, I felt free, and confident, to come and go as needed. Sometimes it's the in-between time – the time between grabbing hold and letting go – that is difficult for me to understand and to know that learning takes on a whole new meaning for me. Marilyn Ferguson, in her book *The Aquarian Conspiracy*, suggested:

> *It's not so much that we're afraid of change or so in love with the old ways, but it's that place in between that we fear...It's like being between trapezes. It's Linus when his blanket is in the dryer. There's nothing to hold on to.*

Going Out Not Knowing: Faith for Our Wilderness Journeys

Through each lifetime run rivers to cross.
What if there's no lifeline, your sinking or lost?
Just believe in your direction and let your heart explore.
'Cause you can't reach new horizons by standing on the shore.
There are mountains you need to climb,
but the mountains standing in our way are only in our minds.
And the risk of going nowhere is the greatest risk of all.
So just listen to the voice that says, "I'll catch you if you fall."

Ann Murray

Going off our porch not knowing what awaits us down the street is sometimes a difficult decision to make because we have nothing to hold on to. As Ann Murray said we run the risk of going nowhere, of leaving our boat longing for the sea and yet afraid. It was like that for Abraham in the Bible. He had to decide whether to stay in his homeland or follow a haunting promise. He didn't have the answer any more than we do. We can just hear his relatives and friends saying, "Abe, you 75-year-old idiot! Forget that crazy trip. You've got it made right here. Enjoy, Abe, enjoy!"

But Abraham and his family moved out and shoved off, destination unknown. The verse in the Biblical book of Hebrews is brief but meaningful: "By faith Abraham obeyed when he was called to go out to a place which he was to receive as an inheritance, and he went out, not knowing where he was to go." Going out not knowing: four words that define our faith. It is tough, sometimes, to realize we have to make many of our first moves on faith alone.

It's difficult for me to remember that the safety net to catch and support me when I fall is already in place. If I listen, the voice is saying, "I'll catch you if you fall." And it's equally difficult to remember that I will be caught, and held, and guided. My heart knows about the safety nets. My life is unfolding in a natural order that I cannot control. I have to let go of the control and let my life happen. I will be loved, protected, cared about, and affirmed if I will provide these same safety nets for others. Allowing my life to unfold – to go out not knowing – means I have to accept the idea that I can't and don't want to know all things – not knowing is part of the mystery and joy of life. Until my hospitalization I, like Abraham, did not know where I was to go. I did not understand my life is always in the process of becoming and I could not know where I was to go. Unlike Abraham, I did not know about the faith that was there to catch me when I fall.

Phil Jackson, in his book *Sacred Hoops*, describes the passage in Castaneda's *The Teachings of Don Juan*, in which Don Juan advises Castaneda, "Look at every path closely and deliberately. Try it as many times as you think necessary. Then ask yourself, and yourself alone, the question, 'Does the path have heart?' If it does, the path is good." To follow a path with heart, wherever it leads, is something we can come to value in our lives. My journey is an unfamiliar path, with an unknown destination. I am trying hard not to look for answers but rather to feel comfortable with the questions, especially the one that asks: "What really matters?" I'm trying to find the paths with heart.

In today's world, we all have feelings of insecurity, and we become frightened of uncertainty in our lives. So there is severe pressure on all of us to drain the mystery, identify insiders and outsiders, and arrive at early closure of our questions. People who are worrying about a job, holding on to their marriage by the fingernails, or struggling to make it alone are trying to make it on faith and in faith. We want to discover what it means to go out not knowing, yet we're afraid. But the poets, along with the theologians, are helpful. Theodore Roethke wrote, "I learn by going where I have to go." I now realize I was learning as I went where I had to go. At those times, I didn't recognize what I was learning and therefore could not apply what I learned to my life. I had no faith in my Higher Power or myself.

If you plant a bamboo tree in the ground, it will be four years before there is any evidence of that tree's growth above the ground. The fifth year, the tree shoots up high above the ground. We have to have faith that the tree is making ready, is developing its root structure below ground. If we do not have that faith, we might dig up the tree just to see if it is growing, therefore damaging greatly the possibility of growth above ground that fifth year. We have to be patient and wait. Four years of having faith is a tall order, but it must be this way.

It requires faith to be willing to bridge the gap between the known and the unknown, to go out not knowing. As we bridge these gaps we enter the wilderness of our lives. These wilderness journeys most often allow us to emerge on the other side with new knowledge, understandings, attitudes, and beliefs – a renewed sense of self. My time in the hospital was a wilderness journey, and there have been many others that I did not recognize. All of my sojourns off the porch to take new jobs were journeys into the wilderness, as are my struggles to find myself. Getting off the porch to bridge this "knowing/not-knowing gap" of experiences and knowledge in our lives does not mean that lessons come to us as soon as we step off the porch. In my case, it has taken years, and I did not recognize some of the lessons I'm learning until later in life. I have learned some of my lessons while on wilderness journeys, but I was not aware of those lessons until I returned to the porch, to that haven of Resting, Refreshing, and Reflecting.

Much of what we need to learn about living life is learned while we're in the desolate, barren, disorienting land of the wilderness. It's in these low places that richness is born. But it seems like we're always trying to move as quickly as we can through these painful, growing experiences – and the reason is clear: it's scary and dangerous in the wilderness. As you read earlier, I've run from most of the storms in my life. The only way I ever wanted to respond to a painful experience was to run as fast as I could in the opposite direction. I looked for new jobs but then was afraid to take them. I took the job as superintendent and quickly wanted to run away. I began therapy sessions in the late 1970's and I have seen several different therapists off and on over the past twenty-five years. The purpose of the early sessions was to help Bonnie and me improve our marriage. We saw therapists together and singly. As soon as those sessions began to get too deep and serious I wanted to bail out. I was afraid to delve too deeply into my relationship with Bonnie. Eventually, those sessions brought to the surface my own issues as a human being – issues I have been describing in my writing. Like the joint sessions with Bonnie, as soon as I was forced to take a serious look at me I was out of there. Never, until my hospitalization, have I been willing to continue the process of finding out about Ed Poole. If we don't embrace and navigate the wilderness successfully, it has the power, like the scalpel of a surgeon, to lay open our spirit in pieces of despair, hatred, bitterness, and cynicism. For twenty years I could not embrace and navigate my wilderness experiences and my spirit was feeling the effects of the therapists' scalpels.

One of the Hebrew meanings for wilderness is "a place we pass through." We either pass through it or perish in it. Wilderness is more than a geographic location. We speak of wilderness experiences in terms of losing a job, feeling isolated, experiencing a death in the family, losing our faith, and giving in to the signs of depression. However, sometimes when we find ourselves in the desert and the only thing we see is sand and the only thing we feel is the heat of the noonday sun, it is difficult to see the possibility of hope.

I'd like to make some points about wilderness experiences.[4] First, people can make a life a wilderness by simply passing through it. They pay no attention to the beauty and wonder around them. A lot of people take what is very beautiful and make it a wilderness by passing through, never looking to either side. I have done this so much of my life. I have been so focused on a goal that I have not enjoyed the process of getting to the goal. My lack of peripheral vision and the need I felt to keep my personal and professional life on an even keel kept me in the wilderness. As I've said, my tunnel vision caused me to miss much of the beautiful scenery along the journey.

Malcolm Boyd talked about making life a wilderness experience by passing through it when he said that one of the most useful functions of artists, prophets, and saints is to ask us, "Did you see that?" There was a man who went to the symphony for the first time. He'd never been before in his life. His tickets were in the fifth row, orchestra section. As soon as the music began, you could tell it was something special for him. He was enamored and totally elevated by the beauty of the sounds coming forth from all the instruments playing as one. Halfway through he turned to the gentleman seated next to him and asked, "How long has this been going on?"

Stoics are people who make life a wilderness simply by passing through it. Stoics guard their emotions because they're afraid someone will hurt them if they allow their emotions to be seen. So they never open up, never become vulnerable. They never have fun because they either are afraid someone will

4 Thoughts from Bob Baggott contributed to this section.

take the fun away from them or don't think they deserve to have fun. Mom was a stoic, and I am my mother's son. I am reluctant to let my emotions show. I remember Mom telling me that life deals us some tough cards but we have to play them. After Dad died, Mom did not enjoy life. Mom told my sister that after Dad died, she just didn't feel she should enjoy herself and life. Like a cheap stereo system, those who make life a wilderness simply by passing through it block out *all* of the highs and *all* of the lows, and go straight down the middle of the road. And yet, the beauty of music is found in all the highs and all the lows – when it all comes together, and that is true of life as well. Much of my professional life was spent trying to keep things on an even keel. I wanted to keep people as happy as I could. As a school administrator I wanted everyone to be happy – parents, staff, students, and the community. I know it is impossible to accomplish this goal – I was unwilling at times to stay in the storm long enough to understand why someone was not happy. I lived this middle of the road so well in my professional life I allowed it to come into my private life as well. When someone in the family was unhappy, I just wanted to smooth it over and make everything all right. Along the way I have missed so many highs and lows in life. I was afraid of the lows – I took the sun for granted – so I missed the highs as well.

The second point about a wilderness experience is, whenever and wherever it is, the wilderness will pass. Often we don't realize this when we're smack in the middle of such an experience. Our journeys often get worse before they get better, and it's most often when we reach this period of saying, "Whoa, what I'm feeling now is worse than before I stepped off the porch," that we retreat back to the porch too soon. No matter how deep is our wilderness journey, we will survive. We forget that the depths allow us to appreciate the heights. Sorrow heightens joy, and depression heightens laughter. We wouldn't always know the joys and laughter if it weren't for the sorrows. In them, we learn to be patient, waiting for the wisdom that will light our way. Difficulties often precede enlightenment, and they pull us inward to find connections in our lives.

Waiting for the wilderness to pass requires patience. Patience is not a passive act but rather concentrated strength. Wilderness experiences will pass, and in the meantime there is sacredness in just holding on.

Our wilderness experiences often yield permanent benefits. There are events in our lives that we wouldn't wish on anybody else – events which we never want to experience again. But we go on to say that, because of that experience, we are stronger. The wilderness we just experienced gave us the ability to respond to the quality of life like we never could before our journey into the wilderness. My stay in the hospital with clinical depression was most definitely this kind of wilderness experience for me. I am stronger today because I spent time in the hospital and experienced for the first time those "3 R's". I had to be patient; I had no choice.

Sometimes when we get together with old friends we haven't seen for a long time, we talk about those early struggles in our adult lives. We may have been starting a marriage or a new career and moving to a new location – whatever it was, and we struggled. However, those struggles gave us our wisdom, our maturity. And when we look back on those struggles, we realize we didn't know how we were going to do it, but we did. And it made us better. These wilderness experiences give us qualities and perceptions we never knew we had. Remember what Churchill said to the British people? "In the darkest hour, hold yourselves so that people will look back and say not simply that it was your darkest hour, but that it was your finest hour." And it's true – some of our finest moments are in the wilderness because that's where we grow, mature, and learn. Every mature person has been in the wilderness.

Finally, I want to talk about the struggles we have while in the wilderness places of our lives. The movie *Forrest Gump*, with Tom Hanks playing Gump, is full of lessons. One of those lessons for me represented something I had not experienced in my life until I was in the hospital. Forrest Gump did not just celebrate surviving; he didn't just celebrate coming out of the wilderness. The film celebrated the struggle itself while we are smack in the middle of the wilderness. It's rare when we human beings are perceptive enough to draw strength from our deepest, darkest nights. It is more commonplace, when we experience a wilderness journey and get to the other end, to say, "I learned from that." But when is the last time, while <u>in</u> the struggle, we said, "I'm learning even now?"

It's a very sacred occurrence when we are aware enough while embroiled in the struggle to celebrate it, to draw strength from it to allow it to teach us, to mold us, to embrace us, to coddle us, and to empower us. And even though we're not there yet, we're learning. Some of the greatest lessons in life are learned in the midst of the pain and the struggle, the distance and the loneliness. It is in those places where we learn who we are. This is what gave Forrest Gump the ability to run through chaos and never even notice it. As he carried friends off the battlefields, he never even noticed bombs were exploding all around him because he grew strength from the struggle itself, not to survive but to learn from it and to help others. The only time in my life where I felt I was learning while in the struggle was when I was hospitalized for clinical depression. The very purpose of the programs I experienced while a patient was to help me learn – why I was there and how I could become better.

The Journey toward Wholeness

Earlier I shared with you the importance of wondering before wandering in life, the importance of becoming centered and self-assured, the necessity of relying less and less on what others think of me and what I do and more and more on what I think of me and what I do. Taking time to wonder before venturing off the porch is understanding the second half of life not in "chronological time" but in "soul time." My journey off the porch is a search for wholeness in my life. I am very much a "whole-to-part" learner. In other words, I have to see the "whole" of something before trying to see the interrelatedness of all the "parts." After seeing this interrelatedness of the parts, I return to the whole – the big picture – and redefine it based on my journey through the parts. The following drawing illustrates this:

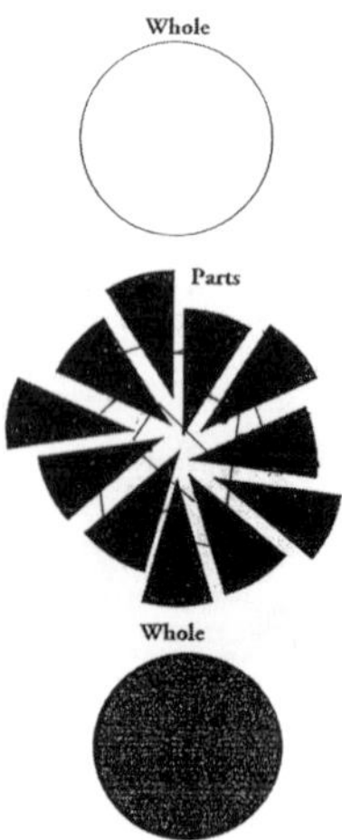

I had been living my life in reverse order. It was time for me to go on the quest for wholeness – for once in my life to wonder <u>before</u> wandering.

In order to "talk the talk" of my whole-part-whole learning style, I created a model for my lessons. The model has an acronym: **SCOPED** and has at its center "<u>S</u>oul-Growing." The other letters represent <u>C</u>areering/Working, <u>O</u>bserving Self, <u>P</u>assing on to Others, <u>E</u>njoying Life, and <u>D</u>eveloping and

Transitioning. Since paying attention to my soul has only been a recent discovery for me, I felt it important to place the entire model within the context of the value of growing our soul throughout our lives. I didn't do this along the way, and it has been an important lesson for me to learn.

I am a very visual learner, and I needed something that would "show" me the wholeness I was discovering while developing my twenty-two lessons. I can remember needing this visual to help me understand the relationships and interactions among the twenty-two lessons. Early in this writing, I suggested that you as the reader would interact with the twenty-two lessons throughout the book. You have and will continue to do so. Each of the twenty-two lessons has a home within the six interactive and interdependent parts of the model. I cannot stress enough how my lessons are interdependent. Parts of my story are found in more than one lesson because the lessons depend upon each other for their strength and credibility.

I seem to be getting the message now that this kind of soul-growing is what I want and need to be doing on my journey. It is my present work that will evolve over time. High levels of interaction occur among the "parts" as they connect with each other and with the "whole." The interaction of the parts gives me a different sense of wholeness than when I first began my journey.

Although the whole takes precedence over the parts, this whole can flourish only if the many parts are honored and nurtured in their various particularities. However, to preserve the whole, cooperation among the interactive parts must take priority over competition.

Even though I am finding it helpful to work from my model, the SCOPED model won't necessarily work for you. This model may even change for me as I continue my journey. But the failure of a model to work in one setting, when it worked in another, should come as a relief, not a burden. This relief tells us we're released from the collective illusion that given the right "prescription" a "cure" will be forthcoming. This uncertainty, due to a lack of prescriptiveness, is good because it suggests a quality of alertness. And, as I struggle with uncertainty, I gain a glimpse of my soul if I know how to pay attention. Soul time for me came very late in my chronological life. This model is helping me during my adult years because our language has few words to describe the critical phases of our lives we experience as adults.[5]

The Second Half of Life

Why is it we have so many words to describe the first twenty-one years of our life? We have newborn, infant, toddler, pre-schooler, child, pre-adolescent, adolescent, teenager, and young adult. One reason for all these descriptors is growth. During the first twenty-one years of our life, we grow so much, and we need words to describe each growth stage along the way. If growth is a reason for identifying our stages prior to twenty-one, why is it that we have only one generally accepted word to define the next fifty or so years of our life? Why do we only have the word "adulthood" to define what happens to us after we turn twenty-one?

Mark Gerzon, a psychotherapist from San Francisco, suggests that the minimal language we have concerning adulthood reveals that most of us believe being an adult after turning twenty-one is one long, stable, predictable period of life. Many believe that when we reach adulthood, we now have it made. We have no more growing to do. However, Carl Jung has said:

> Wholly unprepared, we embark upon the second half of life... We take the step into the afternoon of life; worse still we take this step with the false assumption that our truths and ideals will serve us as before. But we cannot live the afternoon of life according to the program of life's morning – for what was great in the morning will be little at evening, and what in the morning was true will at evening have become a lie.

The compass for the second half of life is held not in our hands but rather

5 Some of the information in this section comes from the thoughts of Mark Gerzon, as reflected in his book *Coming Into Our Own.*

in our hearts. The issues with which we deal in the second half of life are not based on chronological time, but on soul time – not physical aging, but our emotional and spiritual existence here on earth. As Jacob said in the Bible, "As youth departs, we have a better understanding of what matters and what does not." Jacob began the quest into the second half of life, a quest to give meaning to his soul. Jung has said, "Conservative tendencies develop if all goes well; instead of looking forward one looks backward, most of the time involuntarily, and one begins to take stock, to see how one's life has developed up to this point. The real motivations are sought and real discoveries are made."

During the second half of life, we desire to rediscover the parts of us we've neglected, those parts we have cast into the shadows, those areas of our lives we have starved by constantly feeling driven to succeed in this life. For some, the journey toward wholeness happens very slowly. For others, it comes more dramatically. Whenever and however we journey toward wholeness, parts of our lives that were absent appear and parts that were present may disappear. If we have experienced a life through words, then words seem to fail us. If we seem to have life under control, then our life seems to be out of control. If we have been passionate, we lose our passion, and if we have been passionless, we find it. If we have encountered loneliness, we find intimacy; and if we have been intimate, we may find loneliness. The journey toward wholeness is the desire to rediscover that which we have sacrificed along the way to reach whatever successful goals we wanted to reach.

The journey toward wholeness comes to us. We cannot avoid it, and there is no way we can put it off. Whether we begin the journey on purpose, with eyes wide open, or we begin the journey with eyes tightly shut, the journey toward wholeness will come. I believe this about wholeness because I have experienced it in my own life. I did not begin this journey on purpose. I did not even know I needed to make this journey toward wholeness. My stay in the hospital, and the time since, has allowed me to see the importance of being whole and how my various parts were in no way in touch with each other. They needed connecting.

The Wholeness is Connecting the Outside Work with the Inside Work

Adventuring in the outer world, and
just as importantly, Inventuring

(adventuring in the inner world)
is possible for all of us
throughout our lives.
The mid-life crisis, which we prefer to
call the "mid-life inventure,"
presents us with an opportunity to
reexamine our lives and to ask the
sometimes frightening, always liberating
questions, "What do I want?" "What do
I feel?" "What must I do now to feel
right with myself?" "What are my dreams
for myself, and what fears have blocked me?"

Richard Lieder, ***Repacking Your Bags***

In order to be Ed Poole, I have to learn to get to my inside and work outward. A part of this discovery refers back to our calling that I discussed earlier. Doing the inside work demands that I quit defining myself through the lives of others. Theater has a way of holding our lives up to us like a mirror, and we can get away with actions on stage that we can't get away with in life. Sometimes we go to the theater, and when we leave, we're emotionally drained. Other times we sit there, and we say to ourselves, "That's me, right there in that character." The search for our identity, to find the answer to the question, "Who am I?" is a difficult journey for all of us. We have to work from the outside in, as well as from the inside out. We realize that the outside and inside work is inseparable. Until recently I had experienced very few inventures during my life. My first experience with an inventure, which I recognized, occurred only a few years ago, while I was a superintendent, and was heightened with an exclamation point during my hospitalization with depression. While superintendent, I didn't stay with the inventure long enough to bring meaning to my life. I took another job to try and ease my pain rather than stay as superintendent and learn how to better understand Ed Poole.

At two places on our journey, we can find help in answering the "Who am I?" question. The first place is from outside us. The outside pressures of society and our culture impose upon us, time and time again, characteristics and roles that we fall into. When society asks, "Who are you?" the pressures emerge. "I am a parent. I am a spouse. I am a friend. I am a student. I am a co-worker." From the outside realities of our life come the pressures to answer this question and the answers are superficial because they define only the surface of our lives.

The second pressure comes from within – a dramatically different place. It comes from that soft place that we call the soul, which lies somewhere between the physical reality of where our life is, and the spiritual reality of not being sure just where it is going to go. The pressure from within comes when we can no longer give superficial, surface answers to very meaningful questions. The soul really doesn't know; it just feels, but I've never been good at feelings. The soul doesn't accept; it embraces, but I've never been good at embracing. I did not learn how to express my feelings – I kept them all inside. My parents never embraced my sister or me. I learned how to embrace when I began dating girls. To this day my sister does not like to be hugged. I wonder if her feelings about hugging stem from the fact that we were not hugged as children. The soul is the place where the pat answers of life just don't work. However, I've spent much of my adult life seeking those pat answers – the ones that require little or no reflecting on my part.

These two places call me to find out who I am, to find my identity. Dwelling inwardly allows me to realize something of the desolation I feel in always looking outside for happiness, contentment, and fullness. Dwelling only outside myself doesn't allow me to take that long, deep, cleansing breath I mentioned earlier, and to say I can be at home wherever I find myself, at peace with my life as it is, moment to moment. Oliver Wendell Holmes said, "What lies behind us and what lies before us are tiny matters compared to what lies within us."

Potential danger lies in letting the outside world define our identity for us. The danger is, if we look outside ourselves for the definition of who we are, we run the risk of not coming to know our soul, our inside. Perhaps we hold our religious beliefs, our sense and personal definition of faith, not because we might die tonight but because we're going to have to live tomorrow. George Bernard Shaw is quoted as saying, "Most people die when they're forty, and they're buried when they're ninety," because they haven't been able to do the inside-out work in their lives. What do we gain in life if the world defines who we are but we're never able or willing to decide that for ourselves?

The following story helped me along the way of finding the inside work that I must do to balance all the outside work I did during the first half of life. Author Sam Keen tells it about his own life. He said he began the search to find meaning in his life with an insatiable need to find destiny and significance. He began the journey with a sense that he had to decide a destiny for him and that his life had worth. So Keen chose academic achievement as the path he would take to find this worth and identity.

He said, "If I go on this road, then I can find myself." He said, "If I can only be accepted to an Ivy League institution," and he was; "If I could only be accepted to graduate school," and he was – with a Fulbright Scholarship; "If I could only earn a Ph.D.," and he became Dr. Sam; "If I could only be a professor," and he was hired; "If I could only write a book," and he did – many of them. And yet Keen continues that with each of these milestones he reached, the "old cotton-candy sensation" recurred. A moment of intense satisfaction was followed by a sense of total and complete emptiness. Keen is speaking not only of himself but also about me. The old cotton-candy sensation is exactly what I felt each time I took a new job and felt that rush of excitement and anticipation – only to find, after a while, the sugar high was gone and I was left once again with all my same problems and unanswered questions.

Keen felt this ongoing cotton-candy rush until one evening, after giving a lecture at Harvard, he found himself alone and desperate in an old hotel outside Boston. This sophisticated and learned scholar said he felt so much emotional pain that he literally was driven to his knees, sobbing uncontrollably. He lifted his fist up to the heaven and said, "What must I do?" I hesitate to share with you what happened next because your mind is going to tell you, "That never happened." But I share it because I hope your soul will feel it, even if your mind doesn't. For Keen said that after he screamed, "What must I do?" with his fists raised to the heavens, there appeared on the wall in front of him four words, "Nothing, nothing at all."

He said it was at that moment he realized that for twenty-five years he had been searching and straining and looking everywhere around him for identity and self-worth, and it had been present all along. Keen's story spoke to me so clearly. I had fallen into the same outward signs of success as did Keen, and I needed to hear God tell me that I really did not have to do anything to find love, grace, understanding, and self-acceptance Those characteristics were already there within me, had been since birth, ready to be brought forth and celebrated.

My own story parallels Keen's in several ways. I listened carefully to my dad's repeated suggestions to get an education. Like Keen, I chose academic achievement to define who I was to those around me and to myself. The doctorate has been my "ticket" to many of the jobs I've had over many years. The degree gave me recognition among my peers. Each new job moved me a rung higher on that academic ladder of success. I was defined by the jobs I held. When I prayed, I always asked God for specific outcomes – outcomes I wanted to see in my life. I wanted certain jobs and I wanted certain events to unfold for my family in ways I wanted them to unfold. "God I want this job. God I want Eric and Tracie to have this or that outcome in their lives." I wanted Ed Poole to control the outcomes of my prayers. Basically I didn't know how to pray. I kept getting in the way of my prayers. My self-centeredness wouldn't allow God to answer my prayers in His own way and in His own time. Finally I have learned to let go and let God, to say "Not my will but Thine be done." Recently a good friend shared with me the Prayer of Jabez: "Lord, bless me indeed. Expand my territory and put your hand in all that I do that I may harm no one."

I think what Keen discovered that evening in that hotel room outside Boston was a gift, a gift we need to integrate into our souls – not just hear it but feel it. Identity is not something that comes only from the outside-in. Our identity is already in place by our having been given life. We have worth and identity at birth, so our identity isn't something we need to go out and find; we need to bring it forth and celebrate it. As we do the inner work during the second half of our life, we need to rely on ourselves for our identity and not continue that reliance on the outside world we've grown to know over the years.

The growth *is* both inside-out and outside-in. The work begins on the inside through the process of self-observing. That internal journey has an impact on our behavior and greatly assists our seeing the whole of our being and our living. However, I believe that a co-creation occurs, with outside experiences also having an impact on our inside work. For me, it was the interaction of both kinds of experiences – outside-in and inside-out – during the months of hospitalization with clinical depression that continues to have a tremendous impact on my ability to understand my journey. My hospitalization drove me to my knees, much like Keen fell to his knees that night in his hotel room. We spent a similar number of years finding our identity through our work. During my hospitalization I finally gave in and gave up. I was sitting alone in my hospital room one night and I said to God, "I cannot do this alone, Lord. Please help me." This is the first time I can remember asking for God's help in my life and I am feeling that help to this day.

Going Where We Have No Plans to Go

I thought I knew where I needed to go in my life. My stubbornness did not allow me to give in and let God carry out His plans for me. I learned much about a willingness to be led from the writings of Viktor Frankl. If you have read *Man's Search for Meaning* by Frankl, you know it is about his experiences while he was in a concentration camp during World War II. Those prisoners in the camps who saw their lives as provisional – only living from day to day – lost their strength, their hope, and their will to live. However, many of the prisoners who felt they had some important task yet to do when released from the concentration camp survived that ordeal. While their physical bodies were imprisoned, they were challenging their spirits to be free, and they were willing to let their spirits lead them where they had no plans to go.

Frankl himself described a picture he held constantly in his mind and heart. He pictured himself in a large auditorium, filled with people, and in this setting he was describing to the audience his experiences as a prisoner. This dream could become a reality for Frankl only if he survived his stay in the camp. The child within Frankl gave meaning to his physical strivings, to those limitations that surrounded him, and provided him a vision of the possible. Freeing that inner child, that inner spirit – the keeper of his dreams – gave Frankl meaning and purpose. Elsewhere in his book, Frankl wrote that "we can discover this meaning in life in three ways: (1) by doing a deed, (2) by experiencing a value, and (3) by suffering." By keeping his spirit alive Frankl was willing to be led where he had no plans to go.

Much of what I have just said relates to purpose in life. I needed to have a better understanding of my purpose – why I was here and what I was supposed to be doing while here. While I was in transition from one career in education to a career in consulting and coaching, and as I was seeking additional direction in my life after getting out of the hospital and continuing to recover from my depression, I wrote a personal purpose statement, which is lofty but has provided a vision toward which I can move on my journey.

At that time I said: "I want to share with others lessons about my life that I'm learning from my perspective of being out on the porch. I want to integrate these porch lessons into the fabric of the work I do with organizations and individuals in the form of coaching, consulting, facilitating, and training. My lessons from the porch will become my model for telling my story to those with whom I work, and, through my modeling, others will be encouraged to identify and bring to the surface their own lessons, be they oriented in the direction of life, work, learning, change, or the integration of these. I want to share my lessons with others in writing."

You won't be surprised when I say I have only begun to live out this statement written a few years ago. I had the statement set in calligraphy and framed. It hangs on the wall in my office. However, I did not pay close attention to that statement until I began talking about my story through this writing.

What I have just described is not a growth and development pattern experienced only by Ed Poole. Perhaps many of you can identify with these feelings.

Finding Little Eddie While Discovering My Spiritual Side

Though middle aged, respected, and
confident, at times I'm just a child...
Tiny. Helpless. Naked. Lost. Afraid.
Yet, in my despair I'm aware of arms
that hold me; gentle arms, but strong.
They remind me I belong to a Father
who will cradle me and carry me
and will never let me go.

Greg Asimakoupoulos, ***Cradled***

Reaching that point in life where I can live from the inside-out (without all the answers), as well as from the outside-in, is giving me the opportunity to discover that little boy in me, often called "the inner child," who has been trying to get out for so long now. Little Eddie had been driven so deeply inside me, making it very difficult to find out who he is. I am growing to value the fact that the boy in me has not really surfaced and "seen the light of day" for very long in my past.

Much has been written in the last fifteen years about "the wounded child." Jungian analyst Robert Stein has said, "Those child wounds to the soul make it extremely difficult...for one to experience an intimate and creatively evolving human connection." Mom and Dad probably never had the opportunity to honor the inner child in their lives either. I didn't even know Little Eddie was there until I was late into my adult life — my, but there <u>are</u> advantages to soul time. I just know there has always been a little guy inside me, screaming in silence to come forth, and, as I begin to live in the soul time of my life, I am discovering him for perhaps the first time. He's yelling back to me, "It's about time!" The journey to discover the inner child is part of the spiritual journey. Little Eddie is the keeper of my dreams. He's the curious child I've wanted to find and the one who encourages me to find happiness, to enjoy life, and to find my spirit.

I don't remember if as a child I was more or less curious than I am at this point in my life. My hunch is "more curious," and that curiosity got dampened as I grew. Robert Coles, author of *The Spiritual Life of Children*, has said that the curious nature of children is borne out of the fact that children are spiritual creatures. Coles also suggested that it is only when we travel through the various stages of life that we learn to suppress this innate curiosity about the spiritual nature of life. I lived by learning how to deny my spiritual curiosity, my inner child, and I submerged it so deeply that it seldom, if ever, came forth.

I can identify so much with what Coles said. I was curious as a child, but I didn't ask many questions. I learned that my parents were busy, so I just kept all that curiosity inside. Eventually I pushed my curious nature so far down inside me that I didn't even know it was there. My church did not encourage curiosity. When all the answers are given, there is no need to be curious. In fact, curiosity is considered a weakness. But Little Eddie was curious, and I was rebelling so much against the beliefs I had been given. They were not mine, so I accepted the beliefs of others. I am more spiritual today, thanks to my journey to find Little Eddie and the recognition of the value of my spirituality.

These days my spirituality doesn't always come from going to a physical place we call a church, a synagogue, or a mosque. It's interesting that in my earlier adult years, I would feel the guilt from my parents if I did not go to church on Sunday. I knew it was Sunday morning and I should be in church. Without judging rightness or wrongness, today I don't feel guilty if I don't attend church on Sunday mornings. My journey toward spirituality isn't understood only within a physical place.

This past Sunday, for example, the weather was perfect – sunny and in the upper 50's, a rare treat for the Midwest in late January! Instead of going to church, my wife and I took our golden retriever for a walk in the forest preserve close to our house. The experience was wonderful, and, during the three-mile walk through the beauty that surrounded us, I felt a connection with my spiritual side in ways that would not have occurred in church. The red berries of winter stood out on the leafless branches. The tall, stately prairie grass brushed back and forth lazily in rhythm with the slight breeze that was blowing. We were, what Bonnie's grandfather used to call, "communing with nature."

I have internalized more from those early years in the church in my hometown than I could ever have imagined. Now I am able to take those beliefs out, look at them carefully, and adjust them to fit the current stage in my journey. Once I gave myself permission to do that adjusting, I was ready to establish my own beliefs and not feel guilty for doing so.

Along the journey of adulthood, whether we desire it or not, our innate spiritual nature will demand to be addressed. It is always there, just below the surface, and sometimes it just comes forth.

How do we come of age spiritually? The answer is different for each of us. Sometimes it is difficult to find the sacred amidst all the ordinary living that we do. How do we encounter the sacred amidst the ordinary? The journey toward spirituality begins as we honor the very quality of life as it is. As we search for the sacred in our lives, we move toward a wholeness not before experienced. The spiritual journey allows us to break down the barriers that we built inside ourselves – barriers that were in place to distance us from the spirit. My early religious experiences actually prevented me from finding my soul. I was scared each time I came up short of the expectations of my church and my parents. I was confused between being spiritual and being human, allowed to make mistakes.

Steven Covey says we are not human beings struggling to be spiritual, but spiritual beings struggling to be human. Alan Cohen, in his book *I Had It All the Time*, suggests, "Our noblest purpose in life is to remember our spiritual nature in the face of suggestions and appearances that we are material only." As we journey, the spiritual child is in each of us. And as with all journeys, but especially the journey toward the sacred, toward working from the inside-out, we become more aware of T.S. Eliot's observation that there comes a time in our explorations when we arrive where we started and know that place for the first time.

Little Eddie is joined with me for life. The gift my inner child has given me is to realize that, as I honor and bring forth Little Eddie, I am expressing my journey toward wholeness. I learned to embrace Little Eddie during that time I was in the hospital – that time when I was most vulnerable. I had time to remember my childhood and to realize I never had a chance to be a little boy, to find Little Eddie. Celebrating my inner child – Little Eddie – will help me live out the life and dreams he has always had for me.

The Curious Child

As children we are so incredibly curious, and it doesn't take much for that childlike curiosity to send a well educated, well meaning adult scrambling for emotional cover. Dave Barry, the syndicated columnist who writes out of Miami, Florida, tells of one such moment where he learned how to deal with his curious little four-year-old boy. They were riding down Biscayne Boulevard in Miami, and they passed a ninety-eight-story building. Barry's little boy, sitting in the passenger seat, asked his dad, "Daddy, how much does that building weigh?" How would you answer that? Dave Barry said he never missed a beat. As soon as his little four-year-old asked his curious little question, Barry said, "It weighs four million, one hundred thousand pounds." The little boy sat there for a moment, and then he said, "Well, that's just what I thought." Barry went on to say it's not the answer we give our child that's important – it's the fact that we make him or her understand we heard the question. Often in life I have found I need to live with the questions because I do not have answers. The answers are not unimportant but without my ability to ask questions, there will be no answers at all. The questions I ask tell me what is in my heart.

For too long in my life, the voice of my inner child was quiet, just as I was quiet. Not only was the inner child silent in my noncommunicative home environment, but the outer child was silent as well. Because I resisted what was being imposed on me, from the outside in as a spiritual journey, I did not have that journey during which I could find my inner child. Yet I know now my child's voice is essential to the process of becoming me because Little Eddie's voice is uncensored and honest.

We have all been children, and the child's inner voice is one each of us will recognize because the child within us remains within us. The inner child holds our personal history and is the keeper of the dream for our hopes and aspirations for the future. Of all the nostalgias that haunt the human heart the greatest of them is an everlasting longing to bring what is youngest home to what is oldest in us all.

During my own soul time, and perhaps yours as well, I am seeking this connection between the child and the adult. Jung has said that, "in every adult there lurks a child – an internal child, something that is always becom<u>ing</u>, is never completed, and calls for unceas<u>ing</u> care, attention, and education" (emphasis added). I like this thought because, once again, I have some *ing* words with which to work. The process of becoming, as a context and frame of reference, gives me the hope to realize that "this isn't all there is" to me in this life. The possibilities are endless if I can stay the course of allowing my inner child the freedom he deserves.

I am also finding that conflicts arise between the inner and outer child. Wordsworth, in "Ode: Intimations of Immortality," said it so well: "Shades of the prison-house begin to close/Upon the growing Boy." In this context, Wordsworth is using the "boy" as a reference for self-respect. This, for me, describes much of my own conflict: the restrictions both society and I personally have placed on myself from the outside, pushing against the organic pressure for growth from the inside. The conflict centered around all of the external signs and symbols, from family and church, to be this good little boy, and I played that role very well. I knew when to be a good boy – at home, at school, in church – and the little boy kept wanting to have his moments in the sun. I don't really want Little Eddie to change. I want him to stay young and therefore hopeful, unfettered, and optimistic. I'm sure Little Eddie felt abandoned and rightfully so.

The little boy inside my father must have felt abandoned as well – two times in his early life. The first abandonment came when his biological parents placed him in the orphanage, and the second was when his first adoptive parents returned him to that same orphanage. What wounds did Dad carry with him his entire life? You know that I do not know the answer to that question because he and I never talked about those early years. As I am taking the opportunity of looking back and reflecting, I can only imagine that his feelings of abandonment must have been great. He must have been so very fearful. "What is going to happen to me? Am I going to be in this orphanage now for my entire young life? Why did those people bring me back here? Why did my brother get to stay, and I had to return? I miss my brother." Dad's inner child had to be so afraid. An orphanage was a block from the church in which I was raised. Each Sunday morning the twenty-five or so children from that home came to my church. I remember listening to them talk about their fears and their hopes. Those conversations took on a much greater meaning for me when I heard the story of Dad's experience as an orphan. From time to time I wonder what happened to some of those kids.

Can you imagine how you would feel? It is hard for me to put myself in that place. I would think that my father was very grateful that the Poole family adopted him and actually <u>kept</u> him this time. Did he wonder if they, too, would abandon him? I regret not taking the initiative to talk with Dad about all of this. I wish I had wondered about it as much while he was still alive as I do now. Much of the time, Dad was absent in his presence at home. We had very little interaction.

In his book *The Child*, Erich Newmann wrote, "Once we appreciate the positive significance of the child's total dependency on the primal relationship, we cannot be surprised by the catastrophic effects that ensue when that relationship is disturbed or destroyed." If you remember, when I asked Mom about how Dad felt about being an orphan, she said she just figured he was so young, the experience didn't mean much to him. I wonder now how that could possibly be the case. I never saw the playful side of Dad. I do not believe the little boy in him was ever recognized. Now that I am learning about Little Eddie I want to know as much as I can about this inner child I'm discovering.

Jean Follain, in *Exister*, wrote: "While in the fields of his eternal childhood, the poet wakes and doesn't want to forget anything." Earlier you read that whenever I retreated to the dark side, my stay there was temporary. And once the tensions between how I was being raised and what I was experiencing at the time became too great to cope with, I always retreated to the lighter side – to those expectations held for me by others.

I never stayed with the dark long enough to understand it and give it meaning. I didn't listen to the sound of my sighing while there, and, since I had no internal meaning for who I was, I did not trust what I was experiencing. I was afraid. I was not willing to be led where I had no plans to go. I had no idea that standing in the shadows is sometimes the brightest spot on earth. The sun was always my friend. I quickly went to find it, never staying long enough in those dark places to bring any understanding to my life. I knew where I should be going and would not surrender myself to my Higher Power to be led other places. The first time I let go of trying to control my life was when I entered the hospital.

My controlling tendencies were triggered by what my external stimuli were saying to me; therefore, I was continuing to use the compass in my hand, rather than my heart, to guide my life.

I used to talk such a good game to those educators with whom I've worked over the years about the difference between "controlling" and "being in control." I, of course, indicated I subscribed to the latter and that I did not like those who were controlling of others. I feel that I did a pretty good job of not controlling those with whom I worked. However, this practice did not transfer to my personal life. I controlled much of the decision-making for the family and I controlled the finances. My family usually gave into my decisions rather than argue with me. My personal life would be healthier today if some of those arguments had occurred over the years. Anne Wilson Schaef, author of *The Addictive Organization*, speaks of controlling as being an illusion: even when we think we are controlling, we're really not. Now I'm convinced that I cannot control the outcomes of anyone's life. At the same time, I cannot control the outcomes of my own life. I can move in certain directions but I always have to keep turning those directions over to my Higher Power to see my next move.

Parents can control their children because the children do not know any better, and youngsters need and want structure in their lives. As children grow, some begin to understand how stilted their growth has been because they have been controlled. So, in the short term, parents do control and need to. In the long term, however, if parents continue controlling their children for too long, some of these same parents lose any possibility of a long-term adult-to-adult relationship and friendship with their children as these children become adults. Early in their lives, I tried to provide direction for Eric and Tracie. As they grew into adulthood, my direction has diminished. I try to give advice now only when asked.

I learned as a child to deny those demons in the dark, to repress my negative feelings. I didn't cry; I muffled my passion; I covered my anger. Keeping people happy with surface harmony, I now realize, came at the expense of emotional honesty. I didn't let my dark side demons go with a blessing. Now when I admit my fears to another person, who will give them honor and reflect them for me to see, the fears become friendlier. Admitting fears involves trust.

The words of Dr. Martin Luther King, Jr. ring in my ears: "Free at last. Free at last. Thank God Almighty, I'm free at last." I was not free because I was not trusting of others. I also had no real trust in any Higher Power, and I had not found Little Eddie. I know now that I did not trust a Being for whom I had such fear, and I rebelled against going somewhere I had no plans to go.

Trusting and Being Trusted

Woven into the above discussion is a connection between the inner child and trust. I have not always been the most trusting person in the world. I did not trust others, Little Eddie, or myself. Sure, I've talked a good game with my graduate classes, educators, and businesses relative to trust in organizations. I talk about it so easily and model it so poorly. Throughout my life I have not been completely trusting of others. One of the reasons I have not always been open and trusting is because too often I asked myself the question: "Now what is she, or what is he, *really* going to do with this information I'm about to share?" When, during my therapy sessions, J.R. told me I was not trustworthy I knew why I didn't trust others. I can establish rapport, not trust. I've talked often about the fact that rapport develops pretty quickly between and among individuals – or it doesn't develop. But the rapport is either there or not there fairly quickly. Trust, on the other hand – I've said – takes a long time to build and can be destroyed in a split second. If I have a long and trusting friendship with someone and that person chooses to share with another very personal and private information about me – and I have not given my permission for this information to be shared – my trust of this individual is shattered and may never be rebuilt. Have you ever had this same experience?

This trust-building process occurs in families and other relationships. The way trust is built in any organization, I now know, is when each individual within that organization is trustworthy.

Over the years, my secrets and lack of honesty have not always allowed me to be trustworthy. You already know this. Until my writing efforts began, however, I didn't realize why I couldn't trust others more than I did. The "enemy" was not out there somewhere, but rather within. If I didn't trust myself, why would I trust others, and why would others trust me? I assumed most folks were just like me — a little secret here, a little lie there. Over time, the barriers to the inner self become formidable. I also didn't trust myself (or others) because I lacked that internal guidance system I needed so badly. I thought the heart was only a muscle that works to keep us alive.

As I think about it all, I've conducted my own fair share of those parking-lot agendas over the years. And I have had those parking-lot agendas because I was not trustworthy. I didn't trust myself to share publicly with others what I was really thinking or feeling. I knew I wasn't trustworthy. I told my lies and I kept my secrets. Someone would share with me a piece of information that was to be held in confidence. I turned around and shared that piece of confidential information with another, especially if I thought doing so would enhance my place in the organization.

Little by little, though, as others would share their innermost stories with me, I began to honor the fact that they trusted me with this information. I didn't pass along to others what had been entrusted to me, and the more I honored what had been given me, the more trustworthy I became. The only way I am becoming trustworthy is by my actions. Trusting others and being trustworthy myself are cyclical events. One cannot be separated from the other. If I am trustworthy, I will be trusted, and, if I am trusted, I will become trustworthy.

As I am learning to become more transparent with my life, I am finding my trust of others is growing. Almost every time I trust becoming open with another, I find the other individual meeting me more than halfway. I have a friend, Tom Halvorsen, who was a student of mine in high school and has since become and remained a friend for over thirty years. Although we live in different parts of the country, we phone, e-mail, and visit as often as we can to keep current in each other's lives. Tom and I learned the process of trusting one another over a period of years. We have laughed together and we have cried together. We have shared with each other the brightest and darkest hours in our lives and doing so has allowed us to remain so close that we often end our conversations with joint "I love you's." My early experiences with males sharing these words made them feel uncomfortable to me at first. I had not said I love you to another man, just in writing to Dad. Now sharing these words with Tom seems natural.

Another reason I can trust more is because of the thousands of men and women whose lives have intersected with mine, briefly or for long periods of time. Those with brief yet powerful intersections were my friends in the hospital, people who again and again had risen above their own despair, who kept repeating along with the Psalmist, "Even though you should slay me, I will continue to hope in you." That, my friend, is a powerful hope. There is goodness in spite of it all.

As I am writing this particular section, I am overwhelmed by the terrorists' attacks on the World Trade Center and the Pentagon – attacks that, as I write, occurred only two days ago on September 11, 2001. How can I, at this moment in time, say there is goodness in spite of it all? What part of a perfect plan for us all would include the senseless loss of thousands of lives? Where are the small victories that we should recognize? What lessons are we to learn from our porch? How do we "go out not knowing" based on faith? How do I trust those who are not trustworthy? How is it possible in a broken world to become whole? Is wholeness a human possibility at all? I have to live the questions because I have no answers. Frederick Buechner in *The Longing for Home*, put it this way: "A great deal of suffering…can be explained by saying that God leaves human beings free to do unspeakable things to each other presumably because, if they are not free to do unspeakable things to each other, they are not truly free to love each other either or to love God, the great double commandment that is laid upon us before all others."

After the attacks fear gripped the country and the world. As a nation we were fearful because we did not know what would happen next. More attacks? More deaths? The author Don Miguel Ruiz refers in his writings to fear as "the parasite," and this term has helped me understand some of the roots of fear. As does the parasite, fear eats away at our very being and can consume us. I have, however, also asked myself the question: Is fear always suspect, or does it sometimes function as an early warning system? Sometimes I get confused in my thinking. I do feel that fear is disabling and needs to be processed for what it is – a current running through the body – not a permanent part of who I am. I must let it enter and exit because it is not me. How helpful this recent understanding might have been throughout much of my life. I did not give my fears the time needed to pass through me and make an exit. I ran as fast as I could to find the nearest ray of sunlight, leaving the fears inside.

When we are fearful, we want to feel protected. We needed this protection as children, and we still need it as adults. However, after the attacks of September 11th, our government assured us that we would avenge the deaths of that day. The government said the enemy was invisible, hiding in the shadows of countries and caves. So, as Deepak Chopra stated in *The Deeper Wound*, a book he wrote right after the terrorists' attacks, "Protection was denied us at the very moment we needed it most." We feel more protected as the days and months proceed since the attacks, and our sense of confidence as a country is expanding. Nine months have passed between September 11 and the writing of this sentence. Time has helped increase our feelings of protection, even with the acts of terrorism that continue in other parts of the world. At this time our government continues to remind us to be cautious and vigilant. The gap between what we fear and what is real still exists in our minds and hearts.

To trust, to be trustworthy, and to allow time for our fears to pass through us mean making a commitment. I am reminded here of the powerful words of Goethe:

Commitment

Until one is committed, there is hesitancy,
the chance to draw back, always
toward ineffectiveness.
Concerning all acts of initiative (and creation)
there is one elementary truth the ignorance
of which kills countless ideas
and splendid plans:
That the moment one definitely commits oneself
then providence moves too.
All sorts of things occur to help one
that would never otherwise have occurred.
A whole stream of events issues from the decision
raising one's favour all manner of
unforeseen incidents and meetings and
material assistance which no
man could have dreamt would have
come his way.
Whatever you can do, or dream you can, begin it.
Boldness has genius, power, and magic in it.
Begin it now.

For me, Goethe speaks of going out not knowing – of trusting the process, of letting go – and letting the divine, the sacred in us all, take over. I suggest that the commitment is enhanced both by trusting and by being trustworthy.

I do believe that the first time faith triumphed over fear in my life – to the extent that I recognized the triumph – was my time in the hospital, during the most extreme period of my depression. I gave in. I was apprehended by my faith, and I knew that putting my trust in others was the only way I would survive. I had never trusted anyone in my life as much as I trusted my fellow patients and the professional staff at the hospital. I don't know if the parts of my story I'm sharing with you would ever have been told if I had not allowed faith to triumph. I had done everything I could to avoid my feelings, so what could I lose by honoring them for once?

You may have a success in life, but
then just think of it – what kind of life
was it? What good was it – you've
never done the thing you wanted to do in
all your life…go where your body and soul
want to go. When you have the feeling, then
stay with it, and don't let anyone throw you off.
Joseph Campbell, ***The Power of Myth***

Be silent toward all that is unsolved in your heart.
And try to love the questions themselves.
Do not seek the answers that cannot be given you,
because you would not be able to live them.
And the point is to live everything.
Live the questions now.
Perhaps you will gradually, without noticing it,
live along some distant day into the answer.
Rainer Maria Rilke

We can't be anyplace other than where we are right now. Sometimes we have to stand still and let it hurt; sometimes we have to stand still and let it feel good; and sometimes we have to just stand still.

Porches make great "viewing points."

The porch gives us a chance to stand quietly in front of the full-length mirror and learn how to "see" something only after we "believe" it. It's a place to learn about "being" in relation to "doing."

*I saw my sailboat in the stars
as I sat on the porch.*

*A fall from the porch is not always bad. I hit the ground
and I'm getting grounded.*

For so long I didn't know how to quietly stand still – to take time to reflect about my life, slow down, and appreciate that the pace with which I lead my life can lead to the grace of understanding my journey. I simply was never good at just "being"; instead, I was exceptional at "doing." Perhaps we've been taught to answer the wrong question – what we want to do is not as important as what we want to be. The period of time in the hospital and since has allowed me to begin to "be." Though I didn't enter the hospital by choice, that imposed time-out has since become a gift. Nathaniel Branden wrote a section in *Handbook for the Soul*, titled "Passion and Soulfulness." In this section he said "doing and being, action and stillness, are dependent on one another. When being and doing are in harmony, when stillness and action are friends to each other, we create an integrated, satisfied soul." Branden's thoughts were a relief to me because they allowed me to see that being and doing are not "either/or" but "both/and." I inherited my parents' work ethic. I <u>did</u> my job. I did <u>not</u> know about letting go of my work so I could understand myself. When I was working I didn't <u>have</u> to think about me. Now I know that life is about the balance between these two concepts. I do not have to separate my doing from my being – I <u>am</u>, however, creating a better balance between doing my job and being the reflective person I now value and cherish.

Some thoughts I recorded while superintendent, before seeing my therapist, reveal the dissatisfaction I felt when I didn't know how to balance doing and being. The thoughts also identify the desperation I felt at the time as I was trying to understand and ease the pain.

I was definitely stranded in the wilderness. I was also trying to find a "quick fix" for my pain because I ran from every storm in my life, instead of turning around and facing it head-on. The inside-out work began as I taped my thoughts. Prior to this, I had primarily worked from my outside paying little attention to my soul and the pushing out that was happening on the inside. The inside-out work began as a result of some thinking I had done, as well as some sessions I had with my therapist. You already know that the work didn't last long. I took another new job and conveniently got busy with that, leaving the porch to dive into my work, just as I had done many times before. I still was not connected to my soul, to the thoughts and feelings hidden deep inside me, so deep I didn't recognize they were there. Emerging from early therapy concerning my marriage came the fact that I was a major problem for the marriage because I did not know Ed Poole. As I began seeking therapy to help me know myself better, I became frightened about what I might find. For years I only flirted with working from the inside out. Until being hospitalized for depression my pattern with therapy was the same for twenty-five years: When I felt enough pain in my life I would see a therapist but when the sessions became uncomfortable I would quit going. As the sessions got below the surface issues in my life, requiring me to reflect deeply about myself, I became afraid of what I might find.

My heart and my head had not yet connected. Ten years ago, as I left the superintendency, I *said* to myself I wanted to move to a new job so I could begin doing the inner work – but you and I know that didn't happen. If I would have recognized my soul and had been able to become centered within myself, I do believe that from my porch I could have better discerned where I wanted to go and why – both personally and professionally. I was emotionally very young. I had matured physically but not emotionally. I now realize that my situation is not unlike that of young people who become addicted to drugs. Their dependence on drugs keeps them from maturing emotionally as well. The numbness from the drugs allows physical maturation but not emotional growth. I was not into drugs, but I was numbed by a head that kept pushing me along my journey fueled by positive reinforcement from my external guidance system. Dependent on external support, I had no heart to provide my internal compass.

I wish I could say that the notes I made allowed me to "stay the course" and continue to steer my boat toward a greater understanding of who I am. It didn't happen; there were too many years to overcome where I ignored all the important stuff, with too much running from too many storms in my life.

SITTING IN FRONT OF A CAVE

The following notes represent perhaps the first time in my life I actually returned to the porch to reflect although at the time I didn't recognize that I was on my porch. Please note that I am typing the words here exactly as I recorded them. I haven't changed a thing. The notes, then, will take you back and forth between two different times in my life, so please keep your seat belts fastened for the quick movements between those several years.

Six months after having taken the job as superintendent, I felt like I was in a cave. In reality, looking back, I had returned to the porch. While in this cave, I was talking to a wise, old man – a sage – someone I had created in my mind to listen to my cries for help. This conversation with my wise old friend turned out to be the first time in my life I felt an inner guide was there to help me process some very hurtful and confusing information about myself. I could be honest with my inner guide because he did not judge.

"What's the matter, Ed?"

"I don't know what is important to me. Being happy? Feeling comfort? Feeling good about my family? Knowing that my family and I are okay? Enjoying what I'm doing? Not having to worry about my job all the time? I grew up being such a pleaser."

"Well, how do you *feel*?" asked the wise old man.

"How do I feel? I feel isolated. I feel like I'm stuck up or off or out or in a corner someplace. I'm not enjoying my work. I've always wanted to be 'a part of,' and not 'apart from' those with whom I have worked. Even as a high school principal, I always felt like most of the staff accepted me. It seems like every topic I deal with here is just so unpleasant, so uncomfortable, and it's a chore or a task I <u>have</u> to do."

The wise old man then asked, "How is this job different for you?"

"Well, in my other jobs I used to complain some about going back to the office at night or on weekends, but I went back willingly because I wanted to get caught up. In all honesty though, wise old man, I also returned to that office to avoid some parenting responsibilities at home. I just didn't feel I was a capable parent. I'm not sure why I feel this way, but I do. Because I have this feeling of inadequacy as a parent, I just figured it was better for everyone if I got out of the way and let my wife handle whatever crisis situation appeared at the time. You know what? Even in those times I was taking the sun for granted and running from the storms. Now I don't enjoy going into the office. I don't enjoy being there. I feel like I'm in a tomb, or chained or ... it's just all so different. I miss all the people – people in general. I couldn't see it. I just couldn't see it."

"Couldn't see what?"

"I had a blind spot," I replied. "Sometimes it seems it's just so hard for me to keep a perspective on what I've got. I distort it or something. I guess it's reality for me at the time, but then when I get away from it, like I am now with this job, I look back on where I was and ask: 'What was I complaining about?' I also know, old wise one, that I have a tendency to record only the 'sunny hours' of my past experiences, to remember only the good parts, and easily forget the frustrations that were there. I have 'selective memory.' Sometimes I feel there's no hope for me in this job. I just simply don't see the match with my personality. Sure there are people like me, with personalities like mine, who are superintendents, but I just absolutely am so frustrated by it. Sometimes when I get this way, I just want to hibernate, pull in, and hide. Stay on the porch. I am so, so, so frustrated right now. Yes, I know with my attitude, it's a vicious circle. What can I say?"

"What do you mean, it's a 'vicious circle'? I don't understand."

"It means I'm getting back what I'm reflecting. My attitude is terrible, so I'm receiving back experiences that frustrate me, reinforce my attitude, and continue not to allow me to find enjoyment in my work. I know I'm responsible for changing. I just don't seem to be able to change. How do I follow my own direction, and not spend all my time listening to other people? Just do it. Do what I think is right. That's what I tried to do in coming here. Up to this point, it simply is <u>not</u> working out." [When I reread this part later, I said: "I had no direction. I didn't know who Ed Poole was. Those other people defined me, so I had to listen to them to find out what I was supposed to do."]

"What do you want to do?"

"I would walk out of that office tomorrow, and not look back once if I had a viable option. I am just so stifled. You want to know the ironic thing, old wise one, as we sit out here in front of the cave and talk? I was afraid of being stifled and smothered by not being able to get out of the principalship. (Ed laughs here) You <u>know</u> what I'm going to say – now I'm afraid I won't be able to get out of the superintendency. <u>Isn't that a laugh!</u>

"Thanks for coming back to talk with me, old wise one. I've had some more thoughts in the last few days. It's interesting how experiences help us put other experiences into perspective. Compared to the parts of this job that I don't enjoy, the parts of the principalship that I didn't enjoy seem relatively simple, and most certainly not so cumbersome at this point. There are just so many parts of this job that I don't like – the legal aspects, the union aspects, and the day-to-day personnel aspects. I guess I rely so much on other people for help in making decisions, and I miss that a lot now. I don't know if that's a reflection of my personal life and business life together where I seem to need assistance in making personal decisions, and need that same assistance in making professional decisions on the job. I don't know. Maybe it just has to do with decision-making period. I'm trying to know how much of what I miss is still the <u>building</u> I left as principal, and how much of what I miss is the <u>job</u> of the principal. Sometimes I think it's that controlling factor I miss. I seem to think I had more control over my time, my life, when I was a high school principal than I do now. Seems like I'm running hither and yon, taking care of a lot of people's personal agenda items, and I now know I don't like that.

"I so much need to be surrounded by positive, happy, growing people, and I am in such a small, small environment here. It's just to the point of being depressing. [Note I made later, after my hospitalization: I wrote 'interesting choice of words.'] I guess I miss the feeling I get by being around young people. And I know of the frustrations I used to talk about in terms of high school students and their silliness, and whatever. I can still recall stepping out into the hall and watching them and feeling young to the point of even identifying with them. I miss that. Given time, I might well get past it, but I miss it right now. It's the social and the people part that I miss."

"What do you mean by the people part?"

"I answered the wise old man with a question: What does it mean to say 'I'm a people person'? I simply don't know. I do know that being a people person has given me support and strength and reserve to call on when things got tough. I guess I need a lot of positive reinforcement for some reason, and I'm not getting it right now. I used to get a lot when I was a principal – from staff, parents, and students. At least I had enough to keep me going. Here, with this collective bargaining law, things seem to be so restrictive in terms of people working together and the way it mandates expectations for the way people work together. All this just seems to run so counter to the natural flow of that collaboration that I think can happen more naturally when you are not doing it by prescription, but just letting it evolve. It most certainly is a 'glass half empty' attitude, and I just don't see it changing."

"I can tell you are really struggling with your life right now, Ed. It would be good if you can keep talking to me, and let me listen." [I made a note: The wise old man was a good listener, and had certainly internalized the old adage that we have two ears and one mouth, and we should use them in that proportion. I hadn't learned that yet.]

And so I continued. "When I think in terms of balance in my life, I don't know how possible that's going to be, getting used to a new job. If I keep moving on to bigger superintendencies, there is going to be more responsibility. I probably should have realized the opportunity for balance was there in the high school principalship, by just letting go of some of that time I spent thinking about the job and being involved in other interests, and doing other things – travel, whatever. I just didn't see it then. There was such a focus on the job. I didn't see the comfort level and assurance that went with the job as an opportunity to free me up to do other things. I just keep focusing so much on the job and career, to the exclusion of so many other things. [Note to me later: Ed, you were recalling your days as a high school principal through rose-colored glasses. You didn't have a balance in your life then, and you weren't particularly interested in gaining a better balance. Remember the work ethic you got from Mom and Dad?] Now I don't see the opportunity for those other things to develop, because, in fact, I <u>am</u> struggling so much with the job. I struggled with the job of being a high school principal, but I don't think it was anything compared to some of the struggling thoughts I'm having right now. There seems to be such pressure for perfection, always striving, fear of sliding or fear of slacking off – I don't know why. So what if I 'slacked off' and got a better balance? I just don't know.

"Well, several days have gone by since we last sat and talked in front of the cave. Thanks for being willing to listen again."

"And thank you," said the wise old man, "for recognizing the fact that listening is my primary job right now."

"I just have to say, I am <u>so</u> unhappy. The sad, sometimes futile, feelings are there again. I just met for an hour and a half this morning with the people in the central office, and we didn't talk about one topic that was enjoyable for me. We talked about the frustrating situation with the principals – how they feel like they 'won' by banding together and sticking with their position of not integrating the new program we have with the existing programs. That's so sad, so very sad. I think in all honesty they do not see any reason whatsoever to change. I guess I'm seeing that it is, in fact, very difficult to mandate that change from the top. You have to have people in the building who are willing to do it. That's a key. Sure, you have to have a superintendent who creates the possibilities and opens up the avenues to allow that to occur.

"But you can only open up those avenues to allow that to occur if you've got people willing to do it. We talked about me taking a real tough, hard line with the principals, saying it's going be this way and this way and this way, and if you don't like it, you may need to get out. I wish there was another way. I miss being in the building. I got a letter from the grievance chairperson today saying that he had not gotten a response from some of his letters to me about this, that, or the other, and if there isn't a response by January 18th, he is going to file a grievance. I just don't enjoy working this closely with the union. I don't even know why I'm so sad and frustrated. I just, at this point, cannot turn it around and say let's look at all of these as possibilities and opportunities and not as frustrations. And I don't know what it's going to take to get me there. I know I'm getting what I'm expecting;"

"What do you mean by that?" asked my wise old friend.

"I'm getting what my attitudes are reflecting, and that's exactly what I'm getting back. I just can't seem to turn the corner and put that behind me, stiffen my upper lip, and smile and get on with it. I am so unhappy! [Note to me later: Those masks weren't working! Notice how many times I have said how unhappy I am?]

"Was my leaving there [the principalship] out of selfishness? Am I just so 'Ed-centered' that I can't see anything else? Why can't I just do this job and not dwell on it so much, and develop interests and aptitudes in other things? Devote more time to Bonnie? Devote more time to our relationship? Why are my job and my work-setting always a priority? Knowing today what I know, if I knew it a year ago, just twelve months ago, I would have never left being a high school principal. That's as honest as I can be right now. I would never have left the principalship. [Note I made to myself later: Ed, that was impossible. You know you had to leave that principal's job; otherwise you would have been into the 'woulda, coulda, shoulda' thinking about trying the superintendency, but then I didn't realize that back when I was making this tape.]

"I disrupted so many lives. Bonnie is just burning both ends of the candle. As you know, wise one, she gets up at 4:45 every weekday morning. As she gets ready for school, I fix her breakfast, which she eats in the car as she makes the hour-plus commute to her school – a trip that is made during the worst morning rush-hour traffic. In the evenings she waits until the traffic has slowed down some before heading home, so she arrives sometimes as late as 7:30 p.m. If snow is in the forecast, she packs her bag and stays with friends. What long days she has, and I feel guilty that she has to have these days – I feel it's all my fault. It would have been so easy just to have stayed there. I know I couldn't have stayed there, but it would have been so easy, so much easier. Why do I have to learn this lesson this way? What is it I'm supposed to be learning? Bonnie still talks about my being selfish, about me, me, me. She also, though, says that I'm such a people person that I ought to be able to utilize those skills to work with the people who are here and not give up on them. Yesterday Bonnie and I were talking about my job and the five principals with whom I work, and I used a word I don't think I have ever used in talking about anybody before. I said four out of five of them are 'worthless,' and that word just rolled off my tongue so easily. I just don't understand – I don't have the commitment at this point, the dedication, the drive to try to figure out what to do with them, and I clearly don't know. I don't get it.

"I just spent this afternoon talking to a couple of board members about all kinds of specific things that I don't have an interest in – personnel issues, follow-up on this, that, or the other relative to leaves of absence. I guess I find myself dealing with the master contract – in front of me more – as a superintendent than I ever had to do as a principal. And I just don't like it. I used to always talk about the fact that I managed the building in spite of the master contract, and now I'm having to look at it every – this is a little bit of an exaggeration – but every time I turn around. It's just driving me crazy. I just had my third phone call from the same board member about picky little things on the agenda, and it's just not being a fun afternoon. I guess a question I am asking myself is: 'Do I have what it takes to do this job?' I don't know the answer to that.

"Am I projecting the hardships of Mom and Dad onto guilt I feel about Bonnie this year – with the drive and the extra work on her part. It used to hurt me so badly to watch Mom cry – so when Dad would say, 'Don't you know you made your mother cry?' the guilt would be heaped on in many layers.

"I am remembering Harold Kushner's book, *When Bad Things Happen to Good People*. At one point he says he is not afraid of dying because he feels satisfied with what he has done with his life. He had the sense that he had not lived a wasted life – that he had lived with integrity, and had done his best. He also felt he was able to have an impact on people who would outlive him. Kushner said, 'It is only when you are no longer afraid to die that you can say you are truly alive. I believe it's not dying that people are afraid of. We're afraid of never having lived, of coming to the end of our days with a sense that we were never really alive – that we had never figured out what life is for.' I think one of my fears of dying is exactly because I haven't figured out what my life is all about. I am remembering the words George Gray found chiseled on his gravestone back in Spoon River.

[Note to myself made later: "Ed, put some time in on reflecting about what you said back a few years ago. You owe it to yourself. Plus be sure to note that whatever your reflections are now are *not* necessarily *the* answers; they simply reflect how you've changed in your viewing points over the last six years. Erik Erikson has written about challenges of the middle years. He said that man needs to teach, and he commented on the mentoring concept of working with those younger. Did I have all that as a principal and gave it up? How does one work with younger people and be a mentor? Was I trying to mentor students as a principal because I lacked this mentoring growing up? The boy who needs fathering is Ed, not the students I had contact with as a principal. The father and the boy are both inside me. How do we parent ourselves in the missing places?"]

"Thank you, my wise friend, for listening."

So, there you have it – some early notes which took me on a path with my therapist interspersed with reflections made years later, and this book is being written a few years after that. For me, this dialogue I've just shared provides an example of several things:

I believe the dialogue illustrates all four of the lessons in this chapter: It touches upon my inability to be anyplace other than where I was at that time, my viewing point in front of my cave, my ability to stand quietly in front of the full-length mirror, and my feelings about taking a fall from the porch.

Secondly, the dialogue demonstrates to me that I was not ready to do the real inside-out work that I professed to be ready to do. I knew that in later years; however, it has taken five **more** years to develop the lessons and get to this writing. I left the superintendency, I took another job, and once again I pushed aside the work of understanding Ed Poole.

I put this work aside because I was not listening to myself or to my Higher Power. Remember when I said earlier that God tries to send us messages to get our attention? I don't think my attention was captured until I went into the hospital. At that time I think God switched from a 2-by-4 to a 4-by-4 and really whacked me upside my head. Yet, it has still taken me five more years after that to begin sharing my story with you. I'm expecting other whacks later in life because, after all, I did inherit Mom's stubbornness.

I hope the pain I was in at different times during the past few years is apparent to you. Looking back and remembering from this viewing point today, I was definitely smack in the wilderness. I wrote earlier that, when we are in the wilderness, we face one of two outcomes: we'll either die, or we'll move through it. Perhaps next year, or the year after that, or ten more years on down the road, I'll look back on what I have just written and say: "Ed, you only thought you were out of the wilderness back then." Acquiring new viewing points is part of the wonderful mysteries of life and the different perspectives we develop when we are in different contexts. I know I've been on a wilderness journey; I don't know if I'm out of it yet. My hunch is that I'm not because wilderness experiences will always be a part of my life.

As I reflect on the dialogue I've just shared with you, I've discovered there is a journey within a journey. The main journey was the dialogue I had with my wise, old friend in front of the cave. Within that journey I made some discoveries from the notes I later made to myself. Although I seem to be pretty hard on myself in those reflections, I feel now that my frustrations were a sign of growth, not a time for ridicule. I was in a much different place when I reflected on those earlier notes, and I'm in a different place as I write this than I was a few years ago. So, why wouldn't I expect my responses to be different? I've learned lessons and moved to a different place in my understanding of Ed Poole.

I said above that I may not be out of the wilderness yet and that I wonder what I will say next year, or the year after that, or ten years down the road, I **hope** that I **will** have lots of different thoughts about my place in the world as I move into the future. If I can cite those differences, I can make two points: I have not stopped learning yet, and, if I view Ed Poole differently in the future, I will see that new viewing point as a wonderful place to be. I will also know that I probably will never be able, with any degree of definitiveness, to know Ed Poole because this "knowing" is a process, a journey of its own. I may know Ed Poole *better*, but I will always have new wilderness journeys from which I will learn about me, if I'm lucky, and continue to get grounded in understanding Ed Poole after I fall from the porch and hit the ground.

I believe the dialogue with my wise, old friend is a part of every person's story. We all have times when we do not understand the place we're in or what we're supposed to be learning while there.

Finally, I also share this moment in my own life because I believe it can show you what misplaced meaning can do to your soul. If we do not struggle to fill that innate feeling with purpose and meaning, we can become a very dangerous spirit.

The Reflecting Poole

During the past year I've discovered a part of my story that is the most difficult for me to tell. The telling is hard because for my entire adult life I have resisted and denied the fact that the personality disorder called narcissism is a part of who I am.

Gazing into the aqua green eyes
I've seen in a mirror, I looked
in and saw within my friend
a reservoir of hope. The
murky depths once clouded by the
shadows of unidentified sinking
objects are surrendering to the sunlight.
The silt is settling and the surface is
calm like a glassy lake at sunrise.
And yet there is activity beneath
seeking order, drifting free,
keeping stress at bay.
I never knew the Administrator Poole
but the Reflecting Poole I'm
getting to know is an oasis
for the soul.

Greg Asimakoupoulos

I dislike the word narcissism. I dislike the definition of the word, and I dislike all the inferences made about the word. However, I have concluded that these three difficulties I have with narcissism are the very reason I now <u>need</u> to address it head-on.

The poem above by Greg Asimakoupoulos describes what he saw as a positive shift in Ed Poole. He was suggesting that he had gazed into my aqua green eyes and had seen a Reflecting Poole, someone who had become an oasis for the soul. Greg was telling me that he felt I was gaining the ability to look back on my life and gain greater understanding from this reflecting. Greg did not know, nor did I at the time, that there is another meaning to finding a Reflecting Pool<u>e</u>.

In Greek mythology, Narcissus looked upon his reflection in the water and fell in love with what he saw reflected back to him. Narcissus was not in love with <u>himself</u>. He was in love with his <u>reflection</u>. Some of the time as I stood in front of my full-length mirror, I was trying to understand myself better; however, I was also admiring what I saw reflected back to me. There is a difference between true self and the self I saw reflected in the mirror.

Narcissism is officially defined by the Diagnostic and Statistical Manual of Mental Disorders IV (American Psychiatric Association, 1994): "The essential feature of NPD (Narcissistic Personality Disorder) is an aversive pattern of grandiosity, need for admiration, and lack of empathy that begins by early childhood and is present in a variety of contexts." Very little research surrounds NPD. What has been done, however, convinces me that personality disorders are a combination of both genetics and the environment.

Being able to love ourselves is a very healthy quality. However, loving only what we see reflected back in a mirror has two drawbacks: (1) We must have a reflection available to us in order to produce the emotion of self-love. If there is no reflection, there is no self-love. This concept was difficult for me to grasp because I fell in love with my reflection and not myself. Seeing my reflection is a first step toward loving myself. If, however, I love the reflection I see I cannot love myself. (2) We have only the compass in our hands, not in our heart, by which to judge whether or not the reflection is authentic. Therefore, we rely on others to validate its authenticity. When I carry my compass in my heart I have done the needed inside-out work to know myself and not come to those insights about myself through the thinking of others.

Nathaniel Branden, a Los Angeles psychologist, draws a sharp distinction between self-esteem and narcissism. Branden defines self-esteem as "the ability to experience oneself as being competent to cope with the basic challenges of life and of being worthy of happiness." He then contrasts this healthy quality to narcissism, "one of the forms that wounded self-esteem takes. It becomes a compensatory device to overcome self-doubt."

We all look around us for positive clues to reinforce our behavior patterns. However, the narcissist needs these positive clues much more frequently and in greater quantity than a more confident person. The narcissist lives his entire life based on receiving positive feedback from those around him. He lives on the outside, not on the inside.

As we grow, we fear the loss of our identity and our uniqueness. This wish to be distinct and special is universal. These needs are healthy. The difference between these healthy needs and those of a narcissist is one of degree rather than kind. We all need to be recognized and affirmed for what we do and how we live our lives. The narcissist, in love with his reflection, needs this recognition and affirmation beyond any adult expectation. The narcissist lives for external validation. His boundaries are defined from the outside.

At one time we have all been narcissists because this developmental stage leads to the final stage of emotional maturity. We all held fast to the delusion that the "world revolved around me." As we matured, we learned very quickly that we are part of a larger whole called society. We abandoned our "me" orientation and embraced an "us" view of the world. In my case, this transition is happening very late in life. I did not mature emotionally as I grew physically; therefore, I experienced an arrested state of emotional development.

Certain characteristics of narcissism distinguish this personality disorder from others. The narcissist becomes easily bored. He changes workplaces, interests, and friends with lightning speed. The narcissist denies those around him their autonomy, their self-fulfillment, and their path to self-recognition and contentment. Narcissists cannot postpone satisfaction. They are creatures of the here and now. The narcissist is a con artist and substitutes fiction for truth, and he keeps secrets. The narcissist possesses a low self-esteem and will rush away from a situation where there is any possibility that he will be rejected or feel abandoned. Often the narcissist felt abandoned as a child, and this feeling is so strong it gets imbedded in his very psyche.

Feeling parental rejection can lead to this strong need for approval. My parents were absent a lot, both physically and emotionally, and I interpreted that absence as rejection. Such early experiences predispose an individual to becoming extremely sensitive to criticism and disapproval, and I have wanted to be a "people pleaser" much of my life. I do not take criticism well.

Narcissism is the epitome of the old Broadway joke of an actor, who, after talking incessantly about himself, asks his friend, "Well enough about me; how did you like my performance?"

I talked with my therapist J.R. about narcissism. In the past, J.R. has suggested to me that I have an "addictive personality," and he is correct. I have always needed to know how others "like my performance." In working with his patients or with the social work graduate students he teaches, J.R. prefers using "softer" words rather than narcissism – words like vanity, lack of humility, egocentrism, and feelings of grandiosity. He feels I exhibit "features" of narcissism. At one point J.R. laughed and suggested I was behaving like an undergraduate who hears in class all these characteristics of various disorders and immediately exclaims, "That's me. No, <u>that's</u> me. No, this time <u>that</u> is <u>really</u> me." Remember what I said earlier about identifying with some of the characters we see in a play? As I look at the contributing characteristics of any personality disorder, I can likely find some of myself therein.

Vanity is a helpful word in understanding my behavior. I have always identified with the words in the Carly Simon song: "You're so vain. I bet you think this song is about you." Over the years I have surely thought many songs were about me, especially if the song contained a message of grandiosity or superiority. Not only were the songs about me, everything was about Ed Poole. When I would have a conversation with someone I was like the Broadway actor – whatever the topic of conversation, I always directed it toward my own accomplishments. I used to think my jobs gave me superiority over others that went beyond job title and reporting relationships. I could not be a good listener because I wanted to talk about me. I could not let my good deeds unfold for others to see. I had to make certain others knew of my good works and I wanted their praise for all the successes I had. Sometimes I wonder why anyone put up with my self-centeredness and with me. I was simply the best in all that I did – that is until I became superintendent. That was one time I felt like such a failure and so incompetent. That experience was humbling for me.

Vanity is a signal, a message telling us something is out of balance in our lives. We are not balanced when we believe we are the universe instead of just a part of it, and we are also not balanced in the other direction when we always put the needs of the collective society ahead of the needs of the individual.

I can take four steps to diminish my vanity. I need to learn to become an active listener. For much of my life, I have considered my opinions superior to those of others. I need to consider the validity of others' opinions, and the best way to do this is to listen, truly listen, to what they have to say.

Secondly, I need to act on the feedback I receive from others. The feedback will do me no good if I have no desire to change my behavior for the better. However, making a change in my behavior is hard because doing so acknowledges that I am imperfect and I may be at fault. As I have listened to what others have shared with me over the years – information about me that was intended to help – I have dismissed much of it because I saw no need to change my behavior. My wife, my children, and my therapists have all wanted to help but for so long I wouldn't let them. Over the years I knew they were right in their observations about me. I was too stubborn to admit this to them or to myself. I have received feedback intended to improve my marriage. I ignored much of this feedback. I was afraid to acknowledge the suggestions because doing so would have put me in closer touch with myself. Until recently I only wanted to know Ed Poole at a very superficial level.

I can especially get help by reaching back to those I have left along the trail of unhealthy relationships – whether family, friends, or coworkers. Some of those along the trail may be happy to help if asked. I have abandoned friends and colleagues when they really needed me. I have been unable to see the other person in my relationships because I focused on myself.

Finally, I need to value and respect others in the same way they value and respect themselves. As I can see the value in others, I can begin to see past my own needs, wants, and desires.

Often it takes an all-pervasive, all-encompassing life crisis to bring some of these characteristics to the surface. My entering the hospital for clinical depression allowed me to realize I have a problem with some of the features of narcissism. Once again the hospitalization was a gift.

Knowing and reading about this personality disorder will not help me heal. Knowing is not feeling, and there will be little healing without the feelings that go with recovery. I have to learn to like and love myself – not the <u>reflection</u> of myself. I need to continue to gain self-confidence and enhance my self-esteem. I want to continue learning those social skills that will help me be more successful in relationships. These are learnable skills.

Stopping at the "narcissistic station" on my journey has been difficult and painful for me; however, I needed to stop at this station to acknowledge the existence of this disorder, for only then can I move toward healing. My parents were emotionally absent from me in my early, formative years. They did not know how to be emotionally present and how to acknowledge my emotions positively. I was reinforced with what <u>not</u> to do because I was always "going straight to hell" as I committed my sins. I was not praised and reinforced at those times when my behavior was deemed appropriate.

I was unable to feel my parents' goodwill as I grew. Without this reinforcement I escaped into a world of my own to reduce the pain. Many of those trips, as you know, were visits to my shadow side.

My parents needed to fulfill both my physical and emotional needs. In addition to providing food, shelter, clothing, protection from extremes in temperature, they needed to affirm my value to them and to my entire family. Attention was as important to me as food and oxygen. I needed to know I existed was valued and loved.

You know by now that I was unable to have my emotional needs met by my parents. Heinz Kohut, author of *The Analysis of the Self*, has said "the crucial question is whether the parents are able to reflect with approval at least some of the child's proudly exhibited attributes and functions, whether they are able to respond with genuine enjoyment to his budding skills, whether they are able to remain in touch with him throughout his trials and errors."

Narcissism has been a recent topic of conversation for my wife and me. During one of these conversations Bonnie suggested, "Ed, what if you assumed that every single person in the whole world had this same personality disorder, and you wanted to try to find ways to help them. What could you do?" I did not understand what she was saying, so I asked her to repeat it, which she did.

I sat there for a moment and then said, "I'm still not understanding what you're saying. Could you use different words?" Bonnie was just beginning to comment again, using different words, when we looked at each other and at the very same moment broke out in one of those loud, healthy, cleansing belly laughs. The reason I didn't "get" what Bonnie was suggesting was because as soon as she said it the first time I was immediately wondering, "Okay, if I'm going to help everyone else in the world, what do I get out of this?" We realized this at the same moment and also knew that Bonnie's point had been well made. She was trying to help me get outside of myself and my "what's in it for me" thinking and reach out to others. I was filtering her comments through my natural lens of "Surely this is all about me, and why would I <u>ever</u> want to do something when there was no direct benefit to me."

As I write this, I am convinced more than ever that my time in front of the cave with my wise old friend was the first experience I had with standing in front of the full-length mirror and being introspective. I was hurting, but I was not sure why. I had some ideas about my pain, but I didn't fully realize that my heart and my head were beginning to have a conversation – for the first time in my life. Turning around and facing my personality disorder – the Reflecting Pool<u>e</u> – is critical to self-awareness and self-acceptance

Now I'd like to continue with those four lessons and to share some thoughts with you back on the porch, rather than in front of the cave.

The lessons in this chapter require us to be patient, to be still, and to wait. This is the time on our journey when we do sit in silence and <u>not</u> feel the deafening clamor of that silence. We are purposefully waiting. And we do this waiting many times throughout our lives. We do not have one <u>major</u> wait time in our lives and then we no longer have to wait. We find ourselves waiting and waiting at many points along our journey.

Lessons We Learn as We Wait

Finding the connections in our lives requires waiting with patience. Patience in our Western culture is a problem for many of us. We don't like to wait. Immediate gratification is what we're after. A friend of mine said to me, "Ed, you can't be anyplace other than where you are right now." Waiting has a sense of expectancy about it. Have you ever thought of waiting as a way of doing, as a proactive process? Sometimes it's a victory just to make it through the day. Sometimes it takes all the courage we can muster just to put in the time. Sometimes it's like the boxer who has just taken a series of heavy blows, and all he can do is hope he can hold on until the end of the round. There's no glory in hanging on; there's no dignity; we just do it, and we do it because that's the only way we're going to survive.

The Irish survived by learning to wait. The Irish prepared for an enemy attack by building seventy-five foot stone towers. They put food and water in the towers and ropes hung down from each tower. When they saw the enemy coming, they climbed up into the towers, pulled up the ropes, and closed the doors. They just waited for the enemy to go away. To believe that waiting is a kind of doing is a gift. I will tell you at the outset that I am a terrible waiter. I'd like to share with you some thoughts about waiting and explain why I haven't been a good waiter for much of my life.

How good are we, really, at waiting? Because it was so close to dinnertime, Johnny's mother told him that he was not allowed to eat his favorite snack – a Little Debbie oatmeal pie. And this didn't sit quite well with the four year old, so he threw one of those classic four-year-old fits. He slammed the door; he threw his toys around the room; he used the words, "You never let me!" – acting much like a man who loses his channel changer – completely out of control. Johnny's mother was quite wise, and she knew this too would pass, that it was a stage. And if she simply let Johnny act it out, in a few moments the tantrum would be over; it would run its course; he would forget about the Little Debbie oatmeal pie; and all would be well. Sure enough, after the rampage, Johnny ran into the closet and slammed the door. And for a few moments there was some noise coming from the closet, but after a while, there was no noise whatsoever. And the mother knew what most of us know. When a four year old is quiet, something is happening that is not very productive. So she decided to reason with Johnny.

"Johnny, are you in there?"

"Yes," came back the reply.

"Johnny, what are you doing?" And there was silence. "Johnny, what are you doing?" And there was silence again. So the wise mother used that parenting technique that has been used for ages: she used his full name when calling him. "Jonathan Reese Martin, what are you doing?"

And as usual, the approach worked. "Mommy, I have spit on your shoes; I have spit on your dresses, and I am sitting here waiting for more spit."

Waiting. Everything we do in life between the beginning and the ending puts us in seasons when we're not there yet and these seasons force us to wait. Waiting is not a passive action; waiting is a kind of doing. I'd like to suggest that, second only to suffering, waiting is the greatest teacher of maturity and spirituality that any of us will ever encounter in life. Waiting helps us learn who we are, if we can value the place we are, and if we can avoid trying to rush to someplace else. The problem is: our society is inflicted with this dehumanizing characteristic known as "instantitus." Whatever it is we want, we want it now. I thought I could know about me immediately, without doing the work of waiting and listening. But I was wrong.

Society values people who take charge of their lives, who don't wait for life to come to them. We have no applause for those who wait; the awards are for those who have arrived. When was the last time you received recognition for not being there yet? In *Report to Greco*, Nikos Kazantzakis describes an experience he had when quite young. He remembered detaching a chrysalis from the trunk of an olive tree. Within the transparent coating, he saw something moving – there was life inside the coating. Because he couldn't wait for the natural unfolding of this process, he blew his warm breath onto the chrysalis. As he kept blowing, a slit occurred which turned into an opening large enough to allow the butterfly to emerge. He noted with detail how each wing sprang forth from its attachment to the butterfly's body. But, eventually the creature grew stiff and died. "I felt sick at heart. Because of my hurry, because I had dared to transgress an eternal law, I had killed the butterfly. In my hand I held a carcass. Years and years have passed, but that butterfly's weightless carcass has weighed heavily on my conscience ever since." As I read this story of the butterfly, I realized it is contrary to where life is really lived because ninety-nine percent of our time is spent not being there yet. We're always on the way as well as always waiting to get there. On our journey from beginning to ending we both act and wait. We have to learn when to act and when to wait.

I'd like to suggest three statements to you. If we can remember these while we're waiting, the "not there yet" time can become a powerful experience.

First of all, do not allow what we are waiting for to block the experience of what we are waiting with – being aware of all that is going on around us, including the messages and gifts that come to us. After C.S. Lewis's friend Joy died, he wrote this beautiful little book titled *The Grief Observed*. The book was actually a journal of the grief process Lewis felt after the death of his dear Joy. The beginning of the book talks only about how disillusioned C.S. Lewis was with a God who did nothing to relieve his pain. And he said, "God did nothing at all. This God that I serve, I want nothing to do with." At the end of the book, Lewis's view changes, and he says, "God did a magnificent thing for me in my grief." So what happened? How did his view change? Lewis said that as he waited for healing, he had already decided what he needed to be healed. And that's what he was waiting for. He says that his expectation caused him to miss what God was actually doing in his life – the phone calls, the cards, the hugs, the food from people around him. And he says that what he discovered as he was going through this was that God was alive and well and working each and every second in his life to give him courage and strength to wait. It was in the ordinary events of life that the extraordinary emerged. The small things in life, as we wait, give us the strength and courage to wait for what is ahead.

During my job as superintendent, I didn't see all of the growth and joy around me. Surely, as I look back on that time, God was working in me and with me. For the first time in my life God introduced me to my inner guide, someone with whom I had carefully avoided having a relationship. The gifts were all there; I just didn't see them.

I must admit to having similar thoughts about the gifts that surround us this past week after the terrorists attacked the World Trade Center and the Pentagon and crashed a fourth plane in Pennsylvania. How could God allow this disaster to occur? That question is unanswerable. However, as our country and the world wait for what is ahead, our news programs and newspapers have been full of stories of heroism, of caring and love expressed by an entire country and much of the world: the blood drives, the monetary donations, the outpouring of volunteers, the prayers sent to families and friends of the victims – people most of us do not even know. Funds have been established and are filling up with dollars to aid the volunteers in New York and Washington and to provide financial relief for the families of the firemen and policemen in New York who lost their lives trying to save others.

In the midst of waiting to see how our country reacts and what it does in an effort to see justice in the world, we see miracles occurring all around us. As a country, we have become more civil toward each other. I see so many American flags flying on cars and trucks. I see indications of a country uniting to deal with this tragedy. It's these small signs that allow us to wait for the time ahead. Right now it's time to be still and receive the strength from our past, our present, and our dreams, unshattered yet altered. One of the greatest tragedies in life is to allow what it is we're waiting for to blind us from what it is we are waiting with.

The relationship between waiting and doing is confusing. I want to distinguish between doing as a part of waiting and doing as a step toward the goal. I can best illustrate this by sharing a quote my mother-in-law often used as she practiced her commitment to Christian Science: "I am the place that God shines through. He and I are one, not two. He wants me where and as I am. I need not fret, nor will, nor plan. If I'll but be relaxed and free, He'll carry out His plan through me." When Betty Jane first shared these thoughts with me my reaction was: "Does God expect me to just sit around all day, waiting for some big sign? If I'm not willing or planning, what am I doing?" Her statement seemed so passive to me. Now I see Betty Jane's thoughts in a much different light. I believe I have to "let go and let God" by making some decisions in my life (doing) and then turning those decisions over to Him, (waiting) for His feedback on those decisions. While waiting I have to be very active – listening and looking around me for the little signs of His reactions to my prayers – like C.S. Lewis did in understanding the death of Joy and like I did in trying to understand September 11th.

It is also possible that a native Arctic bird discovered that what it was waiting with became very important. Some Arctic explorers wanted to bring home a few native Arctic birds. The explorers and their captured birds were on a large ship in the middle of the sea, and at one point on the trip one of these birds escaped its cage and in ecstasy flew out over the ocean in search of land. The crew was certain that exotic bird would die. The next morning as the crew was standing on deck, they saw this speck on the horizon. As they watched this speck, it came closer and closer to the ship until they realized it was the exotic, missing bird that had escaped the day before. That small, feathered prodigal dropped exhausted onto the deck, and that ship which had felt like a prison the day before now became a place of refuge. Do not allow what it is we're waiting for to keep us from experiencing what it is we're waiting with.

One of our great twentieth-century American novelists learned the lesson of what he waited with as he waited for healing following surgery. During the First World War, an Italian army surgeon, with only a scalpel and a simple pair of tweezers, took out, in a four-hour surgery, 237 pieces of shrapnel from the leg of soldier 0134, a very delicate operation. After the four hours, the operation was deemed a success, at least from the surgeon's standpoint. Unfortunately, the young soldier was faced with months and months of a grueling, painful experience as he learned to walk again. As he waited the soldier created a framework that he would follow whenever he wrote a novel: in every one of his novels, he would have a good person face an enormous obstacle.

When this happened, the reader would see what this person was really made of. The obstacle would not break him, it would not bend him; instead it would define him. Clearly the formula worked. Some years later, *For Whom the Bell Tolls* was printed, and then *The Old Man and the Sea* was published. Soldier 0134 was Ernest Hemingway. In a BBC interview, this boisterous, flamboyant, spontaneous, crude human being explained, while sitting on his porch in Key West, Florida, what he had learned from his life and what theme he held up every day. His answer: "What I learned goes all the way back to those days of rehabilitation. I learned that in order to be healed, I had to become part of the process. I had to become involved and be active in bringing about my goal."

That's pretty simple until you take a look at the books of Ernest Hemingway. In *The Old Man and the Sea*, Santiago endures eighty-four days without catching a fish. And all the young fishermen laugh at him, believing "the old codger doesn't know how to fish anymore." Each and every morning Santiago takes out that salty old skiff, goes out onto the ocean, and follows all the sea birds and flying fish, hoping eventually he will come upon that prize. Eighty-four days and no fish, but each and every day he becomes involved; he goes out in search of the prize. Santiago's goal was to catch fish. Waiting to accomplish his goal meant Santiago had to go out onto the ocean every day – he was active as he waited.

While waiting, we also need to remember a second lesson: we should view the period between beginnings and endings not as a "weight" but as a "wait." There is a difference. Webster says that "weight" is a burden that lies upon something. But if you take the word "wait" and break it down, it means "way to it." It is moving forward; it's active. We are moving until it comes. Waiting, then, is a kind of doing because you know it's eventually going to end. It is a part of life.

The third lesson relates to the period of time right before my stay in the hospital. In most cases A-type, success-oriented personalities, when becoming depressed over our lives, others' lives, or even structures around us, avoid the diagnosis of clinical depression by working even more. We turn the depression not into silence but into even more of that which is sucking the life out of us. And that is what I had done for many years. I kept striving for success after success. The stress and anxiety I felt was my "silent" depression that had been there for some time. It was only falling and being caught in the safety net of a loving family and caring medical professionals that I was able to bring the depression out into the light and recognize it for what it was.

The journey into and out of the hospital was a very difficult time for me. So, about three weeks after my release from the hospital, I went to Northern California to visit my son Eric and my daughter-in-law Stacy. At the time, I didn't know exactly why I wanted to make this trip. The true understanding has come much later. I knew I missed Eric and Stacy, and I felt I could get somewhat grounded if I spent some time with them. They have the ability to do that for me. I love Northern California, especially the Bay Area. The trip was not only a family reunion but also a spiritual journey for me. I was relaxed; I was in reverent awe of the beauty of that part of the country; I laughed; and I played. That trip allowed me to realize that one of the most wonderful and powerful gifts we can give ourselves while we are waiting is to renew our connections with family, friends, and our Higher Power. Once these connections are broken, we're lost for life.

With this thought in mind, I would again like to revisit with you the terrorist attacks on our East Coast this past week. There will be a period of time between my writing this and your reading; however, I imagine most of you remember where you were and what you were doing as the events of September 11 unfolded. For those of you who are old enough to remember where you were the day John F. Kennedy was assassinated, I'm sure this recent attack on our country will also be remembered along with November 22, 1963.

I hope you can remember the passionate desire we all had, immediately after the 9-11 tragedies, to visit and communicate with our families and our Higher Power – reconnecting to seek comfort and to try to gain understanding. Religious leaders throughout the country marveled at the high attendance figures they experienced on the first day of worship after that attack. People needed to reconnect with their Higher Power and their places of worship were where that reconnection occurred. We are waiting; however, this time we are also "weighting." At this point in our country's and the world's journey, we do not know the outcome of our next steps, so we must wait with patience, realizing that a tremendous amount of activity is occurring. This time, as we wait, the world feels the "weight" of our decisions.

As we wait to know some of the outcomes of 9-11, the fear is that our country will revert to its old ways – being less civil toward each other, less willing to give of self, and less concerned about the problems being felt by our neighbors. I know we just have to wait to see if, over time, the feelings, attitudes, and behaviors shared immediately after 9-11 will continue. I hope they do.

Music has always comforted me as I wait. I have several favorite albums of inspirational music. I found myself returning again and again to this music, as I have been silent, waiting to see how our country and the world respond to the tragedy of September 11th. If you have concluded by this time that I like music, you're right! I have loved music from the time I listened to Mom and Dad singing in the church choir and from my own experiences in high school and college choirs. I have since been in some church choirs myself and have dabbled in barbershop quartet singing. When I was growing up, I learned to play the trumpet.

Listening for the Silence

An ancient Maasai saying suggests, "Life cannot be hurried." Fredrick Nietzsche has said, "One must have chaos in one's self in order to give birth to a dancing star." That chaos Nietzsche described involves the inner work of the soul, being still as we wait to see the dancing star.

We need to practice sitting in the stillness – aware of only the present moment – to notice what is happening in us right here, right now, both inside and outside of us. As we walk and eat and travel, we need to be where we are; otherwise, we'll miss most of our lives. We need to overcome the habit of filling our entire lives, inner and outer, with busyness. The first step is one of self-emptying, of letting go preoccupations with the future. We need also to let go of whatever happened in the past that we are still harboring with either resentment or nostalgia.

Remembering is one thing, but harboring is entirely different. When we harbor within us a thought or feeling, we are allowing negative feelings to grow. As we sit still and breathe freely, with each inhalation and exhalation, we feel our mind clearing and our body melting into relaxation. Hearing the left-over chatter of our inner world, we allow the sounds to float into the distance until they become fainter and fainter. Feeling our mind clear and our body relax as they float on the breath and the breath floats on them, we let go of the past; we let go of the future; and there is only now.

In the silence, we hear a sound emanating from deep within us; it is the voice of our soul, calling us to live courageously, to let go of the pride connected with our activities. A word, a phrase, comes to us speaking of this inner freedom and joy. We repeat it softly under our breath – the words carrying the breath and the breath carrying the words – in perfect rhythm. As we sense we are better for having taken this time to be in the here and now, we learn to appreciate being still and standing quietly in front of the full-length mirror of our lives. The best place for me to hear my soul's voice is by the ocean.

When I walk along the beach, with the water barely over my feet, I am most at peace with my inner and outer worlds, able to be in the present moment. I'm not sure what it is about the beach and the ocean, but I have always been able to reflect when I walk the beach, looking for shells, watching the waves come crashing onto the shore. Every time I'm in a group and the facilitator asks me to imagine myself in a quiet, reflective place, I always put myself on the beach. I love being by the ocean and being in the present.

Annie Dillard, our great American essayist, went to the wilderness area of Virginia to listen to her soul and to find herself. She was a journalist with *Harper's Magazine* in New York. But she was burned out, she was tired of everything; and she needed to get away. She went to Hollins College nestled under the edge of the Blue Ridge Mountains, and there she stayed on a farm for a year. A creek ran through that farm, and foothills and mountains surrounded it. For an entire year Annie studied that creek. She observed the birds and the wildlife. She walked in its fields. She kept a diary, and her diary became *Pilgrim at Tinker Creek*, which won a Pulitzer Prize. Said Annie, "I finally experienced the present fully. I caught the grace of God in a cup of water that was being filled."

As I sit quietly on the porch, listening in the silence, I try to know that time is all I have. In the silence of the full-length mirror, I may want to dance, to grieve, to remember, to regret, to forgive, or to forget. The silence, as I said earlier, can be deafening. All sorts of thoughts and feelings run through me. I sometimes want others to do the work for me. I ask my Higher Power to do this or that; I share my wants, but ultimately I must choose from among the doors that are opening for me. Porch-sitting is in many ways connecting with the natural world – being aware of the sights, sounds, smells, tastes, and touches that put me squarely in the now and allow me to wonder peacefully. My connection to the natural world is the ocean and the beach. I carry my porch with me when I go there.

As I sit in peace on the porch and wonder, I think of what it means to be mindful of the present. Wonderful thoughts about "continual mindfulness" are found in the book by Jon Kabat-Zinn *Wherever You Go, There You Are*: "I came to the conclusion then that 'continual mindfulness' must mean, not a sergeant-major drilling of thoughts, but a continual readiness to look and readiness to accept whatever came...We only struggle when we have moved our sights from the present moment. Within the now lies all peace." Our mind can change our sense of reality. In *Calling the Circle*, Christina Baldwin said, "Consciousness is the tool of our liberation. What a miracle: you and I, bumbling through our personal issues, our pain and recovery, have discovered the tool of our liberation."

Accepting where we are at any moment, standing still for that moment, and looking into the full-length mirror of our lives are all essential events in our journey toward wholeness. But doing so is very hard for me. As I have become accustomed to instant answers, it is difficult to accept delayed gratification, even though I know I must.

I have not spent much time sitting in the silence of the porch and facing my problems. I have taken the sun for granted most of my life but I am beginning to realize that there is no running away from anything. I was on the Outer Banks off the coast of North Carolina for a vacation one summer. My wife and I were there with our son and daughter and their spouses, along with twenty members of my daughter-in-law's family. One morning we were watching an amazingly beautiful sunrise over the ocean. The sun was going in and out of the clouds, and behind the clouds the sky was a bright orange. One of our fellow vacationers suggested, very simply, "Just like in our lives, sometimes the sun has to fight through the clouds as it's rising." I have learned that sometimes I have to fight through the clouds in life – by turning and facing myself in the full-length mirror – to find that sun toward which I've so often navigated.

No matter how many jobs I took or what I tried to do in my private life to see change, the pain, uncertainty, and fear found me. I didn't realize that I carried my head and my heart around with me. It was <u>me</u> I couldn't escape from, no matter how hard I tried. I didn't know I could be home wherever I was, that my porch was portable and could be left and returned to at any time. My porch, wherever it is at any given time, has become the place for standing still, for doing the inner work, and for looking into the full-length mirror. However, I had to realize I could return to my porch; I could seek the comfort of the known in order to try to understand the unknown.

Not a Point of View, But a Viewing Point

As I return to my porch and its stillness, I am beginning to distinguish between a "point of view" and a "viewing point," a phrase I've used at various times in earlier chapters. Some of my best viewing points are on that edge of the porch Mom cautioned me about while I was growing up. The differences are more than a subtle shifting around of the words – point of view and viewing point.

Having a point of view about something does not provide me the flexibility I need, as discussed in Chapter 3, to chart my course, my journey. It connotes rigidity, a clinching of my teeth, and a desire to be understood before I try to understand others. There is no stillness for me in a point of view. I am doggedly trying to convince you that my thinking is right. I am certain I still do not fully understand all the differences, but I will share with you what I believe at this time.

Honoring viewing points allows me to assume and exhibit that flexibility I have found I need to bring meaning to my life. A viewing point helps me deal with and understand ambiguity. I can better live with the questions of a viewing point and can stay longer in the rushing whitewater of confusion because out of that confusion will come a guided decision as to which door I should next open as I get off the porch. A viewing point helps me to create a healthy detachment from my thinking and to get away from the consumed ownership of this thinking. If I can just "get up above" my viewpoint and metaphorically look down upon it, I can become detached and therefore open to others and to my Higher Power.

In order to get up above a point of view and create a viewing point, I have often engaged graduate students and other colleagues in the "helicopter exercise." I ask them to imagine they are in a magic helicopter, flying above their school, the building in which they work, their place of worship, or their home. This magic helicopter allows the participants to remove the roof of that building and look down upon the activity going on there. Based on the topic of current discussion (empowerment, teaming, change, religious beliefs, family life, etc.), I then ask them to talk about what they would like to see as they look down from their magic helicopter. Riding in this helicopter somehow frees up those responding to dream, to dare, and to consider the possibilities. Gaining a viewing point from the porch, as I stand in the stillness and the quiet, allows me to feel this same sense of freedom to be and to become.

A viewing point from the porch allows me to foster a wide lens of observing, rather than a more myopic lens of protecting and challenging. I am able to "see" something after I "believe" it. Viewing points allow me to internalize better what I'm observing and to truly believe in what I'm viewing and therefore to "see" it. A point of view for me has always resulted in a very narrow approach to possibilities. I often thought when others approached me, "My mind is already made up; don't confuse me with the facts." Up above the porch, removing the roof and looking down, gives me a much wider view of the possibilities.

Because I am at a viewing point, I can anticipate more. I'm scouting for options, rather than protecting a current situation or position. If you remember a part of your American history course in high school or college, you'll recall that the scouts were the very first to venture off the porch. They had to find and make the trails for the others. The scouts were the first to experience change. They were followed by the trailblazers, then the pioneers, and finally the settlers – those who were least willing to risk and wanted to make sure everything was safe out there before they headed west. In today's environment, it is the settlers, not the scouts, who are <u>most</u> at risk because changes are happening so rapidly in our world. The settlers are not only going to be left behind, but they will never catch up and their world will become unknown to them.

I have been a settler in my life. Often I have not taken risks because I was fearful of leaving the porch. If I got too close to the edge, I would move back and lose my viewing point. If I took a risk by moving to a new job I often fled from what my risk-taking provided me. My time on the porch helps me to scout for options in my life and to understand why I am looking for those options. I could not have become a scout if I had not begun the inner work of finding my soul and my spirit time of life.

There is a portion of the movie *Dead Poets' Society* that provides a wonderful example of viewing points. Robin Williams is a teacher who returns to the preparatory school from which he graduated to begin his teaching career. At one point in the movie, Williams is in front of the class, standing on top of his desk.

"Why do I stand up here?"

"To feel taller."

"No, Ding!!! Thank you for playing, Mr. Dalton. I stand up on my desk to remind myself that we must constantly look at things in a different way. You see the world looks very different from up here. You don't believe me? Come see for yourselves. Just when you think you know something, you have to look at it in another way. Even though it may seem silly, or wrong, you must try." Robin Williams was talking about viewing points. Marcel Proust used different words to express the same idea when he wrote, "The real voyage of discovery consists not in seeking new landscapes, but in having new eyes."

Even though the porch is becoming a viewing point for me, I never saw the whole picture of life. I am only now beginning to see that whole as I encourage my soul time of life. It has taken me this long to realize that life is not always greener on the other side and that I needed new eyes at times, not a new journey. Forrest Church, in his book *Holding On (And Letting Go)*, said, "Just where you think that the grass would surely be green, it may be dying…I am no longer startled by this. What startles me still, though it no longer should, is precisely the opposite. Often, just where you'd think that the grass would be dying, it is green." Gaining new eyes has required me to stand still, listen, and wait.

As I have said before, all those times I went off to new jobs, thinking my troubles would disappear with a new start, they didn't. I was seeking new landscapes but seeing with the same eyes – I wasn't able to "see it after I believed it" because without new eyes I never believed it. **R**esting, **R**efreshing, and **R**eflecting – all done in the silence of my porch.

I have talked about "seeing" and "believing." Author Rainer Maria Rilke said it well: "Once the realization is accepted that even between the closest human beings infinite distances continue to exist, a wonderful living side by side can grow up if they succeed in loving the distance between them which makes it possible for each to see the other whole against the sky." Allowing us the grace of seeing others whole against the sky suggests to me that we can better see the wholeness of ourselves and others when our seeing follows our believing. We have to be at a point in our lives where we're ready to see something.

Richard Bode, in his book *Beachcombing at Miramar*, described this readiness when he said, "After all these reflective days combing the sands of Miramar, I understand that we see only what we are ready to see when we are ready to see it. There is a perpetual dawn rising within us. If we are awake to it, it continues to rise gradually, imperceptibly, throughout our lives. With each passing day we shake the sleep from our eyes." Another way to reflect Bode's thoughts is once again to remind myself that I "see" something only after I "believe" it.

As I pitch my tent on the porch and wait in the stillness, what am I listening for? What can I learn? One conclusion I've reached is that, for me, taking that leap into the future off the porch is taken on the faith that I will be caught. The safety net for me – in getting off the porch, knowing when to return, charting my course, and putting the wind in the sails of life – may not have been either the people in my life or my work. The net wasn't anything my parents either said or didn't say. The safety net for me all along has been the thinking and reflecting I put off but am finally beginning. I had to begin this journey to realize that my safety net has always been there.

Taking a Fall and Getting Grounded

The safety net has been the reading, discussing, and writing I've been doing while waiting quietly on the porch and gaining greater understanding from some of the inner work I've been doing. This net has always been there for me. Earlier I suggested that I have always put off writing because I felt there was something else I needed to read and reflect upon – some words and thoughts from someone else. I now know that a part of the hesitancy was because the reading and reflecting provided my safety net until I felt confident enough to write.

The inner work that has resulted from the active part of waiting is helping me understand what I want to do, and understanding this is part of what safety nets are all about. My family members who have preceded me have given me their blessing to continue this journey, which I am seeing from the viewing point of their shoulders. They are now providing the safety net I could not find while they were alive.

The hospital provided a safety net for me. The time I spent in the hospital because of my depression was a "bottoming out" period in my life. The net was there to catch me. During this time it was painful for me to get off the porch. For me it represented a "fall" from the porch, but this time, when I hit the ground, I began the process of getting grounded – the safety nets were in place. There is another of those ing words I like so much. I will always be getting grounded; I will never get grounded – a journey, a process, not a destination at which I must arrive.

I would like to share with you a piece of Saul's story, found in the Old Testament of the Bible, because it provides an example of what can happen when we hit the ground but don't get grounded. Sometimes we can learn about ourselves by watching the pattern of another's brokenness, of another's fall from the porch to the ground. However, in this instance, Saul did not get grounded; ultimately his spirit was destroyed. I tell the story because it represents some of my journey of moving toward getting grounded in life.

When Saul hit the ground, a deep feeling of despair settled over his spirit. Three issues contributed to Saul's feeling of despair. Despair settled in over Saul partly out of his unrealistic expectations. Saul dreamed too idealistically and didn't recognize the slow pace at times with which change occurs.

Secondly, despair settled in over Saul because of the lack of support he received from others. The imbalance of criticism over counsel took its toll. Saul was not given the emotional support from the very people who initiated the process in the beginning. Much of what Saul received was criticism and abandonment because the people of Israel lacked the heart to help. It is no wonder that the young Saul was demoralized.

These first two descriptions of Saul's despair – unrealistic expectations and criticism – might not have been enough to overcome Saul's spirit. The third factor of despair was the breaking point – it was Saul's own self-image. For some reason, Saul seemed to move through his life clapping only one hand. He was never able to celebrate the gift of love, not because of what he could do, but because of who he was. It was Samuel Miller who said, "Our peace is our place." Saul, like me, was never able to experience such peace because he was never able to accept his gift of place.

I can readily identify with this story of Saul. The same three characteristics of despair that Saul felt are similar to my own experiences. Saul hit the ground, but he didn't get grounded, due to unrealistic expectations, criticism, lack of support, and his image of himself. My expectations were unrealistic in my life primarily because I sought perfection and I wasn't getting grounded; therefore, the expectations of others for me were not my own. I did not know about the inner work I needed to be doing. But, unlike Saul, I felt supported; I was just looking outside myself for my compass. Likewise, until recently, I could never take that long, deep, cleansing breath and realize the gift of place in my life. I didn't know where I was <u>supposed</u> to be, but I knew it wasn't where I was at any given time.

Like Saul, criticism damaged my self-image. We have all experienced criticism in our lives. And, depending on its origin and its delivery, criticism can be healthy for our personal growth. My issue with criticism has been that I wanted everyone to like me. If I thought someone was being critical of what I did, I panicked. What did I do wrong? How can I correct it? Being liked often took precedence over making the right decisions in my life. At times I deferred to the wishes of parents in school-related disciplinary matters concerning their child if that deferment would keep them happy. Even if I knew the decision was not in the best interests of the student I made it anyway.

I've talked about my perceptions of myself, which haven't always been very affirming. For someone who has achieved a goodly amount of success in my life, I have never felt very good about me. I was like the clay that was never centered on the potter's wheel, and I spun off in many different directions.

Like Saul, I felt abandoned as a child – physically and emotionally. My parents had to work a lot and were not home much. Where I part company with Saul is in the areas of getting grounded and having support for my journey. Since I hit the ground with my depression, the support from family and friends has been unbelievably important and critical to my process of getting grounded in who I am and what I am supposed to be doing on this earth. Earlier when I shared those parts of two notes Mom sent me while hospitalized with depression, I felt her support, care, and love for me during this difficult time in my life. I have not expected the changes in me to happen overnight. After all, what took over fifty years to evolve is not magically going to go away. My time on the porch with my "3 R's" – Resting, Refreshing, and Reflecting – has allowed me to begin to get better acquainted with who I am, stripped of all my titles and pretenses. For now, I have been very grateful for this time to stand quietly on my porch and find out some interesting points about me. I am hoping my process of getting grounded can continue; however, part of getting grounded is also trying to let go of outcomes and learn to be me.

Chapter 6: Learning To Be Me

Little did I know that the answer to
changing my life did not lie in
learning how to protect myself from
life. Rather the answer was in
learning how to become strong enough
to let a bit more of life in.

Vern Bittner, ***Letting Life In***

Ed, you need to learn how to be a schmuck, like the rest of us.

J.R

The porch helps me see I'm my own White Knight

What you do on the porch shouts so loudly people can't hear what you say.

I designed some beautiful masks while on the porch.

Ed, you have got to learn and live humility.

This chapter suggests that I am responsible for my own decisions and actions, and that no one is going to rescue me but me. I want to continue to learn how to connect my beliefs with my behavior. And the more I can learn to know and be myself, the easier it will be to understand the lessons in this chapter. I have to tell you though, it's very hard for me, because of my lack of humility, to match my behavior with my beliefs.

Learning to Be A Schmuck Hasn't Been Easy

Throughout my life I have not been good at practicing humility. I was a good representative of the person R. D. Laing described in Knots. I just pretended I knew everything.

There is something I don't know
that I'm supposed to know.
I don't know what it is I don't know,
and yet am supposed to know,
and I feel I look stupid
if I seem both not to know it

and not to know what it is I don't know.
Therefore, I pretend I know it.
This is nerve-wracking since I don't
know what I must pretend to know.
Therefore I pretend I know everything.

R.D. Laing

J.R., one of my therapists over the years recognized this pretense and concluded that I didn't know humility. At first J.R.'s conclusion about my humility stirred a lot of anger within me. How could he say that about me? I've always, after all, cared about other people. Still, J.R. persisted and, in fact, he suggested that I either be a bell ringer for the Salvation Army or collect garbage during a holiday season. The former would have been doable; the latter was pretty drastic, I thought. But, too angry to act, I promptly ignored both suggestions.

However, upon reflecting about what J.R. said and moving past some of my anger, after my hospitalization I volunteered some time with the local Chamber of Commerce in my town. I shared this experience with J.R., feeling very proud of myself for doing what he had suggested. I didn't follow either of the two requests J.R. made for my volunteering, but at least I had entered the world of the volunteer community. J.R. laughed. Explaining his laughter, he said, "Ed, even when you volunteer, you go right to the top of the organization." I felt like I couldn't win. He then said, "You won't learn to be a schmuck like the rest of us by volunteering at the Chamber of Commerce." I understand better now what he meant, but I didn't at the time. My humility was a big issue for J.R. at that time, and not for me. Now my own sense of being humble has become an issue for me. Coming to that conclusion is the result of my time on the porch for Resting, Refreshing, and Reflecting.

Life Seems Easy When We Take the Sun for Granted

I have always had positive experiences and opportunities come to me rather easily in my life. Unwilling to recognize and face my issues and problems, I expected life to be easy, comfortable, and to treat me favorably. With these feelings and behaviors, I expected life would bring me success and recognition. Mom was convinced until the day she died that my grandma Jolly (Mom's mother) "spoiled me rotten." Of course, each time she said that, I vehemently denied it – but always with a smile on my face. In reality Grandma did spoil me, and I loved every minute of it. Mom and Dad didn't spoil me directly; however, I grew up my mother's son by usually getting my own way. I got my own way by controlling others by what I said and what I did. If that doesn't facilitate an oversized ego, I don't know what would.

My high school years expanded my ego and diminished my humility. I achieved success academically and socially. Out of a class of 462 I was in the top ten in both academics and popularity. I had the "right" friends and faculty and students knew me. I reveled in all this popularity and attention. I became a legend in my own mind. One of the main reasons for my academic success was because I always chose easier rather than harder courses. I made many of the same choices in college. Even though my undergraduate experience in college was more difficult, I was still successful. My graduate programs were relatively easy, and I certainly fit the title "Easy Ed."

The best example I have of looking for the easy road to travel occurred during my freshman year in college. During that year I took a geology course. My undergraduate college sets high on a bluff overlooking the Ohio River. This part of the country provides some of the most vivid geological sites available anywhere to geologists as they study the history of our earth. My professor, Dr. Harold Wickwire, always took his geology classes on a very long field trip – investigating caves and rock formations along the river. A major course paper was to be written about this trip. In order to give me a sense of structure and expectations for the paper, I borrowed one written the year before by a fraternity brother, Steve Caldwell. As I began reading Steve's paper, I wondered "What the heck. Why 'borrow' the paper? Why not just 'use' Steve's paper as my own?" So I retyped the paper, taking off Steve's name and inserting my own. Little did I know that each year Dr. Wickwire took his classes to slightly different places – to avoid what I just did. When he read my paper, I received an "F" and got a "D" in the course for that semester. That was the first "F" I had ever received in my academic life and I received it because I took the easy way out.

In my professional life, I usually got the jobs I wanted, when I thought I wanted them. Each time I thought I needed to be off doing something else, that "something else" was there. I never had to struggle much to find the job I wanted. Remember, however, that at those times in my life, I was operating from the outside in – climbing up that ladder of success even if it might be leaning against the wrong wall.

Experiences in my personal life have also come easily for me, partly because I have also taken the sun for granted in this part of my life and partly because I have been controlling of others. For example I controlled Bonnie by expecting her to be the major disciplinarian of Eric and Tracie. I controlled my family by expecting them to follow me on my journey, with little regard for their own journeys. I ran from the storm of dealing with our children by going to work. I ran from other personal storms by always seeking the sun. Each time I ran from a storm and ended up in a different job and community, I came to expect the old problems and issues to emerge. When they did, I fell into my old patterns of control – control growing out of fear. And, because I became fearful when the same old issues faced me, I began once again to look out for me. In so doing I usually got my way – a new job, a different community, another renewed attempt to gain comfort by imposing myself onto the lives of family and friends. I felt life was supposed to be this way – easy, successful, and full of me, me, me. I don't believe I truly turned around and faced my problems in life until my hospitalization for depression.

Trying To Learn Humility

I lived for my own pleasure; I was the leader of the blind.
A passenger on the road to fame, I was a legend in my mind.
Ah, but when the truth came to me, well I sadly did confess.
Just a pile of rags before God's eyes, in my righteousness.

Anne Murray, ***Elijah***

I struggled to become humble because I didn't want to. And I didn't want to because I was operating from a false definition of humility. I felt if I was humble, I could no longer use the "Marlboro Man" we see on the billboards along the highway as my image of manliness. I would become more like that unfortunate and inaccurate image I initially internalized for my father – weak and timid. I added my own special ingredient into the mixture for being a man – getting what I wanted and being a "me-firster." Everything was about me. My own self-centeredness prevented me from any serious attempts to be humble.

I'm taking another view of humility these days, but I have a ways to go in internalizing the concept. One of my new viewing points suggests that being humble is being human. Because I was a human "doing" for so long rather than a human being, I missed this sign post along the way. Being human means accepting the "both/and" of our being – sinner and saint, male and female, devil and angel. Being humble also means being honest – little wonder I didn't recognize this aspect of my humility either. In *Markings*, Dag Hammarskjold said, "Humility is just as much the opposite of self-abasement as it is of self-exultation. To be humble is *not to make comparisons*. Secure in its reality, the self is neither better nor worse, bigger nor smaller, than anyone else in the universe. It is – is nothing, yet at the same time one with everything."

In the book *How Can I Help?* there is this interesting little story about being humble and about the problems with comparing myself with others:

> One day a rabbi, in a frenzy of religious passion, rushed in before the ark, fell to his knees, and started beating his breast, crying, "I'm nobody! I'm nobody!"The cantor of the synagogue, impressed by this example of spiritual humility, joined the rabbi on his knees, saying, "I'm nobody! I'm nobody!" The shamus (custodian) watching from the corner, couldn't restrain himself either. He joined the other two on his knees, calling out, "I'm nobody! I'm nobody!" At which point the rabbi, nudging the cantor with his elbow, pointed at the custodian and said, "Look who thinks he's nobody!"

Being humble means we do not compare. I have compared myself with others much of my life – as a husband, a brother-in-law, a father, a son, a community member, and an educator. Perhaps because of my own ego, I usually came out ahead when making these comparisons. Grandiosity is sometimes viewed as an opposite to humility. As my inside grew smaller because I didn't dwell there, my head – my ego – was getting larger and larger. I lacked humility in my earlier years, but I was sure grandiose in my comparisons. My grandiosity overcompensated for my lack of an internal locus of control. I did not know about my need for soul time, so I only understood myself through an external comparison with others, and I needed to come out on top of all these comparisons.

Being human not only means I don't compare myself with others, but also my humanness gives me permission not to have to choose between "all and nothing." As I become humble, I learn to rejoice in the reality of my "mixed-up-ed-ness" with "both-and" thinking, rather than "either-or." Ernest Kurtz and Katherine Ketcham, in *The Spirituality of Imperfection*, suggest, "when we come face to face with the reality of our own imperfection…the masks we see in theaters…intertwine." I learn to both laugh and cry. Being human allows me to embrace the ambiguity of life.

As We Gain Humility, We Match Our Words With Our Behaviors

Humility, which inspires us to kneel before
God and next to our neighbor,
emerges as an essential virtue.
Even as pride separates us from one
another and God, humility breaks down the
barriers between us…
The essence of successful going forward
is humility – a recognition that
success in the past has no
implication for success in the future.
Michael Hammer, ***Beyond the End of Management***

As I grew, I observed that my parents were very humble. They came from meager beginnings and always appreciated everything they had. They were considerate of and helpful to others. It was I who began the journey toward self-centeredness. Because my parents were humble, appreciative people, my porch reflected humility but not openness. And I wasn't humble enough to see this. I did not always recognize their humility because much of the time my parents' humility resembled the rabbi's in the story you just read.

Since my hospitalization I have begun to learn about limits to my life, about becoming powerless, about losing control over outcomes and wanting to surrender to what is happening. I had suddenly, for one of the first times in my adult life, lost control – my future was unfolding, and I was unable to make it unfold on my own terms. I became vulnerable and transparent for one of the few times in my life although I had talked a good game for many years. During this time, out of all these feelings and realities, a tiny seed of humility was planted and it seems to be growing. As I realize the value in being humble, I am opening up new beginnings – charting my course with flexibility.

In every one of my fifteen commencement addresses to high school seniors, I talked about the importance of "being yourself," of "getting to know who you are" so "your behaviors will match your beliefs." And in every one of those speeches, I told the seniors to remember that "what you do shouts so loudly, people can't hear what you say." I also made those comments, by the way, for all the parents who were in the audience. The words sounded so good;

the problem is I forgot to follow that advice myself. At times in my life, there has been a vast chasm between what I said and what I did, and my behaviors shouted so loudly people were not able to hear what I was saying. Even if people were listening to what I said, they were also watching my feet to see where they went.

I would like to indulge your patience here and share with you some thoughts from just one of those fifteen commencement addresses because it demonstrates to me that I was not ready to match my talk with my behavior. This particular set of thoughts is indicative of reflections I shared with graduates at all the commencements, and, knowing what you have learned about me thus far, you will quickly realize that what I shared with them included thoughts that I in no way had internalized for myself. What I was doing in my life when I shared these words was shouting so loudly the graduates couldn't hear what I was saying to them. You will also notice the thoughts reflected below are similar to those I've shared with you earlier in this book. It only took me <u>twenty years</u> to realize how those thoughts **<u>really</u>** applied to me. Up to this point, I was talking a good game. Here are those words:

> "As I think about things that are important to share with others on a day such as today, several different thoughts come to my mind because as I think about commencement, it seems to me this day is full of mixed feelings. It is a day to reflect upon four years in high school, four years of accomplishments. It is a day when we are forced to look in two different directions at the same time – looking back and at the same time, looking forward.
>
> "As you look back, I'm sure it's natural to do so with a great deal of pride, some sense of disappointment in not accomplishing everything you wanted to perhaps, but with a sense of having done your best. Looking forward there is anticipation, eagerness to see the challenges that are there, yet with some feelings of apprehension. Today is an ending and also a beginning.
>
> "It seems to me that part of the challenge in thinking beyond graduation day is that of being willing to go out from this point not knowing. Life beyond today for all of you is going to be full of questions, more than answers. Life is going to be full of uncertainties. One of the important things you have to be willing to do is to take risks, to dare, and to feel comfortable enough in yourselves and the foundations that you have acquired to allow you to do that. In being yourselves, you will have to know that *what you do shouts so loudly people can't hear what you say.* (Emphasis added)

> "If someone asks you to try something, to be willing to put yourself on the line and risk something, to take on a new responsibility, you can always say, 'Thank you very much, but I'm too busy, or I'm not interested,' and in so doing you will probably avoid many a sleepless night. But, unfortunately, you will also miss some of those mountain-top experiences that come only when we are willing to risk and to dare. We have to risk, to leap, to leave, or to stay.
>
> "Leaving school and leaving home, as you have known them up to this point, means moving out into a transitional period characterized by many mixed feelings. It is frightening, scary, and risky. At the same time, it is exciting, promising, energizing, and self-fulfilling. It's painful to leave the security and knowledge of places we've been – whether it's school or home – as we have known them. We experience grief. The losses are real. There are endings, but again there are beginnings. This period of change, transition, and passage will be a time of vulnerability – the order and structures of yesterday are being dismantled for a time, and each of you is going to be without your protective, as well as your restrictive, shells.
>
> "There is not an easy road map you can follow, no inside track to discover the exact paths you need to take. Going out not knowing is realizing you are moving into a period of time when you need to be willing to listen less to others for your validation and to become more and more interested in your own self-validation. Going out not knowing means that your life is going to continue to be a series of successes and failures, just as your high school careers have been. But the most important question that each of you will have to continue to ask is: What am I going to count, my successes or my failures? Going out not knowing means the importance of realizing it's not where you've been that is important, it's where you're going. It's not who you've been that's important, it's who you can become."

Well, there you have it, part of a commencement address I gave twenty years ago. Could I <u>talk</u> a good game or what? Those innocent seniors had no idea it was just that – talk – and I as well didn't fully understand that it was all talk. I had done such a good job of avoiding the real me because I created this fantasy that I actually <u>possessed</u> all those characteristics I encouraged the graduates to acquire. For me, it shows so very clearly that I had no idea how to internalize these thoughts into my own life. Matching my beliefs with my behavior is perhaps for me the most difficult lesson to internalize.

Did you notice some similarities between what I said to those seniors in high school and what I am saying to you <u>and me</u> twenty years later? I could talk to others about these ideas, but I couldn't talk to myself or live them myself. I wasn't ready; I had done no internal work at all; I had not begun the process of discovering my soul.

Unlike me, Albert Sweitzer did match his words with his behavior. He was a major humanitarian figure in the last century. He held doctoral degrees in medicine, music, philosophy, and theology. Sweitzer reached the point in his adult journey where the search for the spiritual part of him came alive. In his memoirs he wrote: "I decided I would make my life an argument. I would acknowledge and advocate the things I believed in, in terms of the life I live. <u>That instead of vocalizing a belief in God, I found it necessary to have my life and work say what I believed</u>." (Emphasis added) I want to make the point that Albert Sweitzer learned because he wanted congruence between what he said and what he did. He didn't just vocalize his beliefs; he lived them through his work and his life.

The Masks That Keep Us from Knowing Who We Are

While on the porch, I became a master craftsman at designing masks for my life – masks that were made for both comedy and tragedy. I had a mask for everything I did and for every role I occupied – father, husband, son, son-in-law, educator, neighbor, community member – everything. Figuratively, I had them all arranged in neat order, on shelves, in my closet at home. I could open the closet and pick the mask that was needed for any occasion. I became expert not only at making them but also at selecting just the right mask for just the right role I was expected to play at a given time. Most of the masks were beautifully decorated, with intricate designs. Some, I discovered, had become too little because I wore them as a child. Some masks were so critical to my ongoing success, that I designed duplicates and hid them away in secret places. They became my oldest, best friends. As a son I always wore the masks that would portray me as the person my parents thought I was. I wanted to continue being a good little boy in their eyes. As a husband and a father I wore masks that allowed me to keep secrets from my family. As an educator I wore the masks of self-assuredness and strength to hide the uncertainty and fragility that I knew was inside me.

In his book *The Magnificent Defeat*, Frederick Buechner suggests that, when we are on our journey through life what is real is not so much the masks we wear or the roles we played in the place we are leaving. Rather, he indicates that "what becomes increasingly real as we travel along is something much closer to the actual face that lies behind all the masks and that gives a kind of relative unity to all the different parts that our life demands that we play…travel can be a very unmasking experience." As I traveled my path I used masks, not to provide unity, but to keep separate all those parts of me that were confusing. I did not know how to unify all the parts of Ed Poole. When I kept my life in different categories I fooled others and myself.

I talked about my masks during a long weekend visit a few years ago with my friend and former pastor, Bob Baggott. Bob and I talked long into the nights that weekend. At one point I proudly told Bob that I felt I was finally going to be able to break all my masks and throw them away. I made this declaration on just the beginnings of my inner work and the understandings that were coming to me as a result of that work. Bob listened and then asked a very interesting and perplexing question, the answer to which I did not have. He asked, "Ed, do you really want to destroy *all* of your masks?" My initial response to Bob was "Yes." I was beginning to feel good enough about myself to get rid of those masks. Bob and I went on to talk about when and where in life we want and need to wear our masks. We decided sometimes the answer to this question is difficult because each of us has both a public and a private self. In *Your Mythic Journey*, Sam Keen and Anne Valley-Fox suggest, "The public self performs for an audience, real or fancied. It is the creation of the eyes that watch it. We learn to put on our masks and costumes to play the roles society expects of us…By compounded example we learn the language and dress that are appropriate to our class and profession." This thought from Keen and Valley-Fox fits perfectly with what I believed about my own masks and why I wore them. I was always on stage, performing for my various audiences – students, parents, community, family.

A wonderful concept called the "Johari Window," developed several years ago by Joseph Luft and Harry Ingham, helps me see my masks as a façade in my life. The window is shown below, with its four cells in the grid involving different variations of what I know about myself and what others know about me.

Johari Window

	What I know about me	What I don't know about me
What others know about me	Arena	Blind Spot
What others don't know about me	Facade	Unknown

In the cell that includes what I know about me and what others know about me, we are in what the inventors call the "Arena." In this Arena area, interpersonal effectiveness depends upon an open and free exchange of information. With greater disclosure, communication increases, and the potential for serious conflict decreases.

Right below the Arena, is the cell titled the "Façade." In this area of the grid, we find parts of our lives that we know about but that others do not know about us. In this area, it is possible to develop relationships with others; however, doing so involves selective disclosure of feelings, ideas, attitudes, goals, and values. If the Façade is large, others can never really know us. It is in this area of the grid that I have used my masks because I have been unwilling to be transparent and vulnerable enough to allow others to know that deep part of me that I didn't know or understand about myself. Masks were my only option, and I pretended that I knew everything.

Immediately to the right of the cell titled Façade is one titled "Unknown." When we are in this cell there are parts of our lives we don't know, and also parts that others don't know about us. We are truly in the unknown area of our life, sometimes on a wilderness journey. Without feedback and without openness on our parts the unknown is likely to remain unknown. Feedback and openness provide illumination for others and us.

The final cell is just above the one titled Unknown. It's the "Blind Spot" because this cell includes areas of our lives that others know about us, but that we do not know about ourselves. We haven't "seen" these areas yet because we don't "believe" them. We have not internalized about ourselves what others may know about us. I have many Blind Spots in my life but, as I learn how to be open with others, I'm growing in my understanding of these areas and moving some of my new understandings to the Arena.

The purpose of using this technique is to discover ways to expand the Arena part of our window and decrease the other three cells. Doing so involves removing our masks and presenting our genuine selves to others. Because I didn't trust who I was and didn't have any sense of what my life should be about, I ignored the problems and issues in my life once again and expanded my Façade. Since I was very much into pleasing others and trying to keep everyone happy, the information in my Façade became very unsettling to me. As I wore my masks I always imagined others were thinking the worst about me – little self-confidence and even less internal control over my own self-esteem created these imaginations. I wasn't my own person; I was whatever anyone wanted me to be because, after all, I had those masks.

In public we often wear our masks. Because I lived many years without looking at my soul, my private self was both limited and endless. My understanding of my self was limited, but the private sides of me were enormous because I didn't share; I didn't open up; I didn't want to let go of my secrets.

After some reflection on Bob Baggott's question, I have begun to analyze it from a different viewing point. This new viewing point has allowed me to combine some thinking about humility and masks – another both/and and not either/or for me. The answer to the question of whether or not I want to throw away all of my masks is somehow related to what I see as an inverse correlation between masks and self-image. I have just said I really did not want to work on being humble when the topic was first presented to me. I was still into grandiosity and inflating my ego.

Enlarging my ego was in part due to thoughts of inadequacy I felt about myself – how I viewed myself. The lack of work from the inside-out didn't allow me to realize I had an issue with self-respect. Now I'm wondering if the number and kinds of masks I needed have been related to my self-image. Did I need lots of masks because I didn't know who I was, because I needed to pretend I knew everything, because I didn't feel good about myself at all, and because I did not know the meaning of the word humility? As I gain a better understanding of humility and rummage through the closet to see all of the masks I have designed, I recognize the connection between these two lessons.

Sometimes, while I appeared to others as having it all together, as being in control of any situation, inside I knew I had lost my way in the world. I gave this appearance in searching for jobs and in parenting Eric and Tracie. I rushed around, frenetically, as if I knew what I was doing and appearing self-assured. After a while, however, this image of myself grew thin to me, not to anyone else. Others thought they knew me through my masks, but they didn't. I am sure they didn't know me because I couldn't know myself. In fact, people had no idea I was wearing my masks. I wore them because there was a frightened soul inside – a soul I didn't acknowledge and, until a few years ago, had carefully avoided. In his book *Beachcombing at Miramar*, Bode said of people like me: "For a while they lead us astray. They loom as heroes, as gods; we invest them with magical powers to make up for the defects we see in ourselves. Then one day we find out that for all our frailties, for all our faults, for all our flaws, they are the weak and we are the strong." Like Bode, I thought the uncertainties surrounding my life – my lack of a definition of who I was – were signs of my weaknesses. I wanted to inhale that long sigh of relief to relax and breathe free not to always be on edge, and to be able to answer the question, "Am I doing the right thing here?" I read and read, seeking my answers through the words of others. I have now come to a different conclusion. I see that to be confused is to be strong. Confusion forces me to reflect upon my situation, to proceed with care, to evaluate my progress, and to make mid-course corrections as I sail along.

Wearing masks caused me to need recognition and applause from other people for who I thought I was and what I felt was important in life. Because I didn't know who I was, I didn't want anyone to see who was behind the mask, and the mask became a defensive symbol to hide behind, much like the false storefronts in the old Western movies. When we looked behind the propped-up wall, nothing was there. When who we are depends on external validation, we betray ourselves. While wearing our masks, others cannot see through, and we come up wanting.

Returning to Bob Baggett's question: "Ed do you *really* want to destroy all your masks?" – for now, my answer to the question is "no." I doubt if I can ever become so transparent, or perhaps *want* to become so transparent, that I am willing to shed myself of all the masks. I will probably always have some parts of me that will exist in the Façade cell of the Johari Window. However, as I get into the soul time of my life, I will wear masks within the following understandings: (1) I will consciously choose which mask to wear. (2) I will recognize that I am wearing a mask, and I will know why I am wearing the mask, what purpose the mask is serving me at that particular time. (3) I will know when, where, and how to return the mask to my closet when I'm finished using it. (4) I will acknowledge to others that I am talking from behind the mask of whatever topic is being discussed. If I do not want to give up all my masks, I need to let others know my words to them are coming from behind the mask. Maybe doing so will allow others to help me understand why I'm still wearing a mask in this area of my life and how I can move that part of me into the Arena.

The best example of the four points I just made is in my role as a university professor. As I work with doctoral students and interact with the politics of a university campus, I sometimes wear masks. For reasons I now understand when I choose a mask, I am not always willing to be completely open with whomever I'm having a conversation. The politics, even on a small university campus, are ever-present. I often keep my honest thoughts and feelings to myself and do not share them in a meeting or a conversation, for fear of how they will be received. Today I am doing much better about being transparent than I was in the past, but I still have my masks. Today when I wear a mask I <u>know</u> I'm doing so. Over the years when I was not myself but the person represented by the mask, I didn't even know I was not being transparent. I became so accustomed to being someone other than myself, that I allowed my masks to define me. At a very conscious level I now know when I can put a mask back in the closet. For me, this is a major accomplishment. There have been times when I could switch masks on the run and not even be aware of what I was doing. It is not uncommon these days for me to at least be honest enough with doctoral students and colleagues to let them know I'm talking from behind a mask. They know me well enough to realize I have my reasons for my lack of openness. Can I improve? You bet! Am I doing better about showing my true self than in the past? You bet I am!

My hospitalization was a turning point for me for lots of reasons. My time as a patient in the psychiatric care unit was the beginning point for open and honest communication and deep reflection. I'm not there yet by any means, but I am making progress. I acquired a new perspective, a new viewing point. I began to emerge from a prison of psychological isolation. All the thoughts and feelings I had kept too deep inside me for all those years began to come out into the light of day. I began the process while in the hospital, and I was afraid of what I found. I didn't know what to do with all these surfaced feelings, so I retreated into yet more work so I would not have time to try to figure out what to do with an emerging sense of self.

The time spent in the hospital was an unbelievably significant event in my life. I had learned to live with the self-imposed guilt and shame of my behavior over the years and I was so afraid to discover me. I had gone against most of the religious principles by which I was raised and had allowed myself to be influenced by those principles. The fear caused me to become active again once I left the hospital. I volunteered at the local Chamber of Commerce. I began teaching part time at a local university and then I became a full-time professor. The major difference now in my life is that I have not filled my time so completely that I have none left for me. The obvious validation of the last statement is my work on the porch and the completion of this book. This time I'm sticking with it and, believe me, my life is different today because I haven't lost the desire to find me.

Wearing masks helped me avoid detection. Others thought they knew Ed Poole, but because of the masks, they knew very little. Masks did not help self-understanding and self-acceptance to grow; therefore, I needed to find a means by which I could begin the transformation process and be less hidden to both others and myself. The means I found is my writing. God has gifted me by guiding my thoughts through this writing process. I would never have acquired the clarity I have today without this writing. Much is still unclear but I know I will be able to continue discovering that which is unclear and seeking clarity to bring greater understanding.

A White Knight With No Horse

Not only did what I say not match what I do, I also did not know that only I could rescue me from myself. I kept waiting for others to come riding up on their white horses and rescue me, because I had not done this necessary work. It is only recently that I've discovered I am my own white knight and that I am not a white knight for anyone else, nor do I want to be.

I now realize that I can give myself permission to get off the porch and I can determine when to return. I pick those parts of my life I'm willing to risk an adventure and an inventure off the porch. I cannot imitate life as I see it from the porch; I have to create my own. There is a line from an Eagles' song that says we live our lives in chains without knowing we hold the key. Being my own white knight means knowing I have the key to unlock the chains around my life. I have always been ready, waiting to be my own best guide on my journey through life. A few years ago I began to realize I needed to be my own guide, and, through this writing process, that is clearer today than when my inward journey began.

How much freedom to be my own white knight do I want? What would I be willing to consider? How do I limit my own freedom, and what sets those limits for me? My culture, my loyalties and obligations, my own needs, my strengths and weaknesses, my knowledge and ignorance, other people's choices – all these variables contribute to establishing limits to my freedom to choose, to become my own white knight. Yet, as I learn to journey off the porch, to be free to sail my course, I can feel a power that calls me beyond a particular relationship, role, or place, to go where I must go and to be who I must be. I am my own white knight.

If I want to be truly free, free to be my own white knight, I have to choose. Not any destination off the porch picked at random or reached by happenstance will do. With passion, I have to head for those destinations that summon me because those will give meaning to my life. But I am free to choose. I have to ignore the warnings from friends, the cautious ones, who might tell me why I couldn't or shouldn't pick a destination. As I set my sails, I have the ability to choose the points on the compass, whether it is in my hand or in my heart. From *First You Have to Learn to Row a Little Boat*, we find, "What's at stake is nothing less than personal autonomy – our capacity to empower ourselves so that we may choose the course of our life rather than have it chosen for us by others whose values may differ radically from our own."

It is difficult and scary to begin the most important part of the growing up process when we're in our fifties. If I'm my own white knight, I cannot depend upon anyone else for my own survival – I am coming into my own, on my own, alone. Herein lies the balance between being alone and being in relationship. We have to understand ourselves well enough through our relationships in order to understand ourselves when we are alone. Relating to others is the only way I can begin the journey toward self-understanding. Others help me define myself by the experiences we share and the conversations we have. I can only say, "That's not me" or "I do not like to engage in this activity" when I am relating with others.

As I am finding my own space in the universe, I am also watching others find theirs. I cannot manage their lives any longer, and I don't want to, much less control them. They are defining and claiming themselves, as am I. If I become a white knight for anyone else, I am severely limiting his or her own life choices. I have done just that for many years with my family. I have limited decisions others could make because I was controlling. Now I want others to take responsibility for their own lives.

At the same time I don't want others to take responsibility for my life. Thoreau went to Walden Pond for two years to know more about what he was doing with his life. He called a time out to the routines of his life in order to stop, listen, and understand. He did not want to answer to others or be rescued by others. He wanted to be himself, and Walden Pond was his oasis.

We do choose the lives we lead. Ralph Waldo Emerson said, "To become a master of change, you must understand the nature of power and become the source of your own power." We can choose to be happy or sad, successful or unsuccessful and as we mature, we realize we must accept responsibility for our actions. One of the side benefits of accepting responsibility for being my own white knight is that it heightens my awareness of personal power. I am in control of my outlook, and my outlook decides my future. In *First You Have to Learn to Row a Little Boat*, Bode writes, "I believe we are born with the power to heal our wounds, not through miracles, but through a silent voice that speaks to us from within ourselves and won't be stilled, a voice that tells us where to go and what to do."

Being "my own white knight" was driven home to me recently when I was introduced to Clair Duckham through an article in my local hometown newspaper. Clair, 95 years old, was preparing to ride his bike in the two-day "Hilly Hundred" in southern Indiana, close to where I grew up. This 100-mile bike adventure is up and down some very grueling hills. I've tried to walk lots of them, so I can imagine what it's like to bike them. Clair has been riding bikes for sixty-five years, beginning with his first bike, a Schwinn Superior, which he bought in 1939 for $67.50. The owner of a bike shop near where Clair lives commented in the article about one of his favorite customers: "Here he is in what would be considered the winter of his life, but he acts and thinks like it's the spring of his life. The guy is such an inspiration."

When asked about his secrets for longevity and the vigor in his life, Clair said, "Never stop…Find things you love to do and make sure you do them – don't just think about it…And never hold anyone else responsible for your happiness. Your happiness can be enriched by the people and things around you, but it has to come from inside yourself to start with." Sage advice from a 95-year-"young" man, who has learned that he is, in fact, his own white knight, and he assumes responsibility for his own happiness.

Clair's wisdom motivates me to take responsibility for myself. Doing so gives me the courage and the freedom to find my own way in the world. Taking responsibility for myself means being humble, choosing with care how and where I wear my masks, and walking the walk by matching what I say with what I do.

Chapter 7: What Can We Leave for Others As We Say Good bye?

You may give them your love, but not your thoughts, for they have their own thoughts. You may house their bodies but not their souls... You may strive to be like them, but seek not to make them like you. For life goes not backward nor tarries with yesterday.

Gibran

Our task as adults then might be to search for whatever it takes to forgive our parents for being imperfect. In some families, that imperfection will be slight, in others, severe.

Thomas Moore, ***Soul Mates***

The only pain she ever caused was when she left us.

Inscription found on a tombstone in the cemetery where Mom and Dad are buried.

Legacies can be left from both off and on the porch, but you can't learn to fly a kite from the porch. We gift each other as we leave legacies.

From the porch, I didn't learn how to say good-bye to my dad.

This chapter pertains to letting go, saying good-bye, and leaving places a bit better when we go than they were when we arrived. Learning how to say good-bye – to those we love, to friends, to colleagues at work – is at times very difficult. In fact, one of the reasons it was so hard for me to say good-bye to Dad was because I did not know how. However, we have to learn how to say good-bye in order to learn how to say hello – another thought about endings and beginnings. Leaving legacies means as we learn to say good-bye, we have this internal desire to leave places, people, and things a bit better than they were when we found them. Legacies can be left from either on the porch or off the porch. Learning how to fly a kite, however, requires us to leave the porch. What is the connection among staying on or leaving the porch, learning to fly a kite, and leaving legacies?

Flying Kites Gives Us both Wings and Roots

Erma Bombeck left me a legacy as she talked in one of her books about flying kites. I used this story each year I presided at a high school graduation. As I thought about her words, I realized it's impossible to fly a kite from the porch. I had to get off the porch to fly my kite, especially considering what Bombeck tells us. As I used her story at my fifteen high school commencement ceremonies, I hoped I was leaving a bit of Bombeck's legacy for the seniors, returning staff and students, and parents. Bombeck said,

> "I was autographing books at one of those little tables in the book department of a Midwest department store when I found myself looking into the saddest eyes I had ever seen."
>
> 'The doctor wanted me to buy something that would make me laugh' the woman said.
>
> "I hesitated about signing the book," Bombeck said. "It would have taken corrective surgery to make that woman laugh. Is it a big problem?" I asked.
>
> 'Yes, my daughter is getting married,' the lady responded.
>
> "Is she twelve or something?" Bombeck asked.
>
> 'She's twenty-four' said the woman biting her lip, 'and he's a wonderful man. It's just that she could have stayed home a few more years.'
>
> The woman behind her looked wistful. 'We've moved <u>three times</u> and our son keeps finding us. Some women have all the luck.'
>
> Bombeck goes on to say, isn't it curious how some parents don't know when they've done a good job or when it is basically finished. They figure the longer the kids hang around, the better parents they are. "I guess it all depends on how you regard children in the first place. How do you regard yours?" Bombeck asked.
>
> "Are they like a used car? You maintain it for years, and when you are ready to sell it to someone else, you feel a great responsibility to keep it running or it reflects on you? Are they like a finely gilded mirror that reflects the image of their owner in every way? On the day the owner looks in and sees a flaw, a crack, a distortion, one tiny idea or attitude that's different from his own, he casts it aside and declares himself a failure." Bombeck continued, "I see children as kites. You spend a lifetime trying to get them off the ground. You run with them until you are both breathless. They crash. You add a longer tail; they hit the rooftop. You pluck them out of the spout; you patch and comfort, adjust and teach. You watch them lifted by the wind and assure them that someday they will fly. Finally, they are airborne but they need more string, and you keep letting it out, and with each twist of the ball of twine, there is a sadness that goes with the joy because the kite becomes more distant and somehow you know that it won't be long before that beautiful creature will snap the lifeline that bound you together and soar as it was meant to sore, free and alone. Only then do you know that you did your job."

After reading Bombeck's words at fifteen high school commencement exercises over the years, I thought I had just the perfect story for ending such a ceremony – a story about leaving legacies from parents to their children. I had to laugh one day when I received a letter from the father of a member of that year's graduating class; in fact, it was my last graduating class before leaving that position. The father was a scientist at the Argonne National Laboratory, which was close to where I lived. In part, John Carpenter's letter to me read,

> "As in the original metaphor, the kite does truly soar higher and freer, the more the flier lets out the string. Indeed the flier must trim the yoke and adjust the tail, as you aver, so that the fledgling can rise up. Perhaps by your purposeful omission, your audience already remembers and comprehends that until the kite can fly at all, the flier has some work to do, running to get the foil into the air, then manipulating its still-short string to bring it into a favorable wind. So far, the metaphor is good, and the analogy well drawn.
>
> "Hereafter, although you make well the desired point of it, you have (or Erma has) wrong the aerodynamics of the kite. The physics is such that, in order to fly at all, yoke and wind notwithstanding, the kite will simply fall to earth if the string is actually let loose. The balance of forces is such that a tie to a fixed point is absolutely required, in order that the kite derives from its windy environment, the lifting force it needs to raise itself up and soar.
>
> "From this I draw the understanding that the flier-parents of their kite-children must always tend the tether, in order that the flight continues. The attraction from the fundament must exist, in order to provide the needed balance of forces. Although the tugging on the string needs only to be steady during full flight, and although it seems to the flier that the kite always tends to get away, and to the kite that the flier is always holding it back, the kite can only fly if there is that connection to the ground. Parents and maturing children may do well to know these truer parallels between their flight and that of the ageless toy."

People flew many kites during those summer vacations to the Outer Banks with our daughter-in-law's family. Several families there had small children, and it was great fun to watch the kite fliers run along the beach, catching the ever-present wind off the ocean and seeing the kites becoming airborne. I did notice that when the kites were at the full length allowed by the string, the flier tied that string to a firm anchor on the beach.

My parents (especially Mom) didn't see me as a kite whose string needed to be unwound so that I could gain height and distance from the porch. In fact, my kite – my life – couldn't fly from on the porch. Carpenter's words made me realize that I do have to get off the porch to fly a kite, but the foundation for me and my kite is the porch, a foundation to which I can return for Resting, Refreshing, and Reflecting. Although I thought so throughout my life, I now know I didn't need to have my parents totally let go of the kite string. In fact, had they done so, the results would have been disastrous, according to Carpenter. But I didn't know that. Mom and Dad must have been very smart, realizing more-so than I, that only by holding ever so gently onto the end of the string, would I be allowed to soar free. Until now, I didn't know that Mom and Dad truly wanted me to soar free, and the only way to allow that was to hold gently onto the end of the kite string – another insight I've gained through writing.

Our role as parents never ceases. The role just takes on new forms and functions as our children and we grow and mature. So, from Carpenter's analogy, my kite string will always have some attachment to the foundation: to my parents and the porch. I'm grateful for that anchor.

Erma Bombeck left a legacy for me through her kite story. The story also allowed me to see that legacies are left off the porch, as well as on the porch. In turn, I tried to leave Bombeck's legacy with those fifteen classes of seniors who graduated, close to 8,000 students. As I have seen some of them over the years, they often will mention "that kite story you read at graduation" – an indication that those individuals received and understood my gift.

Legacies Are Left, and Legacies Are Received

To find the best in others; to give of one's self;
to leave the world a bit better, whether by a healthy
child, a garden patch or a redeemed social condition,
to know that one life has breathed easier because
you have lived – this is to have succeeded.

Ralph Waldo Emerson

Passing on legacies is a wonderful part of living, demonstrated by Bombeck's kite story. However, sometimes the legacies that really count have to be left off the porch, a place where we can really help someone gain his or her wings, take flight, and move to greater heights, just as the baby robins did at our house this past spring. Those baby robins and their mother left a meaningful legacy for me. They also had their foundation, our porch, to provide their anchor.

As we leave legacies, legacies are left for us. My daughter, Tracie, phoned on August 27, 1996 (three weeks before I went into the hospital) with words of encouragement, support, and love. She knew I was struggling with my job and whether or not to resign. She phoned again on August 26, 1997, and read me some wonderful words. She then said, "What a difference a year makes." And she was so right. What a year I had experienced after my hospitalization – a year that was indeed a gift. The card she shared with me said, "I am leaving you with a gift – peace of mind and heart. So, be not troubled." My son Eric also sent me a note as I was experiencing that difficult time in my life in late 1996-early 1997; it was a quote from John Muir, after whom that beautiful, peaceful, and spiritual redwood forest is named just outside San Francisco. Muir said, "Go now and then for fresh life. Go whether or not you have faith. Go up and away for life; be fleet. I know some will heed the warning. Most will not, so full of pagan slavery is the boasted freedom of the town, and those who need rest and clean snow and sky the most will be the last to leave."

I was almost "the last to leave." Until I fully realized the seriousness of my depression, I was still trying to find the sun and avoid yet another storm cloud. Eric's thoughts through John Muir helped me greatly. Legacies are left, and legacies are received.

As we leave legacies for those we love and care about, not only do the legacies take on special meaning to those important people in our lives and continue through them, but the legacies can also come back full circle to those who originally imparted the legacies. Those who initially felt the legacy being left for them become the new "imparters" of their own legacies – sharing and leaving legacies with those they love.

My mother-in-law, Betty Jane, held a special place in the lives and hearts of our son and daughter as they were growing up. She gifted us while she was alive and left us legacies after her death. She died when Tracie and Eric were in their early and mid-twenties, and she continues to hold that same special place in their hearts and minds. Betty Jane's legacy to all our family grows stronger with each passing year as we all record the sunny hours of her influence on us.

The full circle of this legacy hit home to me as I reread a letter my daughter sent to her grandfather a few years ago on September 7, the day before his wife's birthday. In the letter, Tracie was not only exemplifying the legacy from her "mamaw" but also returning her own wonderful viewing points of that legacy to her "papaw." In her letter, Tracie mentions Jamie, who is Tracie's cousin. Tracie was helping her grandfather celebrate the legacies her grandmother had left us when she wrote her letter.

> "Dear Papaw:
>
> As Mamaw's birthday approaches, I find myself thinking about her a lot. Actually, I think about her a lot all the time. I still miss her very much. Often something good or exciting will happen, and I think about how much I wish she were still with us. But, at the same time, I know she is smiling right along with us.
>
> Thinking about her birthday on September 8th, I wanted to take some time to share some of my happiest memories with Mamaw and with you. One of the things I remember most about Mamaw is her laugh. She had the kind of laugh and the kind of smile that spread to anyone around her. I also remember her waiting on the porch for us when we would come visit. I remember the way she would get up in the morning and go out and 'talk' to the birds. I remember being out under the big pine trees and having Mamaw show us which birds were which. I remember the way she used to play the piano and sing. She had a beautiful voice! And what a cook! Some of my favorites that I remember the best are big pancakes, chili, fried chicken, and of course, chocolate chip cookies! I also recall many Christmases spent decorating her homemade Christmas cookies.
>
> Jamie and I were talking the other day about the many happy times we spent together at your house. We talked about riding the little white horse up and down the sidewalk in front of your house. We also talked about the four of us fighting over who would get to sit on the little step stool at big family dinners! I can remember coming to spend a week with you two and taking a very fun trip to the zoo. I also remember being very excited just to be able to spend a week with my Mamaw and Papaw all by myself!
>
> I remember lots of visits either to you or from you. When you came to see us, Mamaw always brought a big grocery bag (or two) full of lots of 'goodies'! I also remember lots of fun family vacations that you and Mamaw took with us. One special one that sticks out is the time we all went to Lake Michigan and stayed at Martie Andrews' family cottage. I remember how much Mamaw loved being back by Lake Michigan. We all spent a fun day shopping and sightseeing in Pentwater on that trip. Trips to California were also fun for all of us. I remember southern California and trips to the beach and up to Lake Arrowhead. Mamaw sure did love water and the ocean! Then we spent fun times up north in San Francisco and Yosemite. She enjoyed all the beautiful flowers and other wildlife so much.

I remember how much Mamaw loved the beautiful flowers in your yard. In the spring and summer she and I would go out and cut flowers to put on the dining room table. She also always brought us a bouquet of flowers when you would come visit.

I also remember Mamaw making lots of things. One Christmas she made Jamie and me matching white and red polka dot flannel nightgowns and matching hats. (That picture is hanging somewhere in your house!) She also used to crochet beautiful Afghans and vests for Mom and me. She made me a doll one year for my birthday that we named Jocelyn, and I still have her!

The one thing I remember most about Mamaw is the values she taught us, and the love she gave us. So much of what I am today is because of Mamaw, and I am forever grateful to her. She is such a special part of my life – she will always remain a special part of my life. I always have and I always will love her with all my heart. I still miss Mamaw, but I have smiled many, many times while writing this letter. We are so lucky to have such wonderful memories of a wonderful lady.

I love you very much, Papaw, and I am very grateful for you too. You have taught me lots, and I thank you.

Love,

Tracie"

Did you notice how many times Tracie used the word "remember" in the letter she wrote to her Papaw? And did you then "remember" earlier in the book when I talked about the importance of remembering past events in our lives? It seems Tracie has internalized this value of remembering much earlier in her life than I did in mine. Tracie's Mamaw loved cardinals. Betty Jane died about six years before her husband, Paul. On the day her Papaw died, Tracie was teaching in her first-grade classroom when she received the news of his death. She said that she looked out her classroom window and saw two cardinals sitting side-by-side on the branch of a tree just outside. That sight provided a sense of comfort and peace for Tracie who had just lost a very significant person in her life.

My daughter also gifted me with a legacy as I struggled with my job a few years ago right before I went into the hospital. She sent me two thoughts, written by others. The one author is unknown.

"Each and every one of us have the ability to reach out, to grow, to change for the better, to set our goals and to begin traveling in the direction of our dreams. If there is any secret at all to being happier in life, it is this: to realize what a marvelous person you are to begin with; to treat that person with love and care; and to understand that if you truly desire for your dreams to take you places you've never been…all you have to do is believe in yourself…and begin."

Tracie also shared these thoughts from S.H. Payer: "Live each day to the fullest. Get the most from each hour, each day, and each age of your life. Then you can look forward with confidence and back without regrets. Be your best self. Dare to be different and to follow your own star…And don't be afraid to be happy. Enjoy what's beautiful, love with all your heart and soul. Believe that those you love, love you. When you are faced with a decision, make that decision as wisely as possible – then forget it." The legacy of Tracie's notes became more apparent to me as I progressed through my time in the hospital and since as I continue to work on enjoying life as it is, loving myself, and learning to be me.

Tracie and I were lucky enough to have been working in the same school district as I was entering the hospital, and we shared lots of wonderful moments together through our work over several years. Tracie sent me the following e-mail six days before I resigned my position, and seven days before I went into the hospital: "Hi, Daddy! How are you? I hope you are hanging in there. I was talking to Mom last night, and she was sharing her concerns with me. I know it's easy for us to tell you what we think. I am just thinking about YOU! I hate to see you unhappy, Daddy. I know the decision you're facing is scary, but I also know that you are not where you need to be. One of your favorite sayings is happiness is not a place it's the trip. Right now you aren't enjoying your trip, and that's the most important part. Maybe I am wrong to encourage you to make a change, but I can't imagine that this is where you are supposed to be. I know that whatever is supposed to happen will! I only want you to be happy. You give too much happiness to others not to have any yourself. Please know that I love you very much, and that is why I am trying to put all of this down. I also worry about you, Daddy! I'll talk to you soon!"

I sent this note back to Tracie that same day: "Hi, Sweetie! You know, 'ya did just fine' with your thoughts this morning. I appreciate them and you so very much! I got home about midnight last night and Mom was asleep, but she and I talked briefly this morning, and she said the two of you had talked last night. She felt the only reason I am staying here is because of her concerns, some of which are valid and should be considered, but somehow right now, in terms of my feelings, I am trying to see what weighs more. I know Mamaw used to say, 'The place you're seeking is seeking you,' but I don't feel right now this place is either seeking me or being sought by me. Your thought about happiness being the journey is so good. And you're right – I'm not enjoying the trip right now, and life is so very short not to enjoy as much as we can along the way. I feel a little like I would be abandoning you by leaving. I have so enjoyed the luxury of working here with you, and the very special joys we have in just being able to see each other on a regular basis. That is something I will miss, but perhaps we can make up for it in other ways. I love you so very much and am so grateful for your love, support, and thoughts right now. This is hard, but it'll get better."

Tracie sent me another e-mail that same day: "Hi! It's me again! Thanks for your note! I can't believe you said that about Mamaw – I said the exact same thing to Mom last night. I just want you to do something that makes you happy – like you said – life is too short not to enjoy it! I would really miss seeing you, too, but please don't feel like you're abandoning me! I would just look at it as we have been blessed to share the 3+ years we have – most fathers and daughters don't have that opportunity (especially if they had the opportunity we did to spend my high school years together!!) I feel like I have already been so lucky to have had the extra 'Dad/Daughter' time we've had! I love you, Daddy. Please do whatever will make you happy! Thanks again for your note!"

You have no idea how much Tracie's thoughts meant to me and still mean to me today. Her comments about my happiness and her belief that I was not abandoning her and her work freed me to leave my job. I truly believe those thoughts and the release they gave to me were the beginning of the permission I needed to enter the hospital.

Giving and receiving legacies have been an important part of my relationship with my son, Eric. He received an undergraduate degree in Marketing from Indiana University. He also fell in love with biking his senior year in college, spending many beautiful days biking up and down the hilly countryside in and around Bloomington, Indiana, the same place Clair Duckham rode in the "Hilly Hundred" you read about earlier.

Upon graduating Eric packed his bags and went off to the Bay Area in San Francisco to work part time in a bicycle shop with his cousin Scott, telling his mother, "Oh, don't worry, Mom. If this doesn't work out, I can always fall back on my education" – just what a mother wanted to hear after four years of paying college tuition. Taking this journey was not what I had envisioned for Eric. I imagined him in his nice suit, going to work every day for one of those

Fortune 500 companies, using his degree from a very respectable business school. But Eric reminded me, "Dad, at my high school graduation you read the poem by Robert Frost that talked about the 'road less traveled.' I'm just trying to do what the poem said I should do in following that less traveled road." With that, he gave me a big smile and a hug. What could I say? Eric was living his dream.

Finally, I had to let go of what I wanted for Eric in his life, much like Erma Bombeck shared through her kite story. Bonnie and I had done our part by providing that college education for Eric, just as our parents had done for us. Once he graduated, however, I could no longer expect Eric to follow the path I felt was best for him. Letting go of my plan for him was one of the best decisions I've ever made in my life. Richard Bode put it so well in speaking of his own son: "He sailed out of his own knowing without any direction from me. In that elusive moment I remembered how I had felt as a boy and forgotten as a man, and I knew I had to set my son free so he might find his masters."

Live, Learn, Laugh, Love, and Leave a Legacy

While working in the bike shop in northern California, Eric discovered a wonderful company in the Bay Area called Backroads. This company specializes in biking, hiking, camping, and walking tours all over the world. Eric got a job as a Backroads leader, partly because he had that experience working part time in the bicycle shop with his cousin. It was after Eric spent six years leading tours for Backroads that the company computer put him and another Backroads leader, Stacy Smith, together for a series of biking tours on the San Juan Islands, north of Seattle. During those weeks of co-leading tours, this young couple discovered some common interests and strong feelings for each other.

About a year and a half later they were married in the backyard of Stacy's beautiful home in suburban Philadelphia. At this time, I had just been released as an inpatient in the psychiatric care unit of the hospital and was there as an outpatient, a category that allowed me to leave the hospital and go to Philadelphia for the wedding.

I was very honored when Eric asked me to be his best man, and at the rehearsal dinner I took off my "best man's hat" and put on the "father of the groom hat" to offer a few thoughts – honoring a tradition in our culture when the bridegroom's parents host that special occasion called the rehearsal dinner as part of the events in the marriage process.

My gift to Eric and Stacy was in the form of a story I told, centering around one of their favorite places, Moab, Utah, and one of Eric's favorite authors, Robert Fulgham. Eric and Stacy called Bonnie and me from a pay phone at a busy intersection in Moab, Utah, on Mother's Day to tell us they had just become engaged. They were in the Moab area for several weeks leading bike tours for Backroads. Robert Fulgham has a cabin outside Moab where he sometimes goes to write. Knowing of Fulgham's love for Moab, along with Eric's admiration of Fulgham as a writer, and the great love Eric and Stacy have for the beautiful Moab area, I decided to create a story that was a mixture of fact and fiction in sharing my thoughts at that rehearsal dinner. Here is what I shared with Eric and Stacy and all of our friends that evening – thoughts that were for them, but also for me, as I was just beginning to understand the journey I had to make.

> "These are some things that are in my heart, that I have wanted to share with Eric and Stacy for a long time, so I ask for your patience for just a few minutes. We need to take a long trip, in a short time, so I want to ask all of you here tonight to blink your eyes twice and then open them. Believe it or not, we are standing at the corner of Center Street and 100 in Moab, Utah.
>
> Many of you know that on Mother's Day Eric and Stacy were standing on this same corner we're on right now, using that pay phone right over there, calling relatives and friends to share the wonderful news of becoming engaged and planning to be married on October 12. Eric and Stacy were so happy, excited, animated, and full of joy, and a crowd gathered to see what all this happy conversation could possibly be about. As many of you know, Robert Fulgham is one of Eric's favorite authors. You may not know that Fulghum also has a cabin in the Moab area, where he goes to get away from a more frenetic pace in Seattle, to relax and write.
>
> Well, as it turns out, one of those who gathered on that corner of Center Street and 100 that afternoon was Robert Fulghum, who also happened to be walking by and stopped to see what all the excitement was about. It didn't take Fulghum long to realize that this couple was sharing with others the good news about their engagement and upcoming wedding. Fulghum stood for a while, watching the excitement on Eric and Stacy's faces, and hearing it in their voices.
>
> (At this point in my remarks, I turned away from Eric and Stacy and toward those in attendance at the rehearsal dinner and asked them to

blink their eyes twice again. I suggested that we had just ridden with Fulghum to his cabin, and we are now sitting with him in front of his computer.) Fulghum starts to write, and we see the following on his screen:

'Today on a corner in Moab, Utah, I witnessed one of the most inspiring happenings I've experienced in a long time. I was walking down the street and saw that a crowd had gathered at the corner of Center Street and 100 in downtown Moab. The crowd was watching a beautiful blond young lady and a handsome red-haired young man. The couple was at a pay phone making call after call to, I would imagine, friends and relatives. I'm assuming the calls were to friends and relatives partly because of the laughter I observed and partly because of what I discovered as I stood and listened. The couple was informing those they phoned that they had just become engaged and planned to marry. No one there was intending to eavesdrop on those kids' conversations – except me of course. I was so overwhelmed by what I saw and heard that I had to jump into my car, get back to my cabin, and capture some thoughts in writing before they escaped.

'Driving back to the cabin, I found many thoughts were just whirling in my mind. I finally imagined that this couple had invited me to their rehearsal dinner, and they also had asked me to say a few words. The words I would say to them were flying through me as I drove. I could hardly wait to get back here and write these words I would share with them at that happy occasion. If I could give this young couple some advice at the rehearsal dinner, as they start a wonderful partnership together, it would be those thoughts that flew past me in the car, that I now would share with them as my 'Five L's: Live, Learn, Laugh, Love, and Leave a Legacy.' The ironic part is that this couple who inspired me to share these thoughts will never know I've written them, unless they happen to buy my next book. If they do happen to buy it, I know they will recognize the setting I've described. So, here are the Five L's:

'The first Live. It became apparent to me that these kids must be living well now because I didn't notice an ounce of body fat on either of them. I would encourage them to truly live life to its fullest. I would ask them not to wake up some morning in midlife and have to say, I lived half my life before I realized it's a do-it-yourself job. I would encourage them to keep a balance in their lives between work and play, and I would also hope they would recognize the total integration of the mind, body, and spirit – an integration our western culture makes very difficult. I would also recommend they see a movie. They may have already seen it, but it has carried a lot of meaning for me in my own journey. It's called *Dead Poets Society*, and the carpe diem thought that is there – Seize the Day – would be a wonderful concept for them to think about often.

'Second – Learn. The drive to learn is innate. I would encourage them to continue learning throughout their lives – as if they had a choice. As we enter the 21st Century, being open to new learnings is increasing on a minute-by-minute basis. Babies enter the world curious, as did this couple a few years ago. My hope is that their experiences with education didn't dampen this curiosity, but rather heightened it for them.

'Third – Laugh. My goodness, was this young couple laughing as I observed them around the telephone booth in Moab! I would share with them that laughter is good therapy for the mind, the body, and the soul. Always find things in life to laugh about and always be willing to laugh at yourself.

'Fourth – Love. To say that this young couple was very much in love would be an understatement. I would want them to know that keeping – throughout their lives – the excitement, mystery, caring, joy, and happiness they have right now will take hard work, every day. It involves being willing to say those three hard words, "I forgive you," and it also involves good communication and mastering the art of listening, and of creating win-win solutions to their problems.

'Finally, Leave a Legacy. Someone whom I love dearly once told me that happiness is a journey, and I know this young couple has a wonderfully exciting journey ahead of them. I can just feel it. Leaving a legacy means that at every single stop along life's journey, you must leave it a little bit better than it was when you found it. I would suggest to them that this means you have major responsibilities not only to yourselves, but also to whatever you define as community, and to society at large.

'Well, that's my story of the Five L's – live, learn, laugh, love, and leave a legacy,' Fulghum wrote. 'And at this point in my rehearsal dinner thoughts for this young couple, if I was feeling particularly brave, I'd probably turn to the couple and suggest to them that these Five L's are an absolutely critical foundation to a happy marriage and a fulfilling life. But, I would also want the couple to know that the Five L's are just that – a good foundation. Most of the rest of life with a partner in marriage is what I would call on-the-job training. With the foundation piece, however, the daily work will be much easier. Gee, I wish I knew who this couple was, standing on that street corner in Moab, Utah, on Mother's Day. If anyone reading this knows of a beautiful blonde girl, and a handsome red-haired young man who got married sometime after Mother's Day, please suggest they read this section of the book – who knows, it might be them and then I could finally find out who they are.'"

Putting together those thoughts for my son and daughter-in-law's rehearsal dinner was meaningful for me at that particular time in my life. I had just left the hospital as an inpatient and would continue there as an outpatient for four months after the wedding. In all reality, the "5 L's" were written as much, if not more, for me than for Eric and Stacy. I needed to hear me say those words to Eric and Stacy. And the words are mine, not Fulghum's.

Legacies From Our Work

Our task is to ensure that when we step
aside, our job, or at least our organization
still exists for the next generation.
Peter Block

Sometimes I save pieces of information, not really knowing at the time why I do so. Later, I revisit those saved treasures, and I understand why I saved them in the first place. As I was transitioning from high school principal to superintendent of schools, I received some wonderful gifts of thought and encouragement from some of the high school faculty whom I was leaving and still didn't want to leave. I would like to share some of those thoughts with you, not because they reflect positively on Ed Poole, but rather, because they reveal how gifted I've been throughout my life by those colleagues with whom I've worked, and what a wonderful legacy of thoughts they gave to me as I left. Although you don't know them, I hope their words will help you develop the same realization I've just shared – I have been blessed.

The most wonderfully surprising discovery I made as I reread people's thoughts was that I had already begun talking about "the porch" way back then. Until I came upon this folder, I had thought my porch thinking began about five years ago. I am beginning to realize the porch is an image within me for many years, unknown until recently. Through a whole series of events that appeared unconnected at the time, this image finally surfaced as I took my golden retriever Katie on those walks to the park. Please remember as you read this next section that, truly, legacies are left and legacies are received.

I would first like you to know some of the thoughts I shared with the entire school faculty when I said good-bye to that group who had been such an important part of my life for eleven years.

> "Two years ago, I was sharing with you why I didn't go to Colorado as an Assistant Superintendent for High School Education. Today, I find myself sharing with you why I have accepted a position as a superintendent, and I hope to do this sharing in a way that will add to your understanding of this decision.
>
> As I've assessed myself and my future, at this time I want to address a totally new set of problems and issues in my professional life. If I'm going to address these new problems and issues, I need to 'get off the porch' to do so." (I then went on to explain the porch metaphor – the first time I had publicly attempted to put meaning to the porch.)
>
> Robert Raines in his book *Going Home* talks in the first chapter about being apprehended, and, when we are apprehended, we leave home. For me, these past eleven years, home has in large part been this school and the people in it. As we leave home, Raines talks about leaving a primary concern for the validation of ourselves by others to an acceptance of self-validation. For much of my adult life, I have longed for validation from outside myself. It's time to do some internal validating of Ed Poole. Raines concludes this section of his book: 'Faith is not managing our destiny, but losing control of our destiny. Faith requires us to learn to trust the process.'"

That spring, as I was leaving a safe haven and venturing out into the wilderness, I was beginning to trust a process I didn't even know existed. Understanding what that process journey was all about came years later. But as I was leaving that job I had no idea how much I would grieve the loss of my dear friends. Looking back, I'm certain many of the tears I shed in the middle of that bed in a hotel in Carlsbad, California, were because I had left the porch and was missing my friends.

Some of the faculty at that high school shared with me their thoughts and feelings as I left. One threesome from the faculty used an Eagles song (Remember, I love music) to convey their thoughts – and they signed the sheet "Joe Walsh, Don Henley, and Glen Frey" The words are to the musical notes from the Eagles' song, "Lyin' Eyes":

Our friend Ed Poole is leaving us too early.
A superintendent's job – he got the call.
He's movin' down the way to Indiana.
And Bonnie is going with him in the fall.
Late at night his old friends will be lonely.

They'll wonder how he's doin', cause they care.
But we know 'old' Ed will keep it going.
He'll probably form a future's team down there.

We can't hide our cryin' eyes,
And our smiles are a thin disguise.
We hope someday he'll realize.
How much he's meant to Central people's lives.
How much he's meant to Central people's lives.

Legacies are left, and legacies are received, including a wonderfully meaningful card Eric and Tracie sent me. The card contained notes from both of them. They saw me struggle with my decision to become a superintendent and had watched helplessly as I sat in the middle of that hotel room bed in Carlsbad, California, sobbing uncontrollably at the news our home had been sold, realizing it truly was time to get off the porch. Together they said: "Congratulations, Mr. Superintendent! We love you very much and we're <u>very</u> proud to have you as our father." Then they each wrote individually: (Tracie) "Daddy, I am so happy for you and so proud of you. You have worked hard for this, and your accomplishment speaks for itself! I <u>know</u> you have made a good decision, and I know you will be an excellent superintendent! Munster doesn't know just how lucky they are, but I sure do. I love you with all my heart."

(Eric) "Dad, I am very happy for you and proud of you. I know, given time, you will realize that you have made a good decision. Naperville will miss you, my man, but Munster sure has a good thing coming in the form of a new superintendent. I am sure going to miss you when I go to California. I could not have asked for a better Dad. You are the <u>best</u>. I wish you all the luck in the world, because you deserve it."

Legacies are left, and legacies are received. One of the assistant principals at my high school was appointed principal after my resignation. Tom shared the following thought with me: "'The grass is not <u>always</u> greener on the other side of the fence; it's only greener if you water it.' (Robert Fulghum, 1990) God Bless You, Ed!" I wish I had remembered this note from Tom. I certainly didn't water the grass on the "other side of the fence" in my superintendency. I focused only on the frustrating parts of my job. For most of the events in my life, time allows me to take activities that once appeared negative and later see them in a positive light. The light brightens as, over time, I gain understanding of those activities. I'm glad I experienced the superintendency because that experience clearly defined for me what I did not want to do as an educator. I was able to water the grass only as I've gained the perspective of time.

As I left the principalship one of the teachers shared with me the following: "Ed, just a note to let you know I admire your 'getting off the porch.' I've learned a lot just by observing and experiencing your leadership these past few years at Central. Best wishes always." Legacies are left, and legacies are received.

After I had started my new job as superintendent, one of the teachers on the Futures Team at Central sent me the following card: "Dear Ed, Last Thursday the original Futures Team came together to hear progress reports from the design teams, and truly, Ed, your presence in that room was very nearly palpable! I missed you as a friend and a leader, yet had the sense that you've left a vibrant legacy via your vision of the future. May the days be good to you!" Legacies are left, and legacies are received.

A teacher shared the following: "Ed, I'm sorry I did not attend your farewell dinner, so I'd like to say thanks with this card. Although we have not always agreed, you have always given me a chance to speak my piece, and have thoughtfully considered my opinions. Especially in the last two years, I have felt comfortable speaking to you. I rarely found your door closed (amazing, considering the number of meetings you must attend) and appreciated your candor. I also want to reiterate how much I enjoyed having Tracie in class. She is a fine young woman in both character and intellect, traits that must in no small part be due to her parents' nurturing. I wish you and your family happiness and success." Legacies are left, and legacies are received.

From another faculty member: "Ed and family…thank you for your leadership over the years. It's a pleasure to hear a person reflect on life's meaning…struggles and all. It's also heart-warming to see love and credit given so freely to special friends and family. Please know that you will be missed greatly. Your new endeavor will be that risky 'stepping off the porch' you've mentioned so often…yet rewarding in the end, I know."

One particular note stood out for me, and I carried it close to me for many months after changing jobs. Then I lost the note, and I thought I would never find it again. But while doing some research for my writing, I dug into an old book that I hadn't seen for years. When I opened the book, out fell the note from my friend. Her words were and are so very meaningful to me. I know I was supposed to review that old treasure one more time, to gain new insights, and to find my lost gift. Here is what my friend said:

"Since I never trust my own words as much as those of ones I read: 'Were it possible for us to see further than our knowledge reaches, and yet a little way beyond the outworks of our divination, perhaps we would then endure our sorrows with greater confidence than our joys. For they are the moments when something new has entered us, something unknown; our feelings grow mute, in shy perplexity; everything in us withdraws, a stillness comes, and the new, which no one knows, stands in the midst of it and is silent' (Rainer Maria Rilke). 'Life must go on; I forget just why' (Edna St. Vincent Millay). My words – My regret is that I will not get to know you – your knowledge and depth intimidate and make me shy. Yet I sense a richness that I feel sad. I don't know or understand it. Thank you for what you've given this place – that must feel good to you. It is a good place; you must be a good man. I wish you what you need." And she signed it. Legacies are left, and legacies are received.

There were others, but I hope by now you do know these people well enough through their words to know that I was truly gifted in that place I left. I was at odds with myself: I felt it was time to leave, but I didn't want to leave this place that showed me such grace and caring. The faculty assumed my departure came because I had give careful consideration for the reasons I was leaving to become a superintendent, but I hadn't, really. I was just moving on down the street to a new house I had found, with my compass still in my hand, not in my heart.

Please remember I shared the above remarks with you to allow you to see how others have gifted me and left legacies for me. I was truly going out not knowing, but also, as it turns out, I was going out not even knowing <u>why</u> I was going. I thought I knew, but as you have read, and as I came to see, the reasons were all outside of me, not within me.

This wasn't the only transition I was to make in my life within a very short period of time. As you know, I got off the porch to approach the superintendency. I went down the street from the principalship and went into the house I thought from the outside looked really inviting. Upon entering, however, I found the insides of the house weren't quite what I had hoped they would be. You've read some of the thoughts and introspecting I did that year as superintendent. And I knew I needed to leave the porch once again to find another house. The new house I entered as a superintendent was not as inviting as I expected because I entered it for the wrong reasons. I was climbing the ladder of success without knowing myself in order to really know why I needed to be a superintendent. Once again I had followed my external guides.

You won't be surprised to read that I was gifted at that time as well with some comforting and encouraging words from Eric and Tracie. That spring Tracie sent me the following: "I am very happy for you, Daddy. I'm sorry that you had such a rough year, and I know things will get better! This is a great opportunity. And remember, the most important thing is that you are happy! I love you so very much, and I'm proud of you for trying all these new things! I can't wait to see you (by the time you get this, maybe tomorrow!) We are going to have a great summer. Congrats!" And Eric shared with me these thoughts: "If I were there I would give you a high five in person. I think this is the next best thing. I am really happy for you about your new job. I could tell when I talked with you and Mom this morning that you were pretty darn excited about the whole situation. I am proud of you. I am sure you guys will be glad to be back in the Naperville area, It sounds like your new job will be great too – including getting to 'hang-out' with Walter Payton [Walter Payton lived in the community in which my new job was located.] Go into it with an open mind and have a good time with it. I know you will do great. Remember that whatever happens – I love you and that won't change. I gotta run. Take care. Congrats again! P.S. stay gold!" Legacies are left, and legacies are received.

As I was leaving the superintendency, I also shared a resignation statement with the faculty and the community – remarks that left a legacy for them. I offer a part of that statement to you, again to suggest that I have been blessed beyond all belief:

> "I know many people were surprised to hear that I will be leaving my position as Superintendent of Schools. Because it's important to me that people understand my thoughts about this decision, I wanted to take a moment to share them with you.
>
> The decision I made to come here was the right decision to have made last year. I know everyone – the community-wide selection committee, the Board of School Trustees, the staff, and my family and I – felt the match was a good one, and we all looked forward to a long and enjoyable working relationship. As the year has progressed, however, it has become apparent to me that Ed Poole and the superintendency are not a match. Everyone has been most gracious, friendly, supportive, and helpful to my family and me as we moved, and as I began my job this year.
>
> I've probably done more introspecting and thinking about myself and my interests and abilities this past year than any other time in my life.

One of my conclusions is that as I'm immersed in a situation, in this case the superintendency, I'm better able to understand and assess it than at any other time.

Of all the characteristics of educational leaders we hear and read about these days – the need to be visionary, to be future thinkers, to involve others in making decisions, to gain commitment from others for long-range goals, etc. – I believe five questions to be the most critical and which I've tried to ask myself this year: (1) Am I being true to myself? (2) Do I exercise introspection? (3) Am I being hopeful about myself? (4) Do I have a passion for the truth about myself? and (5) Do I see frustration, tension, and growth as essential parts of the change process? You may have a different personal list for leadership than I have, but my own belief system says if I can achieve satisfactory answers to these five questions for me, I can do a better job of providing leadership for others and myself. I want to thank the community, the staff, and the Board for all the kindness and consideration extended to my family and me during our time here. I wish the very best to you as you continue down your well-chosen path of excellence."

Six years later – right before I left the hospital as an outpatient – I was gifted with the legacy of a farewell party given by my colleagues at my former workplace. At one point in the evening, I had an opportunity to share some thoughts with another group that had been very supportive of me. In part I suggested that some cultures have more holistic ways to deal with clinical depression without this treatment taking place in a hospital. I noted that our culture does not have such holistic tendencies, so I shared with them a bit of my experiences as a patient. I also told them that God knew I was coming to see them that evening because at our group gathering that day in the hospital we had read the following meditation:

> Treat your friends as you do your pictures, and place them in their best light. Taking our friends and loved ones for granted, expecting perfection from them in every instance, greatly lessens the value we have in one another's life. We need the reminder, perhaps, that our friends are special to our growth. Our paths have crossed with reason. We complete a portion of the plan for one another's life. And for such gifts we need to offer gratitude.

Once again, I was blessed with friends who were trying to understand my difficulties with depression by wanting an opportunity to say good-bye and to show their support as I was struggling in the wilderness. Legacies are left, and legacies are received.

The Legacy of Family

I have tried to make some changes in how I raised my children compared to how my parents raised me. Some of those changes have been successful and some not. I believe that if each generation, in leaving legacies with their children, can improve upon the raising of their children, then, as their own children grow, get married, and have families, they can, if they so choose, try to alter some of the ways they raise their children. Believing in and attempting to bring about change – to try to make a more meaningful life for all – is all about leaving and receiving legacies.

Legacies are left, and legacies are received. My wife Bonnie has given me the best and most meaningful "living legacy" I've received in my adult years. She has been my biggest cheerleader. Our marriage is a legacy for both of us, but the marriage has by no means been perfect. I've always made myself feel better by suggesting that there are <u>no</u> perfect marriages out there, no "perfect tens." Maybe there truly are some, but I've not seen them. All of the married couples I really know have been and still are struggling with life and with married life in particular.

At times Bonnie and I have both laughed and cried about the possibility of going our separate ways. And sometimes we've been close to doing just that. But, somehow, for some reason, we've hung in there together. And for that I've always been grateful. I've been very fortunate in having a God who has continued to send me a very consistent message throughout the years: "Ed, ya big dummy, you can mess up other parts of your life, but if you get out of this marriage, the loss will be overwhelming." God sometimes uses other words to get my attention, but the message is still the same. Every single time either of us has talked about leaving our marriage, I hear this message from God. There have to be good reasons for that, and, for once in my life, I've tried hard to listen. I can remember one of Bonnie's great aunts, as she was going through the receiving line at our wedding, stopping directly in front of me, looking me straight in the eyes and saying, "Ed, you lucky devil." That's all she said, but down deep inside, I've always felt she was speaking the truth.

Have there been times when Bonnie would have been justified in saying, "That's it! I'm outa here"? Of course there have been those times – more than I care to count. But Bonnie has always stayed in the struggle with me, wanting above all else to preserve our marriage and to work through our problems. For many of our married years, Bonnie has been the one to initiate the desire to improve our marriage. Those initiations have been in the face of many disappointments I've given her as a husband.

I've known seventeen people who are now or have been gifts to me during my life and about whom I can honestly say, "These are just the finest of human beings." Those seventeen are Bonnie, our son and daughter and their spouses, Bonnie's brother Bob, his wife Betsy, and their children Jamie and Scott, Bonnie's parents, my parents, and my sister Mary Belle, brother-in-law Norman, and their children, Eddie and Janice. They are and have been just genuinely good people. They all have their "warts and bumps" as do we all. But when I get beneath those, I find truly wonderful people.

One of the initial attractions to Bonnie and her family was what I understood her family life to be all about and what I saw in her family as parts that were missing in my own family. The Miner family became my "adopted family" as I was dating Bonnie. When we were in college, I could go with her to visit her parents and gain a feeling of comfort at what I observed transpiring between parent and child. I liked that. In some ways, my father-in-law was able to father me more than my own father. I don't admit this out of anger but out of gratitude that Bonnie's dad was there and talked with me. Paul (Bonnie's dad) had this outer crust of exactness, right and wrong and black and white. And he was, as I understand it, a strict disciplinarian with his own children as they were growing up. However, when Paul allowed someone to get underneath that exterior, he or she found a wonderfully warm and caring person. He loved his son and daughter like you wouldn't believe. But he loved them so much that he allowed them to do their own stumbling and failing in life, get up, and move on. As a parent myself, I know how hard at times that must have been for Bonnie's mother and father.

I've heard many stories about Bonnie and Bob being sent to opposite corners of a room, to face their corner, and try to keep from turning around and giggling at each other. One time when Bonnie and Bob were in the second and fourth grades, they threatened to run away from home. So Paul promptly went upstairs and packed a suitcase for each of them – the biggest and heaviest he could find — and put those two bags along with his son and daughter on the front porch of their home and closed the door as he went inside. He had made his point. Bonnie and Bob did not leave. They must have felt like that exotic bird I described in Chapter 5. You will remember that the bird was on a ship being taken to the explorers' native land. The bird discovered that the ship that had once seemed like a prison became a place of refuge. As Paul put those suitcases and his son and daughter out on the porch, Bonnie and Bob must have felt they were in a good place after all, right there at home on their porch.

Bonnie has given me the legacy of presence and support for me. For much of my adult life, I've been the one "front and center." I've had the high visibility jobs. But each time I listen to the Bette Midler song, "Wind Beneath My Wings," I realize that Bonnie has been that wind for me. She has always been a strong supporter of Ed Poole, whatever I was attempting. And she did so, knowing full well my weaknesses and failures as a husband and father. She was willing to pick up and move every single time I thought I needed to be climbing that next rung of my career ladder. She never complained. She took those moves in stride, especially those times I went early to start a new job and she was left to sell a house, pack up our belongings, and make the physical move to our new community.

Being the wind beneath others' wings is a role Bonnie plays well in every part of her life. A few years ago, Bonnie was recognized as "Teacher of the Year" in her school district, a district of approximately 1,500 professional educators. I'd like to share some of the criteria used each year to choose this outstanding teacher because I think the criteria so eloquently describe Bonnie as wife, mother, educator, friend, and community member.

This annual award is in memory of the Gaworski family – a local family who, over the years, saw many of its members go into teaching. The principals of the various buildings nominate teachers for this award. The winner is an outstanding teacher who is an "unsung hero." She or he has been an outstanding leader all along although not officially recognized as a leader, such as president of the teachers' association. The winner is someone who works behind the scenes to support others in their quests for growth and improvement. The winner is someone whom others can count on as "always being there" to listen, support, and make suggestions when asked to do so – someone who is a good listener, solid as a rock, and is willing to share her or his experiences with others.

Unknown to Bonnie, I was invited to attend the ceremony where she received this award from the superintendent of schools. As one of the Gaworski children, herself a teacher in the district, read the criteria for the award, I couldn't help but realize those criteria describe Bonnie perfectly. I have seen those qualities in her as a mother, a wife, and a friend to many. Others have seen those same qualities in her role as educator. This consistency in perceptions amazed me. I had thought about these criteria relative to

Bonnie for many years. I just needed someone to read them to me, as part of a teaching award, to realize they apply to all parts of her life. Bonnie is truly the embodiment of someone who knows and practices the consistency between what she says and what she does.

I just shared with you my thoughts about how each generation tries to improve, for its family members, parts of its own early years as a child. The one part I focused on trying to improve was my relationship with Eric and Tracie. I think all of my immediate family members would agree that some of these improvements in relationships were there and evident and purposeful on my part. I still to this day tell both Eric and Tracie that I love them, and they say the same to me – it just seems natural. And whenever we are together, our initial thought is to hug each other long and hard – and the same with Stacy and Chris, my daughter- and son-in-law.

You also know there have been times when I have doubted my ability to be a good parent. Remember the Sunday trips to the office? I think at times I have been envious of Bonnie for the closeness she has had with Eric and Tracie. Bonnie has truly been there for them all of their lives, just as she has been for me. As I have had those feelings of envy, I have also realized that those feelings are a self-fulfilling prophecy of sorts. Now it seems perfectly natural that in many ways Eric and Tracie would feel closer to their mother – after all, she has always been there for them.

For many years, I showed my love for Eric and Tracie the same way my parents showed it to me – from the role as family provider. Sure, I've been fortunate to make higher salaries than Mom and Dad, so I was able to provide even more "things" for my kids than were provided me. However, the role has still been the same – when in doubt, buy 'em material gifts. It was when Eric and Tracie were in college that I realized, finally, that this show of love was very limiting and that actually my kids would appreciate their father showing his love for them in different ways. I saw my parents working hard and providing for me as they parented me. Their role as a good provider was so very important to them. I did much the same with Eric and Tracie over the years.

I've tried, over the past ten years, to show my love, caring, and concern in different ways. I don't run to the office now when a tough parenting task comes along. If you are a parent of grown children, you fully realize that the job of being a parent never ceases; it only takes different forms and functions as your children are on their own journeys. I can honestly say that, from my viewing point as a father and father-in-law, Eric and Tracie are definitely making improvements in their own marriages over what they must have observed as children growing up in their own homes. They are more attentive to and considerate of their spouses. Eric and Tracie have a better balance than I between work and play. To be able to make these observations makes me very grateful and happy. And I say, "Way ta go, kids! Keep it up!"

The legacies I share with my children have been a higher priority than those I share with Bonnie as my wife. Until recently I hadn't fully realized that I didn't attend to my relationship with Bonnie as much as I did my relationships with Eric and Tracie. I worked hard at improving the legacy I want to leave with my children. I haven't worked as hard at improving the legacy I want to share with and leave for Bonnie. Although parts of my marriage are an improvement over what I observed growing up with Mom and Dad, other parts are pretty much the same as I saw at home as a child. At times, I've viewed Bonnie, and my relationship with her the same way I viewed that relationship between Mom and Dad. She's been the stronger of the two of us, and I've been less than that. Knowing a bit, as you do, about how I perceived that relationship with my own parents, you can realize how frustrating it has been for me to see myself as I saw my father. At some level, however, I've played out my life with Bonnie as I saw my parents playing out their lives together. Bonnie and I got the job done working together to make our lives and those of our children better than what we experienced growing up.

Bonnie has felt much of the pain of my adult life, but she has helped with the struggles. Has she contributed to my struggles? Yes she has, and Bonnie would acknowledge that she has. But she has been the wind beneath my wings always and has stood as a tower of strength during my struggles. Any marriage is a fifty-fifty, give-and-take relationship. It's just that many times I've done more than fifty percent of the taking from Bonnie. You will recall my propensity to be a "me-firster" in my life when I thought it was all about me, me, me. Bonnie has felt my pain, and she has hurt many times herself, both for me and because of me.

Because I wanted to be different than my dad, I insisted for years that I handle all the financial issues for our family. Only recently did I relinquish to Bonnie the control over the money. I have to admit a big relief has come to me, a relief I never anticipated. Once again, I have thought about my dad and the fact that every Friday he came home and gave his paycheck to Mom. And once again, I am now realizing that Dad was a lot smarter than I have been all these years. As I have said, I never gave Dad the credit due him over the years. I wish that earlier in my life I could have viewed his actions from a different viewing point, a different frame of reference: "Way ta go, Dad."

Have I been blessed? Most certainly I have – as a husband, a father, and a son. Has the life as a marriage partner and a parent been hard at times? Most certainly it has, but I try not to take the sun for granted as much these days by running from every storm of those relationships. I hope I can continue to do so.

Legacies are left, and legacies are received. I want to share with you now the obituary of the death of Archie Jolly, Mom's dad and my grandfather, on December 22, 1918: "His life had been one of devotion to home and family, for to him there was no place like home. He was an obedient son, a devoted husband and father, a faithful friend, a kind neighbor. He had been able to oversee his farm work most of the time until the last days when it became evident he would soon be called home. After some parting words to his family, he said, 'All is well with me, and I am ready for my Savior's call.'"

How much of her father I saw in Mom through the years. Much of her father's legacy was left with Mom, and she in turn left it with me.

My Legacy from Dad through Mom

As I said earlier in the book, I recently took a couple of days off work and went back to my hometown to talk with Mom. I wish I could have had this conversation with Dad, but since he was dead, my next best chance to fill in some of the gaps in my understanding of Dad was to talk with Mom about him.

I always knew there was never much communication among our family members as I was growing up at home. However, I was still surprised that there were many parts of Dad's past that Mom also didn't know because they didn't talk about certain issues either. Most of those issues centered around Dad's adoption and his life before Mom and Dad married. That revelation should have helped explain some of the poor communication between myself and my parents when I was growing up; however, until recently that obvious fact wasn't internalized – it was just out there somewhere on the periphery. For my visit with Mom, I wrote down questions I wanted to ask her. I have selected portions of that conversation to share with you. The notes that follow represent, *in absentia*, part of a legacy from my father to me, and they also provide part of the legacy from Mom to me.

E (Ed): You know it's only recently that it's been acceptable for men to sit down and try to come to grips with some of these issues – issues that surround boys as they grow up at home. And so I sat down the other day and came up with some questions that maybe we can talk through. Just to talk a little bit about Dad. One of the first things I thought about was – he was so young at the time (of his adoption), but did Dad talk much with you about his time in the orphanage in Indianapolis?

M (Mom): No. See, he was only four years old when they took him out, and he never did talk about that.

E: How old was he the first time they took him out of the orphanage? Was he out very long with his brother, or was that just a short period of time?

M: That must have been just a short period of time. He never talked about that, either. Harrises took both of them out of the orphanage, but then they couldn't keep but one of them. They put your dad back in. That's when the Pooles took him, but I don't know how old he was.

E: I wonder if that had any effect on Dad? It must have affected him in some ways, if he thought he was going to be adopted, and then he was returned to the orphanage without his brother.

M: Well, when he was that young, I doubt if it would have that much of an effect – a child that age, you know, wouldn't think about it. (In talking about this time in Dad's life I have said, earlier in the book, that here is the difference between my own and my mother's viewing point of this critical time in a child's life. I would say that <u>because</u> he was that young, this whole period of time had a tremendous effect on Dad, both then and as he lived out his life.)

E: And Dad never did know anything about his real parents?

M: No, he found that one brother, you know. {Note I made at that time: It's curious, but we went to Tulsa, Oklahoma, to visit Uncle Johnny when I was about nine or ten. If he and Dad talked at all about their early years, Dad never shared any of those conversations with the rest of the family. That was the one and only time I saw Uncle Johnny. He and Dad had very little communication beyond that one visit.]

E: What did Dad remember, or did he talk much about his early life with Grandpa Poole?

M: Well, I think it was kind of a hard life because Grandpa Poole was a contractor, and he didn't always have work.

E: Did Dad talk much about that?

M: He just never did talk much about anything.

E: He was just a really private person.

M: He never went into that stuff.

E: And never talked much to you about it?

M: Huh-uh.

E: Did you ever wonder about some of those things?

M: Yes, I wondered, but I just hated to ask him. I know one time, I think Grandpa Poole had the contract to build that high school at Scipio (close to where Mom was raised). And they lived down there, north of Scipio on the highway. And they fished a lot because that was cheap food. I have heard him talk about that. And, then they had lived along the river in a tent at some time or another, or creek, or something. I don't know where Dad was working at the time, and I heard him talk about fishing a lot and eating the fish they caught.

E: How'd you meet Dad?

M: I met him when he was teaching Sunday school classes at the Methodist Church in Scipio. I used to go there with one of my girl friends.

E: What was Dad like those early years when you first met him? How would you describe him? What was he like? What did he like to do? What do you remember about him?

M. Oh, I don't know. We always had fun together.

E: What did you do for fun?

M: Ride around in a car; go to church. We always went to church, all the Sunday school meetings. We went around to different people's houses and made ice cream and ate ice cream – it was a lot of fun.

E: So a lot of social activities were centered around the church and doing things with people there?

M: When we lived with Mom for two years after we were married, we had ministers who were preaching at Oak Grove come and stay with us – you know a week at a time – them and their wives. We always enjoyed that.

E: What kinds of jobs did Dad have those early years – right after you were married?

M: Well, he worked in the canning factory up here, and he cut his foot. We were going to go to the World's Fair in Chicago, and he had cut his foot, and he couldn't go. But he wanted me to go ahead and go anyway. And I went.

E: What kind of job did you have when I was born?

M: When we first moved up here, I did housework for a while – just wherever I could get it, because Mom was living with us, and Marie passed away, and Leona stayed there for a while. [Marie was my Mom's sister, and Leona was Mom's niece.] And Harley couldn't hardly make ends meet, with everybody here you know. And I did house work – different jobs. And I went to work with the theater, and I worked there for – I don't know how many years – but a lot.

E: Yeh, a lot. You were still working there when I was finishing high school because I used to go to the shows all the time. But now, what kind of job did Dad have during that same period of time, when Leona moved in with you and Grandma was there?

M: Well, he worked at different jobs too. When I married him, he was driving a truck for the Mayflower company, and he had to make such long trips, clear over to the East Coast, and he didn't like being away from home that much, so he quit that job, and he worked at the Farmers' Market for a while. And he worked for his dad some on building. He worked for the state highway on building roads, and he worked on the railroad. He just had a lot of different jobs until finally…

E: What do you remember – like the time between I was three and five, right before I went to school – what do you remember about Dad during those early years? Because of those jobs, was he gone a lot?

M: He was gone a lot. That was the trouble with most of those jobs. They took him away from home. Yeh, he was gone a lot.

E: Do you remember if he and I – because he was gone a lot, I don't remember if he and I did things together.....

M: Not a whole lot. I remember when you kids were little, he took you and went over to Thompson's where he was working – showed you off over there.

E: I can remember going to Thompson's, I guess, and I remember the plant there where they processed the milk, but he must have worked a lot of long hours.

M: He did, and he was a good worker. He always brought his money all home – he never spent any of it foolishly, but you just didn't make very much at that time. 'Course, expenses weren't near as great like they are now either. I guess maybe I was a little too stingy, but, when I was young, Mom and I never had anything. I always saved every penny your dad made, and he'd get quite a bit of overtime at different places. I'd always take that and put it with the house payments so we could get it paid off.

E: When I was young, did Dad talk at all about being angry or sad or upset about his time in the orphanage, or his time with Grandpa Poole or anything?

M: No, he never ...

E: He just kept all that inside him?

M: Yeh, he never talked about it.

E: I just bet from time to time he wondered about that.

M: I imagine, but he just kept it all bottled up inside. He never said anything about it.

E: Dad was a really private person, wasn't he?

M: Yeh, well, I don't like to talk about things to people either. I'd just rather keep it all inside of myself, you know.

E: What did people used to say about Dad?

M: Oh, he was a good worker. Everybody always thought he was a good worker. I remember Grandpa Poole telling you one time if you were going to be a schoolteacher you'd have to learn to talk a little more.

E: Yeh, I know. I was pretty quiet. I think sometimes because Dad worked so hard, when he was home he was real tired, so I don't know – you tell me if you think I'm off base here – but it seemed like in the evenings when we were all home, we tried extra hard to be quiet because we wanted Dad to be able to rest…

M: Right

E: We didn't raise a lot of ruckus. Seems like I never got called down a lot anyway as a youngster for just being loud and boisterous, and I guess what I did, Mom, was kinda develop a world inside myself or something because we just didn't talk a lot. Is that how you remember it? [Note: Did I use the excuse of Dad being tired and wanting quiet as a convenient excuse for not talking?]

M: Yes, I think so. Like you said, he was always tired and worn out.

What Legacies Have Been Left by Mom and Dad?

Recently, I debriefed myself on that conversation I had with Mom: "So, Ed, you've retyped a conversation you had with Mom. What did you learn?" I made these observations:

Mom did leave me a legacy through the conversation we had that day. That conversation affirmed a lot of thoughts and feelings I've had over the years. Rather than just turn on the tape recorder that day in Mom's kitchen and begin talking into it, I purposely chose some questions I wanted to ask to provide structure to our conversation. To that extent, the conversation reflects my own biases, but there was specific information I wanted about parts of the lives of both my parents.

I grew up in a noncommunicative family, period! No one talked much to anyone else. Mom and Dad were both private individuals, and they were that way with each other. I was not able to acquire positive communication and relationship skills growing up.

My father was strapped with having other people for whom he had to provide, besides his immediate family. Living with Grandma Jolly for the first two years they were married, then having Grandma and my mom's niece move in with them, and having my sister and myself – I can't think of a time when there was just the two of them, except after I left for college.

Dad was most definitely in the provider role, and he played the role well. However, because Mom's dad died when she was six, and she lived with her mom while her two older brothers moved to Indianapolis to find work, I also believe Mom saw her role as that of provider, to a large extent. She worked from the time I was very little until I got out of college.

So, for much of the time, I had an absent father and an absent mother, both physically and emotionally. A lady down the street babysat for my sister and me.

"I'm scared to death I'm turning into my father."
Kevin Costner, ***Field of Dreams***

A fortunate few males experienced a close and warm relationship with the fathers of their youth. A few more have found their way in adulthood to at least a buddy relationship with their dads, and a few have actually made peace with their fathers about the pain of their history together. Most of us, however, live with the old resentments, deep pain and silent yearnings for our fathers. We live with authority conflicts, wobbly self-esteem, unconfessed dependency upon and resentment toward our wives or mothers, and self-doubts about our own capacity to father.

As you know in 1991 I began some introspecting. I was miserable in my job as superintendent and I didn't know what to do to lessen the pain. During this time I: renewed sessions with my therapist on a weekly basis; spent time visiting with Mom to find out more about Dad; attended a two-week workshop designed to help participants better understand our maleness; and spent time "sitting in front of the cave" to try and understand why I felt as I did about my job.

Under ideal conditions the phases a boy experiences in his journey toward manhood are as follows: (1) The son's first bonding is with his mother. (2) The son's step toward becoming an individual is taken away from the mother and toward identifying with the maleness of his father. The strength of the parents' bonds to one another allows the mother to surrender the intimacy she has had with her son; the strength of the son's bond with his father flows into the son.

(3) In adolescence, which may extend into the late 20's or beyond, the son is helped to leave home and become his own man. Again, the strength of the parents' bond allows them to let him go. (4) Because he carries strong nurturing father images with him, the son moves into the adult world of work and is capable of self-nurturing in his marriage.

I do not know many men who are this healthy. In my case, the phases went as follows: (1) I was overly bonded with Mom and didn't connect with Dad. (2) Because I was too close to Mom and didn't have Dad around to help me separate from her, I pushed away from Mom to try to form my male identity. (3) Lacking a close identification with Dad, I adopted other male mentors in my life. During most of my early years, until I got into college, I ran with an older group of males. I played in a dance band comprised of young men between six and eight years my senior. I became attached to some of those men. (4) My relationship with Bonnie has been one of self-protection. I was interested in taking care of me; I was selfish; I was controlling; I maintained my independence. When things got stormy at home I became an absent father myself. I married the girl who has taken such good care of me. Over the years I became very dependent on Bonnie and, in some ways, we have become co-dependent. I married the girl most like my mom.

In an interesting custom among some African tribes, at a particular point in the early lives of the males, their fathers leave the village and make camp in a remote setting far from home. The mothers gather their sons together in the center of the village, and, yelling and screaming, literally chase their young sons away from the village and to their fathers waiting for them. The fathers and sons then spend a long period of time creating that critical father-son relationship. It was deemed time for the sons to pull away from their mothers and draw towards their fathers. After chasing their sons out of the village, the mothers return and compliment each other on what a fine job they did chasing their sons away. My mother never drove me toward my father, and so the father-son bonding didn't occur. Instead of "leaving" Mom and bonding with Dad, I remained very dependent on my mother and her control over me for much of my life.

One of the student assistants in the building where I have my office is married and has a five-year-old son. Recently Rosie was lamenting to me the fact that her son doesn't want to do things with her anymore. When Charlie's dad is out in the garage working, he wants to be there. When his dad goes in the car to get something, Charlie wants to ride along. Rosie was feeling like a failure as a mother. I told her the story about the mothers chasing their sons toward their fathers, and I assured her that because Charlie wants to spend time with his dad, she is doing an excellent job as a mother. She should feel grateful this change in Charlie is occurring. I told Rosie that this transition did not happen to me, and I felt a dependency on my mother most of my life.

Mom was unable to provide me the direct emotional side of her. She was quiet, and a very private person as well. She and I did not learn to share.

Leaving home to go to college meant leaving Mom. Often our inability as men to let go of our mothers seems like a consolation prize for the absence of a reassuring father. Perhaps I had trouble letting go of Mom because of Dad – and this may have affected how I relate to Bonnie. For better or worse, the men of one generation play a big role in determining how the men of the next generation will live their lives, as a parent and a husband. I first thought my issues were with Mom and then they switched to Dad – I see now that it is not possible to deal with one without dealing with the other. It was difficult to leave home to go to college, because I was so dependent on Mom and she kept me on the porch. Leaving home for college was so hard that, in fact, at the end of my first semester as a freshman, I packed up all my belongings, came home and was prepared to sit out a term and transfer to another university. During that winter break, I talked with several people who convinced me that I had not given college a chance. I repacked my bags and returned to my freshman dorm in time to begin the second semester. As early as my freshman year in college, I was running around looking, looking around as I ran, and not knowing why.

I had this half image of Dad because I did not really know or understand him, and I had a Mom upon whom I was very dependent. I felt guilty leaving her/home. Maybe that is what has been so hard about "leaving home" these past few years – getting off the porch. I still (albeit at a different level) carried around this half-image of Dad, and I was afraid to leave home (the porch). I didn't want to venture out. As I'm creating a fuller image of Dad, it has helped with the venturing out and with understanding some of the why's. Bonnie talked about leaving me several years ago, when our marriage reached an all-time low and I did this same "clinging" to her – out of hysterical fear – that I felt with Mom. Because I transferred my dependence on Mom to a dependence on Bonnie, I allowed Bonnie to mother and nurture me, and I didn't want her to leave. After all, what would I do?

My mom was a mother to Dad when he was sick for those many years. I also watched Mom's role with powerless Dad when he was sick, and that role must have fit the early stereotype I had of Dad – weak and dependent. Mom was a mother to Dad a lot. She always "took care of him" – finances, food, clothing, decisions. When Dad died, Mom lost not only her husband but also her full-time job of caring for him. Did she have time to mother me when she was mothering Dad, being a wife, and working hard? Did Mom take the place of Dad's mom, whom he never knew? Has Bonnie taken the place of my mom, whom I never knew? I have to answer both those questions "yes."

Much of Mom's early life was strongly connected to her church. Mom's church was her own oasis in her wilderness journeys. An early religious experience was not part of my dad's journey. When Mom and Dad were married, however, Dad – like me – always returned to "Mom's world of light" and began attending church on a regular basis.

As I write, I'm discovering the legacies from Mom and Dad to me. One cherished legacy is the effort they made to allow me to have a better life than they experienced, either as children or adults. For as far back as my memory takes me, both Mom and Dad – but especially Dad – taught me the importance of a good education. They both saw education as the path toward a better life. You know a little about their own childhoods and adult lives, so their emphasizing to me the importance of education was remarkable. It might have been easier for them just to assume I would move off the porch and out into life with an educational background like their own.

Where and how did they discover the importance of education? Did they know it themselves when they were young but never had a chance to take advantage of going to school and learning? The path my parents consciously chose to help make my life better than theirs was through education. I firmly believe it was this choice by Mom and Dad that instilled in me the desire to make education my chosen profession. By leaving me this legacy, Mom and Dad provided the opportunity for my kite to soar, and thus gave me the freedom to discover a different world than they knew.

Setting Sail and Saying Good-Bye— Finding Peace With Our Fathers

Recently, I attended a conference in Houston, Texas, a conference for those whose lives are involved in coaching others, both those on business journeys and those on their personal journeys. Also at this time I began my own consulting firm, called *Setting Sail: Harnessing the Winds of Change*™. I had remembered George Gray's epitaph in the Spoon River cemetery, so the consulting firm uses a sailboat as its logo. The business cards have that logo imprinted on them. At this conference, as I shared my business cards with others, they asked me, "Oh, do you sail?" And I answered, "No, I haven't really sailed that much. Sailing is a metaphor for my company, an indicator of how we can allow change to happen in our lives."

At this conference, I met David Sheridan, the captain of *Messenger*, a 30-foot Hunter sailboat. Being a sailor, after seeing my business card for *Setting Sail*, David asked me the same question others had asked, "Do you sail?" When I gave him the same answer I had given the others, he said if I could get to the Twin Cities, he would take me out on his sailboat. I jumped at the chance. David sails *Messenger* on Lake Pepin. As I road there with David, I noticed we were on huge flat farmland. Miles of rolling freedom unfolded before me. I saw the silo towers farther to the east above the tree line, and to the west we cut back toward the lake, our car coming to a stop on the edge of a sheer cliff. There is a three-hundred-foot drop off the edge of the cliff.

David uses his sailboat to train people in leadership skills, teamwork, and collaboration – quite a unique setting, I thought, for allowing others to experience, firsthand, some of the major concepts and issues facing American businesses.

During this long weekend visit with David on his sailboat, I was privileged to participate in a Native American spiritual healing ceremony, which David held on *Messenger*. For this ceremony, we were asked to bring something to "give back to the water" as part of that ceremony, something we wanted to let go of. So, I wrote a letter to Dad and, at the appropriate time, put the letter in a beautiful bowl, burned my letter, and scattered the ashes on the water. My letter to Dad is dated September 27, 1997 – eight years after he died.

> "Dear Dad,
>
> As you can see by the date, I'm writing this much too late to ever have had a chance to give it to you to read before you died. But, knowing the life you led as a father, husband, and Christian, I would expect you'll catch up to the letter in the not too distant future.

I'm writing for a few reasons. I didn't really get to say good-bye to you the last time I was with you in the hospital in Columbus, a couple of days before you died. I also have been carrying around so much anger and frustration concerning you, and it's time to let go of that. I need to ask your forgiveness of me, and I need to say, "I forgive you, Dad."

You probably know the number of times I think of you, Dad – more often as I get older. I hope you don't mind, but I've decided to do some research and see if I can find out some more about your biological family. For some reason, the lack of that information is creating a big hole inside me that needs filling. If I don't find out any more than I know now, at least I will know that; I will also know that I tried and probably at that time will let go, but I can't right now.

How much that early part of your life must have bothered you as you grew up. I talked with Mom about it, and she said she always figured it didn't bother you much because you were so young when sent to the orphanage, adopted that first time, returned to the orphanage, and then readopted by Grandpa Poole. Mom doesn't realize, nor do I completely, that because you were so young, that series of experiences had to have had a very lasting impression with you. How good it would have been to have talked about that.

After you died, I went to Columbus and spent a day with Mom, both of us talking into a tape recorder. I found out what you already know – our family just didn't talk much, did we? I know you and I never talked much, but I thought you and Mom probably did. She said no. She always figured you didn't want to talk about your past, or many other things I expect, and so she remained quiet herself and never asked. There is much about you that Mom just doesn't know.

I know how hard you and Grandpa Poole had it when you were young. Mom told me about your coming back from St. Louis and living in a tent along the riverbank around Scipio and North Vernon, fishing for your food, and hitchhiking the twenty-five miles to Columbus to look for work.

Mom said she knew the people with whom you worked would always describe you as a hard worker, and I know how important it must have been to you to have that kind of recognition. I am very grateful for that work ethic. Hopefully the best parts of it rubbed off on me, but I think I may be a bit lazier than you! I know it wasn't always easy to find work, but somehow you did and provided so well for your family, which I also know must have been so important to you. That provider role was one you wanted to do well, and you did. We never wanted for much. I created problems for our family as I got older because I wanted as much "stuff" as some of my friends had. I know now that's not how life is.

I also think there must have been a real human, emotional side to you that I never saw because you kept it so well hidden. I know that the emotional aspects of my life are something that are there and constantly apparent and important to me. I don't know that I got that from Mom, so it must have been you – thanks!!!

Sure, I wish now we could have hugged, kissed, and said "I love you" and seen more of each other. Fact is, we didn't. I've tried to create some of that with Eric, Tracie, and Bonnie, but it's hard, and I'm not sure how good at it I am. I know we hug, kiss, and say, "I love you" on a very regular basis. I know I thought for a long time – until about a year ago – that my demonstration of love to my family was through the "things" I got for them, the money I gave to them, and the "doing." Sure, I got that from both you and Mom as the two provider role models I had, as well as Grandma Jolly. Only recently I've discovered that the "being" part has to be balanced with the doing.

I used to hide out at work on the weekends when I felt a difficult situation existed at home concerning the kids or Bonnie because I wasn't sure how to handle it as a father and a husband. That probably wasn't wise, but I did it. I also know Mom did more of the disciplining of me than you – partly because you were not around much and also perhaps because you didn't want to. I can understand that now. I know the good ol' guilt trips you gave me about making Mom cry when I pulled one of my many escapades at the time left me with some "stuff" to work through. I also know being raised on guilt wasn't all that uncommon with our generation.

I've been frustrated about your later years because of your illness and not being able to spend more time with your grandchildren and all of us. I can remember how frustrating it was for you to have us come visit and not be able to join in the fun. I just wish it could have been different—Eric and Tracie missed something, as did we all. In my heart, I know you would have loved to have played with your grandchildren.

So, Dad, before this letter turns into a "woulda, coulda, shoulda" piece, I just want to say thank you for all the blessings we had as a family. You never had us out of your thoughts in terms of our best interests, and I know you overdid it many times in providing for us – in jobs that were very hard in terms of physical labor. Did you make the most of your gifts? Of course you did. Did you encourage me to try to better myself? Of course you did. I also know that you did your job in giving me birth

> and those first few early years. The living part has always been up to me – so I no longer want to use you as an excuse for my own living and not living. I want to take responsibility for that and am trying, more and more all the time, to do just that. It's hard. I do love you, Dad, and your memory. Please forgive me for holding you up as a convenient excuse all these years, and not doing my own work. Thank you for everything.
>
> Good-bye, dad
>
> Love,
> Eddie"

The Native American ceremony provided a tremendous way for me to talk to Dad and to share thoughts and feelings I wish I could have shared while he was alive. I didn't take that opportunity then primarily because I didn't know how and was afraid to try. I think I became just like Mom – I figured Dad didn't want to talk about all these things, so I never approached him. He may have wanted very badly to talk to me about what I wrote, and much more. He probably didn't know how either, and so we were two ships passing in the night.

On *Messenger* for this ceremony, we were all introduced to a timely story. A Native American grandfather was talking to his grandson about how he felt. He said, "I feel as if I have two wolves fighting in my heart. One wolf is the vengeful, angry, violent one. The other wolf is the loving, compassionate one."

The grandson asked him, "Which wolf will win the fight in your heart?"

The grandfather answered, "The one I feed." I was just beginning to realize this dissonance in my heart about Dad and me, and until I wrote my letter, I had not yet decided which wolf to feed.

It would be inaccurate to say that the journey on *Messenger* and the beautiful ceremony I experienced with the Native Americans on board that evening provided a complete relief from my frustrations. It didn't, but it helped so much.

The ceremony helped me accept the innocent mistakes of my parents, just as I hope Eric and Tracie are doing of mine. As I grow older during my soul time of life, I gain some better understandings of why Mom and Dad raised me as they did. At this point on my own journey, I hope to think in terms not of forgiveness but rather of understanding, appreciation, and acceptance because by now I have lived long enough to make some of the same mistakes as Mom and Dad. Having made some of those same mistakes with my children that Mom and Dad did with me allows me to see how unreasonable it is to expect perfection from a human parent.

One of the most unique legacies I found was left by author Frederick

Buechner who was asked by his son to write his brand new grandson a letter to be opened on his twenty-first birthday, August 25, 2015. As a part of his letter to his grandson, Buechner said, "Maybe we can never know each other's stories in their fullness, but I believe we can know them in their depth for the reason that in their depth we all have the same story...We search for a good self to be and for good work to do. We search to become human in a world that tempts us always to be less than human or looks to us to be more. We search to love and to be loved ...My birthday wish is that after wandering through many a street for many a long year to come, you may find your way at last to the fountain in the square." I thought Buechner's son had a wonderful idea. What a nice way to leave a legacy.

I wonder sometimes if Mom and Dad knew that I will never fully realize how much they loved me, not only because of their own failures as parents and people but also because my sister and I can't know all the ways our parents loved us. I feel when Mom and Dad died, their legacy gave me permission to allow their love to live on in me and through me to my children and my wife.

Finishing the Unfinished Business

As I think back to the questions I asked myself during that time I was in the superintendency ("Is this all there is?" or "Is this as good as it gets?"), I now realize those questions didn't have so much to do with my job and the uneasiness I felt about my work as they did in finding meaning in my life. Often, to understand our male feelings about love and work, we need to discover the unfinished business with our fathers.

According to Sam Osherson, in his book *Finding Our Fathers*, if the father is not around to provide a good model of manhood, the young boy is in a vulnerable position: needing to create a distance between himself and his mother, without having a clear model of the male gender upon which to anchor his changing identity. Osherson goes on to say that the relationships sons have with their fathers begin to shape in subtle ways how the grown sons respond to their own wives and children. He wrote, "At home, some men become determined to avoid the passivity or dependency they saw in their fathers." The separation struggle in men is great. I carried around as an adult the weight of dependency and emptiness because I was grieving as well as reliving a time when going to Mom didn't seem appropriate and when I couldn't or wouldn't go to Dad. My identity struggle as a father myself was because I wasn't all that sure how to be a father and to be present for Eric and Tracie.

I have concluded that at the very same time I have been trying to make peace with my father, I've also been trying to make peace with my spiritual Father as well. Perhaps some of the anger over the years was with that Father, and those wounds need healing also. Until recently I did not have a deep identification with my Higher Power – I had not examined my own beliefs. As I live in the second half of my life, acceptance and appreciation for my spiritual Father are becoming more a part of me.

Recently, as I've thought of the porch and my interest in understanding its importance in my life, I realize that the porch represents my unwillingness to deal with all that is inside me. I have had many convenient excuses not to do that hard work. Hopefully some of those excuses are fading. Today I am more aware of the disconnect that existed between my head and my heart. I relied on the former without realizing the importance of the latter. But somewhere along the way, I bumped into a very unsettling truth: I felt powerless to take control of my life. I had made Bonnie my mother as I became my father in this passion play of life.

Looking for the Sun While Avoiding Closures in Life

I've always had difficulty with closures in my life. Part of what gets in the way as males is our conflict about separating from our fathers. We often separate from significant figures by gaining distance from them without working through our feelings. One point my therapist J.R. and I discussed was my inability to bring closure to some parts of my life – and really a lack of interest in doing so. Instead of bringing closure, I always "cut and run," leaving the person or group hanging. I remember too well how good it felt at the time to find the sun and leave the storms. I couldn't complete the cycle. I didn't know how to turn to face my demons and let the pain stay with me long enough to learn from it. I've had difficulty with closures all my life.

Richard Bode was talking about the closures in the cycles of life when he said in *First You Have to Learn to Row a Little Boat*, "And so it was that in our parting the blue sloop taught me the most valuable lesson of all. I had lived through a cycle of learning and caring, and having learned and cared I had to shed the past so I could begin the cycle over again."

Self-acceptance and forgiveness, in the final analysis, are the same. Each allows us to connect with others. I have to know and accept who I am before

I can accept and forgive others and myself. This has been a major problem of mine all my life – not knowing myself and accepting myself with all my warts and bumps has kept me from being able to say those three words, “I forgive you.” – to myself, my family, my colleagues, and my friends. These three words have probably been as difficult for me to say as the three words, “I love you,” were for Mom and Dad to say to me.

It is interesting to me to see the strong connections between leaving and receiving legacies on the one hand and being able to say good-bye on the other. During this part of my journey, I have been able to see how very blessed I have been during my life and what wonderful legacies have been left for me. A part of these realizations is helping me learn how to say good-bye. As I grow in my understanding of who I am, and the legacies I've received it is becoming easier to say good-bye, especially to Dad. Through this writing, I have a better appreciation for the legacies Dad left for me.

Chapter 8: Skills for Our Journey

For every parcel I stoop down to seize,
I lose some other off my arms and knees,
And the whole pile is slipping, bottles, and buns,
Extremes too hard to comprehend at once,
Yet nothing I should care to leave behind.
With all I have to hold with, heart and mind,
And heart, if need be, I will do my best
To keep their building balanced at my breast.
I crouch down to prevent them as they fall;
Then sit down in the middle of them all.
I had to drop the armful on the road,
And try to stack them in a better load.

Robert Frost, ***The Armful***

We need to turn our face to find the wind direction, until we can feel the wind equally in both ears. We need to face head-on into our problems and wait to "feel" the problem equally on both sides of our head.

David Sheridan, Captain of ***Messenger***

We need toolkits when we venture off the porch.

"May I help you with your bags?"

These lessons describe the skills we need to begin, and continue, our journeys. One of those skills is knowing what we need to pack for the trip. I don't know about you, but I've kept the same bags packed most of my adult life. If you have children, you remember well how you had to pack for them when your family took a trip. Then, do you remember when they wanted to begin packing their own bags – what a disaster that was for a while?

Tools for Our Journey

I had no tools for my work on the porch, and I had no skills to help me get off the porch. Until recently, I certainly didn't know when and how to return or even if I wanted and needed to return to the porch. As you might imagine, the "tools" for our toolkit will come in the form of ideas for us to consider as we go on our journeys. Some tools have been sprinkled throughout the writing thus far. In some instances, it seemed more appropriate to integrate the tools with the lessons and, in other cases, to put them in this chapter. As you finish reading the book, it may be helpful to return to the various chapters and make a list of those tools and skills you find there that will prove helpful to you as you continue on your own journey.

Life itself is a journey, and each of us has a different amount of time to travel. Our "car" was delivered the day we were born. As we secure our road maps and make certain our car is well maintained, remember that we are the drivers and in control of which paths to take.

Here, then, are some additional tools for our journey:

1. The writer who has provided me the most clarity of the value of using myths to help us understand our lives is Joseph Campbell, who has identified for us the "hero's journey." In putting these two concepts together, the tool I would suggest to you is the acronym M.Y.T.H.: Make Yourself The Hero.[6]

Initially, as I thought about this acronym, I became a bit concerned about the word "hero" because, as you know, my ego uses the word to describe myself. However, Campbell's use of the word hero doesn't mean "superstar." For Campbell, heroes are not ego-centered. A hero begins to trust her or his life, its purpose and its direction. A hero is always in a transformation process.

Heroes do not lose their composure when the frenetic pace of life becomes too real, and this sense of calmness is an encouragement to others. Moreover, the hero's journey is circular. We always have the opportunity to revisit previous parts of our lives, and to use these insights for our current journey. Heroes learn to trust the process, seeing the "dark night of the soul" as an invitation for remaining calm, standing still, and allowing growth and change to occur in our lives. Challenges and tests come to heroes – strong spirits are tested early. What we do about those tests, how we respond, is the call of the hero.

The hero is willing to learn from all situations and all people – the wise and the foolish, the obvious and the unthinkable, children and animals. Heroes also know that to understand their calling in life, they have to listen to the inner self and their outer experiences. I have spent most of my adult life ignoring my inner self, listening only to what others had to say.

2. The tool of "enlightened self-interest" is important to pack in our bags. When we are operating out of "self-interest," we are looking out only for ourselves, without concern for others. We are very much "into ourselves" and are "me-firsters." We do not care how our decisions might impact the lives of others; we just know what is best for us and don't really care that much how our life decisions affect those around us. I've been operating from self-interest much of my adult life. I thought I deserved all the good things happening in my life, and not often did I think about how my life impacted the lives of those around me.

However, as we practice "enlightened self-interest," we continue to take

6 Janet Lueck contributed the idea for this tool.

care of ourselves on our journey, but we do so in terms of how our journeys impact others. We make our decisions in terms of what might be best for us, but we also consider how our own decisions impact others. I have often used this concept as I have worked over the years with members of various leadership teams. If each team was representative of various subsets of an organization, I always hoped that, as the members made decisions for their part of the organization, they would do so from an enlightened self-interest posture, meaning they had considered how their subset was an integrated part of the whole and how their decisions might impact that whole.

Below you will find a series of squares that can be cut along the lines shown for each square. I have often used this activity, called the "Five Square Puzzle," with a variety of groups – school faculty, parent groups, graduate classes, etc. In each small group there are five participants. Each participant receives an envelope containing various pieces of these five puzzles but in a very disorganized manner, meaning different parts from the five squares have been put into each envelope.

The task of the five-member group is to have an equal-sized square in front of each member at the conclusion of the activity. The rules for this activity are as follows: (1) The activity is completely nonverbal. Once it begins, group members may not talk until the five squares have been assembled. (2) No member may take a puzzle piece from any other member. (3) The only way any group member can change the number of puzzle pieces in front of him or her is if another member gives up one of his or her own puzzle pieces to any other member in the group. (4) Four group members may not "dump" all of their puzzle pieces in front of the other group member and expect him or her to construct all five squares.

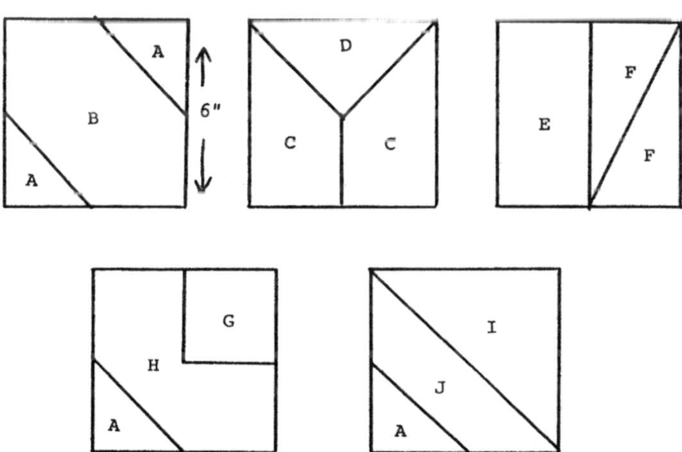

Obviously one square can be constructed from the available parts in many ways, still several ways to put two equally sized puzzles together, fewer ways for three to be assembled, very few ways to put four equally sized squares together, but only one way to assemble all the parts so that all five squares are of equal size. This activity can be used for team building, consensus building, and enhancement of the skill of enlightened self-interest.

I mention the latter use because very often one or more members will have "their puzzle" constructed in front of them – feeling very good about themselves for having completed their part of the task. Those who have completed what they see as "their puzzle" exhibit some interesting nonverbal behaviors: they often fold their arms across their chests; they may even push their chair away from the table, indicating noninvolvement; and sometimes they cast a disparaging glance at their other group members, as if to say, "Hey, I'm finished with mine. What's the matter with you guys?" Eventually, however, some members who have already constructed their square realize they will have to "break it apart" and give some pieces to another member in order for that member to be successful in constructing a square. Giving up pieces of an already-built square is difficult for some because, after all, their job is done – or so they think. This activity is a good example of how we need both to know and to practice enlightened self-interest during our life journeys. For some of us, enlightened self-interest is a difficult concept to internalize; however, it is an essential tool as we venture off the porch.

3. As strange as it may seem, the skill of knowing how to dam a creek in order to make a swimming hole is also an important tool for our bags. If you have ever tried to dam a creek in order to swim, you know you need good tools. You need good rocks, good mud, good scraps of wood, used tires if you can find them, and then anything else that might be available. In damming a creek, however, a delicate balance must be achieved between making the dam strong enough so it won't break and also making it porous enough to allow just the right amount of water in and out so the ecosystem is not destroyed. Without the movement of water, the new swimming hole cannot reinvent itself; it cannot nourish itself; it cannot rebirth itself. And because of this, the same water stays in the swimming hole day after day until it becomes stagnant and begins to smell like a pot roast that has been left out of the refrigerator for ten days. The water becomes stagnant and dies.

In our daily lives of comings and goings, we may encounter very good people who are approaching life the way we may approach the damming of the creek.

We find people who are working feverishly to harness their lives, to dam their lives with some form and shape, and to hold it in a manner that they can feel it, look at it, and say, "This is my life." The lessons learned in damming a creek are the same lessons we can learn in life. If we dam life up and do not allow for change, for continuous flow, for new and fresh ideas and people to flow through, our lives will stagnate, and we will ultimately die – emotionally and spiritually.

One of the real dangers in life is that our insecurities and our fears of all the change that is happening around us will cause us to clutch at life for all its worth, causing the dam to be so strong against change it will stop the flow. As we try to keep our lives the way they have always been, we do not allow that natural flow. Tragically, the clutching we think will preserve us runs the real risk of becoming a strangulation hold, of choking out our breath and our vitality.

The lesson learned in damming a creek is very simple: we cannot stop the flow of life. If we want to live, we have to be willing to ride along with it – through pain, through disappointment, and through change. We have to be willing to try to survive, even if we don't think we can, because that is how life moves. Sometimes we have to be still and let the river carry us where it will.

In my case I was unwilling to give myself over to the river of life. The dam I built for my life was so very tight that I had become stagnant, especially in my understanding of myself. For many, many years I let everyone else except me determine the flow of my life. There was no internal mechanism that allowed me to compare the thoughts of others to my own desires and needs. The quest for wholeness is not something to be found out there; it's something to be dealt with and created from within. The only way my ecosystem was saved was by doing the work of understanding who I was, what was important to me, and how I should proceed based on these understandings. Once I unlocked the gate to my inner self, like the dam holding back the reservoir's waters, my life began to flow. You know by now that until I began the long-overdue inner work, my life was close to permanent stagnation. I did not ask those critical questions that pertained to who I was and what I should be doing with my life.

Sometimes we don't ask the questions because we lose the comfort zones we have in life at that time – whether the comfort zone is in our job, our parenting, our relationships, or our marriage. We keep our lives dammed up, like the lesson from the creek. We must be willing to move along with life; we will not only survive it, but we will learn from it.

4. As we pack our toolkits, we need to do so from a viewing point of "considered opinions," rather than just "opinions." Are you accustomed to having

others share with you their opinions about "whatever"? I certainly am. However, I've learned over the years that those whose opinions I truly value are the ones who have taken the time to form a "considered opinion" about the topic under discussion. Those with considered opinions have taken time to sit on their porch and reflect, and they have wondered before they wandered. They have gathered together some information about the topic so their knowledge base has been expanded. They are centered in their lives, and they are practicing enlightened self-interest. Now I have all the time in the world to sit on the porch and listen to these folks. When my ego spoke for me I did not listen to even considered opinions.

5. There are four tools we need to have in order to move forward on the journey toward being in relationship with others:[7]

We must realize that before we are truly in relationship with another, we must first have a relationship with ourselves. Psychologists have been telling us that for years. I'm not talking about a narcissistic-type feeling about myself. I'm talking about the ability to accept who I am as a human being, to make peace with my past, to embrace the present, and slowly move to the future.

We must approach being in relationship not with what we're expecting to get but with what we're expected to give. To do this, the relationship must become a matter of will and actions, not just feelings.

We must be willing to face our shadow side. There are places in the corridors of our lives that only we know exist, parts of us that we have never opened up to a single person. We know it's in our heads, and we know it's in our hearts, but no one else knows it. And in order to grow in the adult arena of relationships, we must be willing to become transparent, to open our dark side and make it known to others. This is where the intense deepening of a relationship happens – when we allow that person to become the guide to our soul, to take us into places we would never go with anyone else.

We must be willing to embrace the spiritual dimension of the relationship. Being in relationship is a psychological and a spiritual journey. Relationship is the invitation to open ourselves to the seen and the unseen, to the larger parts borne out of our contact with one another.

6. As we venture off the porch on our quest for wholeness, we can take some tools with us.

While we are on the quest for wholeness, we need to get out of our comfort zones. When we expand those zones our road will be full of both pain and bliss, and our enemy will be shallowness. If it feels safe, it is probably not the right path. If it scares you, it probably is. Our culture makes it easy to run from

7 The thinking of Mark Gerzon and Bob Baggott influenced the 5th, 6th and 7th tools.

pain. We learn to take the sun for granted by running from every storm.

While on the quest for wholeness, we need to listen to our dreams because our dreams are ways of reminding us of what we've forgotten. In our quest for wholeness, dreams are our personal guide. We've starved and neglected so much of our lives, and those areas are stuck deep down in the hidden rooms of our psyche. They can begin to emerge only if we dream.

While on the quest for wholeness, do not pretend you're not confused. Confusion is the mother of all change, and if we do not question, we'll not have the quest. The greatest ability we can have is to live in the questions and not have the answers.

While on the quest for wholeness, be careful not to sacrifice those very people, institutions, and activities that brought you this far, for they are what will give us the strength and personhood to deal with the quest..

While on the quest for wholeness, be sensitive to the words of God's spirit. God speaks to us through events. God comes to us through the inner spirit — through what happens to us each and every day.

7. There are six additional tools we take with us on the quest for a calling:

You must not only hear the call, but you must also heed it. As soon as you hear it, you have to begin to act, to reinvent it.

Don't decide too quickly that it's the wrong calling. Don't get back on the porch right away because you think the talents you have don't need to be used. Bill Moyers tells the story of driving out of the parking lot of a Baptist church when he was young. He says he just knew he was called to be a preacher. He just felt it. So he decided to attend seminary. He attended Southwestern Seminary, he graduated, and then he never became a minister. He said, "Perhaps I had the wrong number." Look at what he's done with his life. I know I have jumped back on my porch too quickly at times in my life. I was afraid and didn't know where I was being led.

Remember that work isn't everything. Few people on their deathbed say, "I wish I had spent more time at the office." Think about it. Said the Indian poet, "God respects me when I work, but God loves me when I sing." How I wish I had known earlier in my life that God loves me when I sing.

Remember that money isn't everything. Do you know that Thomas Jefferson, in writing the Declaration of Independence, changed the last phrase from Life, Liberty, and the Pursuit of Property, to Life, Liberty, and the Pursuit of Happiness?

Learn to celebrate what you have been given. Each of us is unique, and we have talents others don't have. Check it out. Bring it forth.

A series of paintings in the National Gallery of Art in Washington, D.C., spoke to our calling in life. The series was entitled "The Voyages of Life." The first painting in the series, entitled "Childhood," depicts a young child sitting in a boat, sailing on a blue, crystal clear ocean. The sky is full of puffy white clouds, and sitting in the back of the boat, with a hand on the rudder, is an angel, all dressed in white.

The second portrait in the series, entitled "Youth," again depicts a beautiful, blue sea, with a wonderful boat on the water. Seated in the boat is a child who has grown up and is now a young adult. The clouds are still white and puffy; the sky is still a beautiful blue. But something has changed. This young adult is now holding the rudder of the boat, steering it, while the angel, all dressed in white, is standing on the shore.

In the third portrait in the series, labeled "Adulthood," the situation has dramatically changed. The sky that was once blue is now very, very dark – no white clouds to be found. The sea that was once beautiful and calm and blue is now roaring. The boat is at a forty-degree angle, and seated in the boat is an adult holding onto the rudder, but the rudder is broken in his hand. The adult is looking up towards the heavens, looking for guidance, with no angel in sight.

The artist is trying to say something about adulthood and the quest for a calling that happens during those adult years. This journey we are on is one of enormous struggles. And the struggles are enormous for me because on my quest it took me a long time to distinguish between an occupation and a calling. My profession is education – it defines the work I do. Until recently I had no understanding of my calling. During my adult years, my sailboat has often been at a forty-degree angle, and my rudder has been broken. I had no sense of direction, the waters were rough and until recently I found no angel dressed in white.

Mathew Fox has written *On Becoming a Mystical, Musical Bear*, a book in which he describes one of the mysteries of life is the mastery of vocation. Because many of us confuse the meanings of occupation and vocation, we narrowly define our vocation as what we do for a living, and we miss the spiritual definition of this term – what we are called to do with our lives. Those who experience corporate downsizing may actually gain from their loss because they are free to leave their occupation and go on a search for their vocation – their calling. As I have said earlier, it is that period of time in our lives that we need more from what we do for a living than just to occupy space.

Perhaps our vocation is not to have just one great revelation and then to live it out the rest of our lives. What if our calling to a vocation comes in a series of momentary vocations? This means that we can have an occupation that all of us, each and every day, are called from into a momentary vocation. If we are called to a series of momentary vocations, we can find meaning in what we are doing right now, within our occupation.

Finding meaning sometimes starts with questions. Why is it that if we see an injustice in the world, we can decide to stand up to it and light a candle instead of curse the darkness? Why is it that we might be compelled at one special moment to share a thought we have with another person? Why is it that sometimes a teacher, who has had a particularly difficult day with one of her students, will take time at the end of that day to sit and talk with that student and ask about his or her life? Why is it that once in a while we have an urge to write a check for something, some social cause, and we have no idea why we're doing it? Conventional wisdom says if you're unhappy, if you're disillusioned, if you're restless with your current place in life, you must go out in search of your true calling. I am suggesting that within our occupations right now comes a calling for a momentary vocation. Each and every day we are called to do good deeds on this earth – to experience moments of grace and beauty.

Karen Bland did good deeds and found her calling within her occupation. Karen was a paralegal. Each morning she negotiated the twelve miles from her home to the city of Miami; she went to the fourth floor of the Northern Trust Bank building, and there she did her job. At five each afternoon, she left the Northern Trust Bank building, got back into her van, and once again negotiated the twelve miles back to her home. And each day, after Karen got home, she went into the kitchen and made over a hundred sandwiches and heated several gallons of soup. And then she took all that food, put it in the back of her red and white van, pulled out of the driveway, and maneuvered those twelve miles back into the city of Miami. And for the next three hours, she drove around feeding the homeless.

A New York reporter who worked for the *Miami Herald* wrote an article on Karen, and he asked her, "Karen, why do you do what you do?" And you know what she said? "My job is in a law firm. My calling is to feed these people." Because of her work, the city of Miami now operates medical vans, clothing vans, and literacy vans – all because of one woman who knew you can have an occupation at the same time you are having a vocation. Life does not have to be either/or but can be both/and – amidst our occupation, we can still experience our calling. When it comes, it always answers the deep vacuums we feel in our soul.

8. I would like to borrow two tools from Steven Covey. The first is to "seek first to understand, and then to be understood," and the second is the importance, in our relationships with others, of moving from dependence, through independence,

to interdependence, all the while avoiding co-dependence. For much of my adult life, I did not try to understand others – I was not a good listener. I have wanted people to know how I feel about a situation before I try to understand their viewing points. I just knew I had the "right" answers to everyone's problems, and when I thought I could be everyone's white knight, I doled out these solutions at will. I am working at not doing that anymore in my life. Becoming an active listener is important to me, and I try to gain an understanding of others' perspectives before giving my own. Knowing now I am a white knight only to myself, I no longer need to rush in and try to rescue folks. Knowing this is a freeing-up feeling for me. I want to help when I can, but it was Socrates who said, "For me not to know is good, because it causes you to pursue." I use this quote with my doctoral students and in my work as an executive coach. Socrates' words encourage me not to give answers, but to ask questions. My students and my coaching clients have everything they need to make good decisions and answer their life questions. If I can listen well and ask appropriate questions, the answers they have inside will begin to come forth.

Covey writes in *7 Habits of Highly Effective People* about a relationship moving from dependence, *through* independence, *toward* interdependence. Our relationships ought not to be just about independence but interdependence. We need to be comfortable in interacting with people when that interaction is healthy and meaningful. It is so easy for people in a relationship to become co-dependent, with neither being interdependent and each actively needing the other for his or her very life. Life is an interactive process during which we begin to understand ourselves as we understand our relationships with others. Becoming interdependent, as we are interactive, allows this understanding to evolve. To become interdependent, we need to have our lives centered perfectly on the potter's wheel. I depended on Mom much of my life. Because I was dependent on her, I never gained my independence from her. Therefore, she and I were not able to achieve interdependence. We never interacted from a base of each of us being independent of the other.

9. On a regular basis, we need the tool of reflection to consider those five questions I asked of myself while I was a superintendent: (1) Am I being true to myself? (2) Do I exercise introspection? (3) Am I being hopeful about myself? (4) Do I have a passion for truth about myself? (5) Do I see frustration, tension, and growth as essential parts of the change process? Some of these questions are more difficult for me than others. Number one and number four are the two I need to nurture. As I open myself to others, I need to be able to accept the truth about myself, not only from others but also more importantly from myself.

10. Convince yourself that you absolutely cannot control outcomes.

Believe me, I have tried to control them, to no avail. Again, my Higher Power does not want me to "sit and do nothing" with my life, just waiting for the next "sign from above" somehow to make itself known to me. That Higher Power, however, does want me to plan and reflect – for me within the context of my lessons – and then remain open to how it all turns out.

11. And, because my Higher Power does want me to do some reflecting and planning, the journey is about both the compass in my hand and the one in my heart – one of those "both/ands" again, and I like that.

12. Always work toward becoming centered in life and achieving balance – much like the potter as she places her clay on the wheel. Joseph Campbell said: "There's something inside of you that knows when you're in the center." Becoming centered emotionally means we acknowledge that love is the most powerful force in the universe. We cannot love others until we love ourselves, and as we grow in our true love of self, we learn how to love others more. Love is the beginning and the ending, the alpha and the omega. Becoming centered spiritually requires us to live our lives holistically. As recorded in the words of Hua Hu Ch'ing, "Join your body, mind, and spirit in all you do. Make choices accord with nature. Rely on yourself. Allow your work and your recreation to be one and the same. Do exercise that develops your whole being. Listen to music that bridges your body, mind, and spirit. Serve others while cultivating yourself."

We Need Bags to Carry Our Tools

For many of us it takes a crisis, mid-life or other,
to get us even thinking about what
we're carrying. And then, unfortunately, we tend
to make decisions from within the crisis. Instead of
pausing to reconsider, in a purposeful manner, what
we've brought along and why, we're
apt to cast everything off and just run.

Repacking Your Bags: Lighten Your Load

These twelve tools can be added to the tools that I have provided throughout the book. With my interest in having form follow function, the function, in this instance, is knowing what tools we need for our tool kits. This time, the form needed to accommodate the tools is the bags we need to pack for the trip. If we do not know what tools we need to pack, we won't know the size and shape of the bags we need. Our bags become the "kits" in which we can carry our "tools."

For me, it has taken some serious unpacking – letting go – and then some serious repacking to begin my journey and to tell my story. As I have unpacked baggage I've carried all my life, I have been able to see events in my life from different viewing points. I've been able to ask new questions. As I unpack, I discover new parts of me and of my journey. Even with our tool kits in hand, we need tremendous self-awareness to know what to pack and what to leave behind. We have to know who we are in order to know what to pack and which tools are needed. In our current lives of rapid change, we will have to unpack and repack our bags often. The skills needed for this task come in part from asking the right questions. These "quest – ions" provide the trail markers for our journey. We need to keep asking ourselves the question: Are the bags that I am carrying still the right ones for my journey?

Personally, I always carry too many bags and pack more than I could ever use on any one trip. My motto is to pack quickly, taking too much, rather than spending time trying to figure out what I really need. I figure all that out after I've arrived at my destination. Remember, I've not been good at wondering before I wandered. The same is true for my life trips.

When I spent that long weekend with David Sheridan on board *Messenger*, I took only two small bags, just what I thought I would need. I was so proud of myself when I checked my baggage at the airport! Going home three days later, I was surprised that there was more space in the bags than when I arrived for sailing. As I put my baggage in the overhead storage area when getting on the plane for the return trip home, I realized I could not remember putting two items back in the bags upon repacking and leaving the boat. I yanked the bags down, went through them hurriedly, and realized I was right. I was stuck. When I got home, I called David and left a message. Of course, he was going to sail for a couple more days, so I couldn't touch base with him right away. When I finally talked to him David confirmed I had left one item but couldn't find a second one. David sent the one item back to me, but the location of the other remains a mystery. Even when I pack correctly and lightly, the trick is to repack <u>the same things</u> for the trip home, or so I thought. Now I cannot honestly remember what item was left that David couldn't find, so obviously I must not have needed it for the trip. It now seems fine not to have retrieved that second item. The skill is learning to take only what we need so we have all we need, but we also need all we have taken with us.

Unpacking and repacking our bags is a process that occurs from the cradle to the grave. Again and again we need to revisit this process in order to continue giving meaning to our journey.

Even with the right bags packed, we can still get lost on our journey – a journey both of adventure and inventure. In today's world, being lost is becoming a familiar place. However, being lost means we need courage to face the newness in our lives and accept our need to continue learning throughout life. In *Repacking Our Bags*, Richard Lieder says this is the "difference between the attitude of a tourist and an adventurer. The tourist merely visits life, checking sites off a list. The adventurer experiences life, immersing head and heart in the totality of it. Ultimately, the difference has to do with a willingness to get lost."

Judith Sills offers this definition of "excess baggage," in her book of the same name: "It's all those things that we can't see about ourselves that keep getting in our way." Sills has described my life. As I mentioned above, my method of packing has been to throw a bunch of stuff into a suitcase and go off on a trip, always having more than I need but sometimes not having what I need. I have packed the baggage I need for my life journey in exactly the same way. I have thrown my tools into bags for my journey – always too much and often not appropriate to what I need – because I had not wondered before I wandered and therefore didn't see those parts of myself that kept getting in my way. Sills goes on to say that baggage is defined as excessive if it meets one of three criteria: it comes between you and success, it comes between you and satisfaction – peace of mind and a sense of well-being, or it makes you harder to love.

We all have baggage in our lives. Sometimes we bump into it while trying to get where we are going. According to Sills, there are "five ruling passions" in our lives that result in excess baggage: the drive for control, the drive for self-esteem, the drive for security, the drive for attachment, and the drive for justice. These five ruling passions, as you now know, have certainly surfaced in my life because these are the passions I have felt a need to satisfy in my life – often not knowing why.

Sills concludes her book by offering these paradoxes of our baggage:

> Baggage is a blind spot. Yet we have moments of blinding clarity...Baggage is an inevitable side effect of personality. Yet it seems also to be an inevitable side effect of life... Baggage is the part of ourselves that gets in the way. And yet who could deny that other people go a long way toward weighing us down too?.. Baggage is something you don't know about yourself. But at times, it is so intrusive that it seems difficult to know anything else.

Tools for our bags and the proper bags to carry our tools are two highly interactive lessons for our journey. However, before you answer my question, "May I help you with your bags?" you may want to be certain I have my own bags packed properly.

CHAPTER 9: THE PAST X THE FUTURE =THE PRESENT

The future is not a result of choice among alternative paths offered by the present, but a place that is created – created first in mind and will, created next in activity. The future is not some place we are going to, but one we are creating. The paths are not to be found, but made, and the activity of making them changes both the maker and the destination.

John Schaar, ***Loyalty in America***

The future enters into us in order to transform in us, long before it happens.

Ranier Maria Rilke

As we learn to get off the porch, we also learn how to get out of the box

The Porch, The Beach, and Carpe Diem – Seize the Day!

When I was teaching United States History to high school juniors, I used to talk about the importance of understanding our past so that we could better understand our present and then interpret the future. Because change is all around us, that formula should now read: The Past x The Future = The Present. Our ability to get outside the boxes that confine us – at work, at home, in our community, in our relationships – and make predictions about the future based on considered opinions will sharpen those discernments we must make while living today. This chapter returns us to the frenetic pace with which we accommodate change in our lives and suggests that the way to make the most out of today is to internalize the idea of Carpe Diem – seize the day.

Breaking the Mold

There's nothing more humiliating than being forced to work in a box. You don't realize what a brain-deadening effect having a cubicle job is until you leave.

Scott Adams, Creator of ***Dilbert***

Below you will find an activity I use with many of my graduate classes called "The 9 Dots and Change." It has to do with how we handle change in our lives. When looking at the nine dots on the left, you will note the directions for the activity. Once you place your pencil on the paper, you may not lift it up, and you must draw four straight lines that connect all nine of the dots. Without exception (unless someone has done this activity before), those following the directions do not realize that in order to draw those four straight lines, connecting all nine dots, they have to project themselves outside the nine dots at two different places. You will notice on the model to the right the dots are connected with four straight lines, with two points projected outside the original nine dots. Students and others completing the activity invariably want to accomplish the task by staying inside the box – the nine dots. They haven't been told they cannot go outside the nine dots to connect the four lines; they just assume they can be successful from inside the box. So it is with life. To be successful, we at times need to get outside the boundaries that are self-imposed.

The lines connecting the nine dots represent the energy of the activity and in our lives – and allow us to give meaning to our lives. The dots are not the points of focus; rather, it is the energy in the lines that allows the dots to become integrated and whole. And so it is with our lives. The focus is the journey between the dots.

It takes courage to break the mold and gain new viewing points on life. Having read to this point, however, you know it is absolutely essential to do so. We cannot solve the problems of today by implementing the solutions we used yesterday. Change will not allow us to do this.

Draw 4 straight lines: (1) without lifting your pencil from the paper; (2) making sure your 4 straight lines touch each of the 9 dots, one time only.

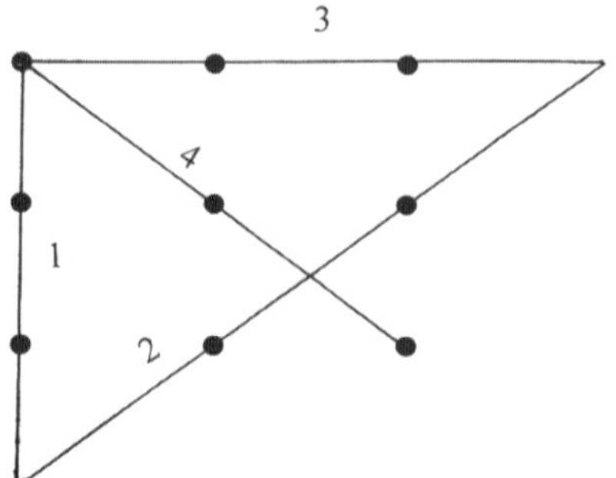

The great Jewish "theologian," Woody Allen, encouraged us to look at the world differently when he said, "Eighty percent of life is just showing up." But when we allow ourselves to venture off the porch, we are invited to "come and see," an invitation to move out of the comfort zone of the eighty percent and learn of the other twenty percent of life. I would suggest that in this place we discern many of life's hidden treasures. To remain stuck in the eighty percent is deliberately to be less than we are capable of ever becoming. And in order to experience and celebrate that twenty percent, we must be willing to get out of the boxes that are confining us in life.

The Desire for Growth and Change

I believe that the need to change – to grow, to expand, to go deeper – does not exist unless we desire it. If first there is not inherent dissatisfaction with where we are and a yearning to understand who we are in our journey, the process of growing outside the box will be a more difficult experience. The reason is that growth does involve promise and enlargement and excitement. But, as we know, growth also entails letting go and facing the uncertainties of life.

Getting outside the boxes in our life is very, very difficult, as shown in the following story about a little boy going to the circus. A father gave his little boy a dollar to go see the circus after he finished his chores. As the clown passed by where the boy was standing, he reached into his pocket, took out that precious crisp one dollar bill, and handed it to the clown. Then the little boy turned around and went home. The little boy thought he had seen the circus when in reality he had only seen the parade. In many of our lives, we settle for so little because we don't know how to jump outside our boxes. The question of how much we desire an anticipated change will help determine if we're willing to venture outside the box to experience that other twenty percent, to see the circus and not just the parade.

Do you remember the popular film *City Slickers* starring Billy Crystal and Jack Palance? It is the story of a New York businessman who was stuck. He had stopped growing. He no longer felt he was edging toward something more, and he could not carry his own personal load. He had become complacent, so his wife encourages him to go and, as she said, "find your smile." Crystal joins two friends, who were stuck as well in their own lives, on a cattle drive between New Mexico and Colorado – thus the title City Slickers. In this film, Jack Palance is the leathery old cowboy who has been on the range forever. And you get the sense that he had forgotten more about life than Billy Crystal would ever learn. One late afternoon, Crystal and Palance are riding horses side by side. For hours Billy Crystal has been asking this leathery, crusty cowboy questions about life! Palance stops his horse. Crystal stops his horse as Palance turns to Crystal and says, "You know, you city slickers are all alike. You spend fifty-one weeks a year getting your rope all tied in knots, and you expect one week out here to change it." Does that sound familiar? And then Palance asks this question: "Son, do you know what the secret to life is?"

Billy Crystal's eyes grow large and he asks, "What is the secret of life? Tell me."

And that old, crusty cowboy, holding up one finger on his right hand, says, "Son, the secret to life is one thing, one thing."

And Billy Crystal asks, "What is it?"

Palance says, "That is something you have to find out for yourself."

I must admit that I am a bit suspicious of anyone who tells us that if we get out of the box and change one thing in our life, happiness will be ours. Life is far too complicated for a change in one aspect to make that much difference. However, I may have bumped into one thought – as I've scurried in and out of my box on the porch – that may be the beginning of the answer to Billy Crystal's question of "What is it?" I think that one thing can be the desire we have to get outside the box and experience that other twenty percent in our lives, the desire to do it, the desire to live and to grow into the deeper meanings of life. The author Brihadaranyaka Upanishad said that "you are what your deep, driving desire is. As your desire is, so is your will. As your will is, so is your deed. As your deed is, so is your destiny."

As human beings, we have a deep ambivalence to change. Because we are by nature static creatures, none of us really likes to change. Yet there is much within us that wants to grow, to expand, to develop, to desire change, and to go deeper into living life. While we enjoy growing, we resist the prospect of change. Sometimes I really do fear that the spindle of routine and staleness is pricking our culture and that we are giving up our dollar for the parade, missing the circus, which is where the real action is – outside the box.

The Calm Yet Ever-Changing Ocean

There is one wave on the ocean
with my name on it, and there is
a separate wave for everyone in this room.
During that instant that I'm on this planet,
I am that wave – unique for only a
brief time – so I must make the most of it.

Forrest Church, ***Life Lines: Holding On (and Letting Go)***

When my wife and I were on the Outer Banks of North Carolina, on vacation with Eric, Stacy, and twenty of Stacy's family, I made it a point to pay attention to the beach and to the waves and winds. I was amazed at the changes that occur moment to moment. The waves and the wind are ever changing. No two moments are the same as we look out over the ocean. The tide is always in the process of coming in or going out. I began to look forward to the changes in the ocean and, through its constant movement, came to know that not only is each day different but each moment of each day is different. I can truly learn to live with and appreciate change while on the beach, and I absolutely love being next to the ocean. Amidst all the change I see while experiencing the waves and the wind in my face, I feel a sense of calmness within, and somehow from that calmness I gain a heightened sense of well being and purpose in my life. I can learn to make my heart an ocean and, with that connection, go beyond the troubles I may be experiencing in my life.

Carpe Diem: Eric, My Higher Power, and Robin Williams

My role model for getting the most out of each day is my son, Eric. Now in his early thirties, Eric has truly lived his entire life by seizing the day. I watched him while he was at home growing up, and I observe him at a distance now, still seizing the opportunities and joys each day has to offer him. As recently as two weeks ago, while I was sitting on the porch writing, I read a card Eric and Stacy had sent my wife and me. Inside the card, each of them wrote, describing the beauty surrounding them while on vacation. Eric's thought was:

I wish every day could be as simple and as
beautiful as today! Actually, I suppose
it can. I just need to learn to be in
every moment that passes by.
It's as simple as that.

More than any other person I know, Eric matches his beliefs and his behavior while centered on *Carpe Diem*. I know I've also learned much from my daughter Tracie, my son-in-law Chris, and my daughter-in-law Stacy, as they each seize the days of their own journeys. My wife Bonnie also works hard at living in the moment and taking advantage of all of life's moments. I have not been so good at seizing every opportunity of the days on or off the porch. But I'm learning from my children and my wife.

Enjoying the moment was brought home to me one summer as Bonnie and I drove back to Indiana from our masters' degree work in Greeley, Colorado. Bonnie describes my driving as a "horse going back to the stable" – I have a direct route and I don't vary from it. That summer Bonnie wanted to stop in Springfield, Illinois, to see Abe Lincoln's home. Reluctantly, I drove the car off the interstate and finally found a place to park in downtown Springfield. When we got close to Lincoln's home, we saw the line waiting to get in – stretching for two city blocks. I hesitated a moment and then said, "There, you've 'seen' Lincoln's home, now let's go." I got my way and we headed home. When we are in Oregon, visiting Eric and Stacy, we often take day trips to see the beauty around Ashland. Wherever our destination for that day, we always make frequent stops along the way to relax and to marvel at the beautiful scenery. Now I enjoy these frequent stops. I wish I could have learned to enjoy the moment earlier in my life.

Our Higher Power gives us one day at a time. But, within each of the days we are given, there is much we can do. We have long enough to find the laughter that follows our tears. We have enough time to pray and to find the silence that allows us to dance together. Within that day we can find the time to help someone in need and to notice the beauty that surrounds us. We have sufficient time to build a bridge of forgiveness or tear down a wall of resentment. And we can find the time to embrace our friends, smile at strangers, play with children, and sing our songs. It is amazing what we can do with each day we are given.

We learned from *Dead Poet's Society* the value of living in the moment, of seizing the day, of realizing there is that one wave on the ocean with our name on it. Some of the dialogue from this movie has played such an important part in my journey. In this scene, Robin Williams is introducing himself to his new group of students at the New England preparatory school. He takes his class out into the foyer of the building, in front of a display case full of pictures and trophies of years ago – a history of the school – and addresses his students.

"In this class, you can call me either Mr. Keating, or if you're slightly more daring, Oh, Captain, my Captain. Mr. Pitts, open your hymnal to page 542 and read the first stanza of the poem you find there."

"'Diversions to Make Much of Time: Gather Ye rosebuds while ye may. Oh, time is still a-flying. And this same flower that smiles today tomorrow will be a-dying.'"

"Thank you, Mr. Pitts. 'Gather Ye Rosebuds While Ye May.' The Latin term for that sentiment is *Carpe Diem*. Who knows what that means?"

"*Carpe Diem*, that's seize the day."

"Very good, Mr. Meeks. Seize the day. Gather ye rosebuds while ye may. Why does the writer use these lines?"

"'Cause he's in a hurry."

"No, ding!! Thank you for playing anyway. 'Cause we are food for worms, lads. 'Cause, believe it or not, each and every one of us in this room is one day going to stop breathing, turn cold, and die, like Mr. Ford over here. Peruse some of the faces of the past. You've walked past them many times. I don't think you've really looked at them. They're not that different from you, are they? Same haircuts; full of hormones just like you; invincible, just like you feel. The world is their oyster. They believe they're destined for great things. Just like many of you. Their eyes are full of hope, just like you. Did they wait 'til it was too late to make from their lives even one iota of what they were capable? Because you see, gentlemen, these boys are now fertilizing daffodils. If you listen real close you can hear them whisper their legacy to you. Go on, lean in. Listen. Do you hear it? '*Carpe Diem*, seize the day, boys. Make your lives extraordinary.'"

I have observed my own kids, and now their spouses, for a long time. I have watched them actually apply some of the lessons from this movie to their daily lives, and I have learned a lot by watching. What better model for them to use than an educator who was trying to get his students, in this very conservative, very staid, and very stuffy Eastern prep school, to break out of their old traditions, to take risks, to get out of the box, and to consider being themselves.

Epilogue: Returning to Where I Began

We shall not cease from exploration
And the end of all of our exploring
Will be to arrive where we started
And know the place for the first time.

T.S. Eliot, ***Four Quartets***

I can see clearly now the rain is gone.
I can see all obstacles in my way.
Gone are the dark clouds that had me blind.
It's gonna be a bright, bright sunshiny day.
Think I can make it now, the pain is gone.
All of the bad feelings have disappeared.
Here is the rainbow I've been prayin' for.
It's gonna be a bright, bright sunshiny day.

Jimmy Cliff

And that's all I know about that.

Forrest Gump

Well, we've come to the end of my journey thus far. The Eliot quote above is appropriate for this particular time in my journey. I feel like I am returning to where I began – on my porch – and enjoying the opportunity of seeing it for the first time, as it is – a haven for <u>R</u>esting, <u>R</u>efreshing, and <u>R</u>eflecting, as well as a place from which I can launch new adventures and inventures. You will notice that the sailboat in the background has its sails up, catching the wind. By anticipating the future, I can adjust the sails as needed to harness the wind and move my life. Having this picture at the ending of this book, accompanied by Eliot's words is also appropriate because, as you know, our journeys are not linear, but circular. We keep circling back to fill in the gaps in our lives, and our journeys have not been in a straight line.

My path is circular, and returning to the porch is comforting for me. I never knew I could make this return, and I certainly never realized I could look forward to coming back to a porch that held such negative meaning for me in my early years. What a sense of relief to have this new viewing point of my porch.

You know me well enough by now to know I am still right in the midst of the struggles of my journey. Every day I realize I still have much to learn about my twenty-two lessons. I do not make this last statement with regret but with anticipation. I want to tell you once again that writing about my twenty-two lessons does not mean I have internalized them to any great degree. I still have much work to do. I may know more of the questions, and I'm learning more about the way to live with the questions and live toward the answers.

I have a few more answers in my life than when I began writing about my journey, but I have none for you. Taking my thoughts and applying them directly to your life would be a mistake and would rob you of your own journey. If, however, I've allowed you to bring forth some of your questions that have always been there and just needed asking, I will be happy.

I've learned that a path chooses us as much as we choose it. I also believe our own unique paths were there even before we were born. In my attempt to understand who I am and what I am about, I am creating my story. Please notice I said I am creat<u>**ing**</u> my story, not my story has now been creat<u>**ed**</u>. You have just read that story as far as I've lived it. My story is helping me understand the larger picture of my life's journey. It has been important for me to look inward to begin discovering what my life is about and to discover the path that was in me as I was born – the path that I have been traveling all my life.

In order to understand <u>your</u> stories better, I first have had to gain a clearer understanding of my own story. The work starts from within. If I don't start the work of understanding my own story first from inside me, I will distort your stories through the lens of the ill-defined understanding of my own story.

For now, unfortunately, it is time to part company. Deepak Chopra said it well in his book, *The Seven Spiritual Laws of Success*: "We have stopped for a moment to encounter each other, to meet, to love, to share. This is a precious moment, but it is transient. It is a little parenthesis in eternity. If we share with caring, lightheartedness, and love, we will create abundance and joy for each other. And then this moment will have been worthwhile." Instantaneously, as I end my writing and you end your reading, our journeys continue. For I must choose those paths which will allow my journey to discover new meanings in my life, and you must choose those paths which will allow you to continue with your own important journeys. One of my realizations in telling my story is that it is difficult to know just when to call a "time out" and invoke Forrest Gump's words noted above: "And that's all I know about that."

Right now, I'm feeling that the writing I had feared and avoided for so long has now become the easier part of this journey. The more difficult task, for me, is actually to live the lessons in my life. One legacy I can leave for myself, and hopefully for others, is to live what I have just written and avoid the thought you read earlier: "What you do shouts so loudly people can't hear what you say." I will tell you, though, parts of my porch lessons will be easier for me to live out than others. I hope I can do this! I have to admit to some fear and apprehension. I'm so good at giving others the same advice I need to give myself. For once in my life, can I actually follow my own advice? As I continue my journey and learn better how to live the questions, I will again someday stumble upon some answers and move on.

As we continue to learn the value of the porches in our lives and the importance of setting our sails to accommodate the changes we experience from our porches, I am honored that you would join me on this part of your own journey. Thank you. I know I will have my own lessons to learn from my *Lessons from the porch* writing experience. I am just uncertain at this time what many of those lessons might be. Maybe those lessons are for another time. I do want to leave myself open to the possibilities that are there for me to continue my own growth.

Lessons Learned

Gradually, if I go with courage and wisdom,
I arrive at my destination, a place called paradise.
It is not a land free of struggle, a realm devoid of
pain or grief. But it is the place where I
feel at home, where I am supposed to be.

Richard Bode, ***Beachcombing at Miramar***

There are some lessons I have learned by writing about the porch. The first lesson is that for me to proceed on my journey, I needed to have the permission of Mom and Dad to tell my story. I don't fully understand the reasons, but you know this permission came to me after Mom died. I believe Mom and Dad both knew this and continue to know this as I stand on their shoulders to finish this writing. And I feel them with me as never before, helping guide my writing. Studs Terkel's book, *May the Circle Be Unbroken*, talks about death in the same view – not as grief or catharsis – but as a very normal everyday part of living that simply has more understanding to give to those still here. And it's that understanding that has come from Mom's death that triggered all the storyteller in me had to say, on behalf of life – my own and hopefully yours as well.

The second lesson I've learned is that I have a different viewing point about Mom and Dad than I did when I began writing. Actually getting my story on paper and going through the reflective process necessary to accomplish that have allowed me to gain an appreciation for and understanding of Mom and Dad – what they did for me while alive and the legacy they left for me in death. I grew to understand better a point made earlier in the book: as we age, we sometimes change from needing to give or receive forgiveness to increasing our appreciation for parents who were not perfect. As I continue to acknowledge my own imperfections as a husband and a parent, my appreciation and understanding of my own parents increase.

I've come to appreciate Dad, for example, in ways that didn't exist before I experienced the writing. He was smarter about parts of life much earlier in his life than I've been in mine. He held his family utmost in his mind and heart. He struggled for almost thirty years with a debilitating illness that would have caused some to stop dead in their tracks – literally and figuratively. He never showed any great outward signs of anger. I wish he could have, but he handled that situation in terms of what made most sense to him.

Dad recognized when he was not happy in a job or when the job had become too much for him. Asking for a new assignment at work when his job got too stressful was a sign of strength, not a sign of weakness – the latter being an impression I carried around for years. I think Dad recognized his strengths much sooner in life that I recognized my own. I spent the first half of life not wanting to walk in his footsteps. Now I wish I could.

I've learned that Mom controlled; she was the strength and foundation for the marriage and for my sister and me. Dad was smart enough to recognize her strengths and allow her to use those characteristics about herself that would move the family forward, economically and educationally. My own stubbornness over the years has not, until more recently, allowed me to make that same recognition of Bonnie. For me to admit Bonnie's strengths means I have weaknesses. You know what? I do. And it's important to get them out on the table and talk about them as a family.

When Mom and I spent that day talking into the tape recorder, she talked about Dad working long hours and always bringing home his money. At one point she said, "Maybe I was a little too stingy, but, when I was young, Mom and I never had anything." I'm old enough now to have been through several cycles of financial ups and downs in my own family. You need to know that, although Mom may have been somewhat accurate in describing herself as a "little too stingy," she did a wonderful job of managing the finances for our family. I did not feel this way growing up, but looking back I most certainly applaud her for taking such care of her family. Remember, when I was at home growing up, it was all about me, me, me and what I needed and wanted. My ego had already begun to grow much too large. Mom couldn't have had much experience in managing finances as a young girl living at home with Grandma Jolly. Somehow she locked in on the importance of being fiscally responsible, and she was. Today my sister and I are enjoying the benefits of Mom's financial planning – a legacy I hope to pass on to my children.

Remember what I've said about each generation working to leave a place better than it was when they found it? Doing so leaves a legacy. Certainly Mom and Dad had to receive their legacies from my two sets of grandparents. You know a bit about the environments in which Mom and Dad were raised and the circumstances surrounding their early years. My parents could easily have repeated for my sister and me life as they found it in their own lives as children. But because my grandparents wanted a better life for Mom and Dad as they grew to be adults, my parents in turn wanted to leave the legacy of a better life for my sister and me. What was there about my grandparents that honored their desire to create better lives for their children? What gave them the courage to break the cultural cycle they had experienced as children? What caused my parents to have this same desire for Mary Belle and me? Legacies are left and legacies are received.

I want to tell you a story about an internationally known soccer player from Uganda, Stone Kyambada, who broke the cultural cycle he had experienced as a child. Stone lived in an impoverished village in Uganda where many of the young men were unemployed and unemployable, with little direction in their lives. Peace Corps volunteers in this village helped those who lived there.

The volunteers asked the boys what they would like to be involved in, and they said they would like to have a soccer team. So the volunteers started a soccer team with a few of the boys, and encouraged them to bring their friends to the practices. Soon the boys came to the Peace Corps volunteers and said they had found their coach. The volunteers were somewhat leery of who this person might be, but they met Stone. He said he really wanted to coach the team, and he did not want any pay for what he did.

Stone began playing soccer in high school and soon became recognized as an exceptional soccer player. When he was 18 he landed a spot on his first professional team, and he played at this level for ten years. By that time he had been chosen to be on the national team – a goal of all Ugandan soccer players since this opportunity gave them the chance to play in Europe and be seen by scouts from the European teams.

Soon after Stone began his international soccer career, he was on a breakaway during a game. A player from the other team cut him down from behind before Stone could score, the contact tearing the ligaments in his knee and ending his soccer career. It wasn't an accident. The player did it intentionally.

In a country where revenge is commonplace, where sixteen years of war and corruption were centered on revenge, Stone just said to this man, "Don't worry about it. You did what you had to do."

Stone's ability to forgive this man was remarkable. Here was a man with integrity, and integrity was exactly what those sixteen year olds needed in order to gain direction in their lives. Stone said, "Some of these boys were druggies, some stole, but they were all wild boys, with no direction at all."

The boys Stone started with had been rejected by their families and their community. They were seen as troublemakers and problem kids. But Stone loved the boys and showed a lot of trust in them. Love and forgiveness formed the foundation for the team. Stone's life taught and continues to teach these ideals. He lives in the same village as the boys – the village where he lived while growing up. The boys know his wife and children and see Stone is living everything he's teaching. That's really the powerful part of what he does, more so than what he says. Stone said, "These boys are going to be fathers. What type of families will they lead if they are left as they are?"

You read earlier the importance of matching what we say with what we do, and you also know the importance of legacies. Stone modeled both these lessons. Stone could have left those young boys as he had found them. He could have lived his life out very comfortably in his village. But he didn't. What motivated Stone to want to break the cultural cycle of those young boys and try to leave a legacy of a better life? His motivation was the same as that of my grandparents, my parents, and Bonnie and me – to leave a place a bit better than it was when we found it.

My grandparents and my parents could have easily assumed their children would simply keep the cultural chain as they had found it. They, like Stone, could have wanted nothing more for those they loved than to have them live the kind of life they experienced as children. At some point in the process of leaving and receiving legacies, family and friends have to take that bold step of wanting their family and others they love to experience something better in their lives. I'm sure the legacies left to Mom and Dad by their parents were to work hard and provide well for your family. Mom and Dad impressed upon me the importance of hard work, providing well for my family, and getting a good education. Bonnie and I are trying to leave these and other legacies with Eric, Tracie, Stacy, and Chris. Each generation <u>does</u> want to leave a place a bit better. Legacies are left, and legacies are received.

The third lesson is the importance to me of sharing my story with my wife, my children, and their spouses. As I said earlier in the book, I want Eric and Tracie to know me better than I knew Dad, and I'd like this knowledge to include Ed Poole as a human being continuing to seek humanness and not perfection. I had good parents – I wish I could have known them better.

A fourth lesson is to make sure I'm enjoying the journey and not focusing on the destination, or the "prize." As you know, I have often focused so much on my destination that I missed the beauty of the trip. The best example of the joy of the journey for me has been the writing of this book. I have so enjoyed the opportunity of sharing my story, my journey, with you. There are times, however, when my thoughts have turned to the destination, the "prize." At these times, I begin to think about getting this book "out there" so people can read it. Sometimes I forget that I want to tell, not sell, my story.

Sixteen-year-old Sarah Hughes provides a good example of enjoying the journey. Sarah was interviewed on the *Today* television show the morning after she won the gold medal for ladies' figure skating at the 2002 Winter Olympics in Salt Lake City. Sarah was so composed during this interview that I became convinced her journey <u>to and throughout the Olympic games</u> was indeed a journey and not the destination.

Sarah said she did not go to the Olympics to win a medal. She went there to have fun and enjoy the experience of being at her first Olympic games. She was relaxed and poised. She had fun doing the routine that won her the gold medal. She was just so honored to be there. Sarah talked about how great it was to stay in the Olympic Village with all the other athletes and how awesome it was to eat meals sitting next to all these world-renowned athletes. Funny, but they probably now think the same about her.

Sarah was just happy to be there. Her goal was to have fun and enjoy the journey. This sixteen year old was so far ahead of where I was at that age. She knew the difference between a journey and a destination. The very symbol she did not seek came to her so naturally because she <u>was</u> having fun enjoying the scenery along the way – a good lesson for me.

Al Carius, who teaches and coaches his sport at North Central College, understands Sarah's journey. In a recent newspaper article, he said, "Letting go and losing yourself in the activity while reacting reflexively, instinctively, will often result in superior performances." Al then went on to describe his personal experience with living in the journey and not focusing on the destination. He described a personal goal he had of breaking 4 minutes and 10 seconds in the mile. He tried everything he could imagine to make that happen, without success. He said, "The fact is, I wanted it so intently that I tried to force the desired result." He tells about traveling with his track club to a meet at the University of Wisconsin. The group got lost on the way and arrived very early in the morning the day of the meet. They had made arrangements to stay at a friend's fraternity house, and Al slept on a couch, getting almost no sleep. When he got up the morning of the race, he and his friend went out for breakfast so they could catch up on each other's lives. Al said he was so immersed in that conversation he forgot about the race. That afternoon Al broke 4:10 for the first time in his life. He ran a 4:09.7 mile, and he said, "I am convinced my mental approach of disconnecting with the outcome had an enormous positive influence." Al, like Sarah, learned that when he let go of the outcome and enjoyed the journey, the outcome took care of itself.

A fifth lesson is connected to our journey toward wholeness. Shel Silverstein, in his book *The Missing Piece*, tells the story about a circle that had a missing piece. A piece in the shape of a triangle had been cut out of it. The circle wanted to be whole, so it went on a journey to find what was missing. Because the circle was incomplete, it rolled very slowly through the world, searching. As the odd-shaped circle moved slowly, it had time to appreciate the beauty of the flowers. The sunshine felt warm to the circle. The sky was blue. The circle whistled and sang as it moved along. Animals came up to talk with the slowly rolling circle, and they all enjoyed such wonderful conversations.

The circle was enjoying the slow-paced journey but still wanted to find its missing piece. It found several pieces, but none of them fit – they were either too big or too little, too sharp or too smooth. Finally, one day the circle found its missing piece. It was happy, for now it was whole again. As it put the missing piece in place, it began to roll faster and faster.

As the circle picked up speed, it began to roll too fast to enjoy the beautiful flowers and the rolling countryside. The circle flew past the animals and didn't have time to talk anymore. Finally, as the circle realized how different the world was when it became whole, it stopped, put the missing piece by the side of the road, and rolled slowly away, once again able to enjoy the beauty on the journey.

When we are missing something — a piece – from our lives, it seems we're on a slower journey because we're trying to find what's missing. Perhaps it's only when we are <u>not</u> whole that we can take the time to enjoy the journey. As the circle became whole, the journey moved too quickly. The good news for us in this story is that we will never be completely whole. We will always be searching for some of the missing pieces in our lives. On our own journeys, we can learn from the circle – we can move slowly enough to savor the beauty and enjoy the trip. The search for wholeness is an ongoing journey. I was happier about my own missing pieces after reading Silverstein's story. Ed, the journey <u>toward</u> wholeness is <u>the</u> journey that allows you to take time to smell the roses.

The sixth lesson is savoring that long, deep, cleansing breath I've been unable to feel – that breath that has left me feeling incomplete but that will relax and calm me – helping me to know and understand where I am and how

I got here. I want you to know I can feel that breath on its way. Telling my story has allowed me to share this feeling with you. The long, deep, cleansing breath is also coming, because I have such a greater sense of appreciation for my mom and dad. Had I not sat on the porch and written my story, my parents would have forever been two different people than they appear to me now. My parents did the very best they could, and always with the best of intentions. I would not be where I am today on my journey had they not wanted the very best for me. They were unselfish and showed their love for me in ways I had not understood before I began this writing.

When that breath arrives and I feel that calming sense of relief, I will be better prepared to recognize, know, and understand the value of those next long, deep, cleansing breaths when they come along. Surely life is more than just one such calming experience. As I find this breath, there will be others to find, which will allow me to continue my journey toward wholeness. Unlike this first one I have not understood, I look forward to those yet to come.

My seventh lesson is helping me understand my vocation – my calling – in relation to my occupation. Making this distinction has been difficult for me throughout my life. Only in the past few years have I understood that we all have a calling in life and more recently that we can experience a number of smaller callings while performing within our occupation. I see my calling, not as something to be achieved but as a gift to be received. The greatest calling I can have is to continue growing into my own sense of who I am as a person. This writing has helped immeasurably in finding the joy of my vocation. You know that when I thought I was ready to change jobs, I went after a new one. You also know my dissatisfaction followed me because I didn't know why I was doing so much job searching. I now realize that, as Wayne Dyer said, I had to be in all those jobs to be where I am right now – teaching in a doctoral program at a university.

Within my current occupation, I'm finding pieces of my calling. I have come full circle – I began as a high school teacher, and I've returned to teach ing to finish my career in education. I'm simply teaching older adults now rather than teenagers. As I reflect upon my occupation, whatever my role has been within my profession, I approached it from my calling as a teacher. I now know this characteristic about my calling in life. I have always been a teacher, whether as a principal, a superintendent, or now a teacher in higher education. At its deepest level, our calling is something we can't not do. We cannot avoid our calling, and mine is teaching.

I love what I do, and most days I have the luxury of experiencing a calling within what I do – just like Karen Bland in Miami. I have an opportunity to give back to my profession, which has given me so much over the years. Some of my graduate students, who have known me over the last several years, have suggested they find a different Ed Poole today. They find me more relaxed and more self-assured these days. I'm grateful for those observations.

I also feel a part of my calling in life has been getting this book out of me and to you. I am learning so much from the experience, and I am so enjoying this part of my journey. By sharing this thought with you, I am not suggesting that the writing has been the calling in my life or that if you read the book you have the answers to your own life issues. Quite the opposite. I am happy to have concluded that the writing and the sharing of my story have been one of many callings for me – all within an occupation I love and understand better than at any other time in my professional career. I feel I can be a better facilitator and perhaps mentor for my doctoral students because I've written about my lessons. I also am saying with much joy that *Lessons from the porch* has no answers for you. As I said in Chapter 4, you should be happy I can make this statement because doing so removes the thought that my journey can be a prescription for yours. You are finding your paths and learning your lessons.

Finally, I want to identify a number of other lessons, about which I need to continue my understanding and acceptance. I have learned it is important in life to take some risks – intellectually, emotionally, and physically. It is important to trust others by trusting myself. Having meaningful relationships with others is critical to our own growth and understanding. I want to try to do a better job of living in the present, realizing I have no control over outcomes. I understand better now the importance of the journey toward wholeness, of making friends with my heart, my mind, and my spirit. I am trying hard to be true to Ed Poole, and I want to continue to understand Ed Poole better than I do now.

At the beginning of the book, I said, "If you can leave the book at its ending, agreeing with me that the journey I'm on is more than worth the price of admission, and can see my story as one of hope, challenges, and growth, I will be satisfied." I truly hope you can say this to yourself because I can. I've said it during the writing process, and I will continue to gain value from my story. If you had stopped reading at the end of Chapter 2, you would have left the book saying to yourself, "Is this all this guy knows how to do – complain? What a crybaby. If he thinks his life was rough growing up, he should have grown up with me." We cannot really compare our stories – it's like comparing apples and oranges. A teaching colleague of mine, Denise Hatcher, has stated: "Although we co-exist on this planet, we can never really know the life of another person because we can never live that person's life and we can never become that person."

The real hope, joy, sense of fulfillment, and heightened understanding come through reading the rest of the book. Up to this point, my story has a happy ending. Without the learning I've done through my writing, I would not see my story as happy. I cannot express strongly enough how this writing has become one of the best experiences of my entire life. You may be able to get in touch with your life's lessons in dramatically different ways than I. I'm a very visual learner, and I had to write my story out, see it printed on the page, read it, and take time to reflect on it before I could make it a part of me. My story is now a part of me; it is deep inside and that long, deep cleansing breath affirms my story within. As I leave this legacy, *Lessons from the porch*, for others, I'm leaving it for myself as well.

I neither regret nor want to change a single stop along my journey's way. As in your own journeys, there have been many peaks and valleys, many bright, blessed days and dark, sacred nights. As I've been given the gift of **R**esting, **R**efreshing, and **R**eflecting, each stop – though sometimes very painful – has contributed to my being where and who I am today. I'm liking "me" a bit better these days, for which I am very grateful. My sorrows have been outweighed by my joys in life, and the sorrows, as I now realize, have been important for my growth and understanding.

As Eric used to tell his bike-riding clients as a Backroads leader, "You have to do the uphills to enjoy the downhills." For much of my life, I thought it was all about downhills. I avoided the physical and emotional pain of the uphills. I now know that true bike-riders relish the uphills because of the challenge ahead as well as the reward of the awaiting downhill.

I have fought some of the stops along my journey, and I have run from other stops, which potentially could have been growth-producing. I will never know. But I do know the places I've been have all contributed in their own way to helping me begin to find Ed Poole. My journey *has been* and *is being* a wonderful gift.

THE DANCE OF LIFE

Each of us who attended church on Epiphany Sunday received a large, bright, blue star – a symbol of the light that surrounds this particular Sunday of the Christian calendar. We each in turn took our star from plates that were passed through the congregation. Each star had a simple word on it, a word we could not see until we picked our star at random and turned it over in order to see the word. We were asked to keep the word we found on our star in our hearts and minds throughout the coming year and to see how that word influences our lives. My star had on it the word "***dance***".

I love to dance; however, only recently have I realized the importance of my being a participant in the dance of life. I've been on the sidelines listening to the music, waiting to see if anyone would ask me to dance. Eventually my thoughts turned to the porch. I remembered the words from Greg Asimakoupoulos: *Did your mother know when she told you not to chance that you'd never learn to* <u>*dance*</u> *with all those opportunities for growth all dressed for the prom? Damn! She didn't. And neither did you!* I think it has been only in the last few years of my life that I have begun to dance the dance of life.

As I continued thinking about the word on my blue star, I was reminded of the words of Thoreau, realizing that, for me, when I "step to the music" I hear, I'm dancing: "If a man does not keep pace with his companions, perhaps it is because he hears a different drummer. Let him step to the music he hears, however measured or far away."

I began to realize that *dance* is a good word to describe our lives. Our lives are a dance. We are constantly dancing a delicate balance among several of life's many paradoxes, such as making decisions that are growth-producing and growth-limiting, honoring our light and shadow sides, taking care of ourselves and taking care of others, leaving and receiving legacies, living on the porch and living off the porch, giving love and receiving love, moving through the wilderness journeys while living in them long enough to learn, enjoying the journey while living toward a destination, taking risks while feeling safe, understanding being in relation to doing, waiting and taking action, wearing masks and being transparent, perceiving, behaving, and becoming. I was also reminded of this delicate balance in the dance of life as I thought about the words of Charles Dickens, from *A Tale of Two Cities*. If you've read the book, you know Dickens talked about the best of times and the worst of times, the age of wisdom and the age of foolishness, the season of light and the season of darkness, the spring of hope and the winter of despair – as well as others. When we are fully aware, savoring each moment, we dance with these and other paradoxes in our lives.

In Chapter 4 you were introduced to some words from Marilyn Ferguson, who talked about change in our lives and observed that often it is that place in between life's changes that we fear the most. As I reflect on my word ***dance***, I am beginning to realize that it is in the stillness of life that the dancing occurs. As I reflect in stillness from the porch I begin to ***dance*** with the insights I gain. If this is the case, then those in-between times mentioned by Ferguson can be welcomed, not feared. We can remember the value of waiting and see this time as positive, as a time to dance the dance of life and continue to bring balance to those paradoxes that surround us every day.

I also thought of a beautiful song by Lee Ann Womak, titled "I Hope You Dance." In part, the lyrics say, "Whenever one door closes I hope one more opens. Promise me that you'll give faith a fighting chance, and when you get the choice to sit it out or dance, I hope you dance." I hope for all of us that we can look forward with joy, anticipation, and wonder to the dance of life and, further, that we continue to be conscious participants in that dance.

Another song came to mind as I was thinking of my word dance. The song title is "Will The Circle Be Unbroken," and several artists have recorded it. The Nitty Gritty Dirt Band recorded the version I like the best. I played their version of this song at Mom's funeral because I wanted to make a point. As members of my tribe have preceded me in death, I firmly believe they have joined in a circle. The circle has to do with family relationships and the opportunity that death has provided them all to stand together and dance. As each family member dies, he or she joins the circle until finally it will be unbroken, and all who are there can join hands and dance.

There is a Jewish holiday each fall called sukkot. In his book *When All You've Ever Wanted Isn't Enough*, Harold Kushner speaks of this holiday. "It comes to tell us that the world is full of good and beautiful things, food and wine, flowers and sunsets, and autumn landscapes and good company to share them with, but that we have to enjoy them right away because they will not last…It is a time to enjoy happiness with those we love and to realize that we are at a time in our lives when enjoying today means more than worrying about tomorrow. It is time to celebrate the fact that we have finally learned what life is about and how to make the most of it."

And So It Is As We Leave

As we leave for now I want you to know that I have learned much from my writing. Carol Pearson has written a book titled *The Hero Within*. At one point in the book, she says, "What if the goal of life is not to prevail, but simply to learn? Then the end of the story can seem very different; and so can what happens in between birth and death. Heroism is defined as not only <u>moving</u> mountains but <u>knowing</u> mountains."

The puppeteer, Jim Henson, had some specific thoughts about how he wanted to leave. Henson died in the spring of 1990, following a brief illness. The master puppeteer who has brought joy and laughter to millions created characters such as Big Bird, Ernie, Miss Piggy, and Kermit the Frog. *Sesame Street* and the *Muppet Movie* are a part of his legacy to us. A few years before his death, Henson had written instructions for his funeral. Upon his death the instructions were opened. It seems his first desire was that his funeral would be a happy time, not sad. Based on the accounts of his funeral, it seems to have been just that. Crowded into the Cathedral of St. John the Divine were thousands of people who had come to pay their respects. Some wore yellow raincoats like the puppets on Sesame Street. Others wore butterfly antennas to bring back memories of other creations. The flowers that filled the 5,000-seat cathedral were in the shape of animals. Big Bird sang a solo, an organist played the Sesame Street theme on the massive cathedral organ, and a Dixieland Band led the worshippers out of the cathedral playing, "When the Saints Go Marching In."

What struck me most about the written account of the funeral were the words Henson desired to be placed in the worship folder. Upon walking into the service, those attending received a program with these words from Henson being the first words they saw. I leave them for you now as I close out this part of my journey and continue on to places unknown.

Please watch out for each other.

Love and forgive everybody.

It's a good life, enjoy it.

I wish all of us well on our journeys toward gaining not only a better understanding of who we are but also of what we are being asked to do while on this earth in order to leave it a bit better place than it was when we first found it. What more could we possibly ask than that?

I want to thank you sincerely for reading *Lessons from the porch*. I hope you have allowed some important questions to surface about your own journey, and, further, I hope you have a desire to tell your story. Early in the book, I suggested that a part of any person's story is a part of all of our stories. I also observed that as we listen to and share our stories, we enter into a relationship with those with whom we experience this sharing.

I would really like to know some of your story. I want to know in what ways this relationship between you and me developed as you read about my journey. I want to know some of your life's lessons and how you learned them. I have a website, www.lessonsfromtheporch.com. I hope that you are willing to go to this website and click on the button *Lessons from the porch*. As you get to this point on the website, you will have an opportunity to do two things: order additional copies of the book, in case you have thought of others who might benefit from reading about my, and your, journey. You can: (1) complete the order form, click the submit button, and I will immediately receive your request. (2) FAX your order form to me at 630/844-5530. (3) Print out the order form and mail a hard copy request for additional books.

More importantly, however, by clicking on the *Lessons from the porch* button on the website, you will have an opportunity to share part of your journey with me. I would very much like to know some of your story because you will help me understand my journey as you share with me your story. You have an important story to tell. I would be honored if you would share it with me. You may do so anonymously, and you may also leave information about how I might get in touch with you. If you leave this contact information, I will be in touch! I envision us forming a "circle of conversation."

In addition to learning your story, I will also look forward to any feedback you might have for me on your reactions to having read the book. As you know, and as I said in the book, learning is a lifelong process. You will help me continue to learn about myself by sharing your reactions to the book. What thoughts did you have as you read? What questions came forth? How did you feel as you were reading about my journey? How and where have you learned your life's lessons?

You may also send me a hard copy containing your story and feedback for me by mailing this information, in care of me, to **STEC Publishing**, ***P.O. Box 3972, Naperville, IL 60567-3972***.

I have developed workshops and seminars for many corporate settings centered on each of the twenty-two *Lessons from the Porch*. The lessons you've read have many applications to corporate America, and I would enjoy talking with you about those applications. Organizations today need to lead both with their heads and their hearts. During the last decade we encouraged our colleagues to think and feel. We finally suggested they did not have to leave their beliefs, hopes, dreams, and stories outside the doors of meeting rooms as they entered.

Thank you, and my very best wishes to you on your journey.

Currently Ed is an Associate Professor in the College of Education at Aurora University, where he teaches in the Doctoral Studies Program. He has also taught at The University of Georgia, Indiana University, Butler University, Northern Illinois University, National-Louis University, and North Central College.

For several years, Ed taught high school social studies and served as a middle school and high school principal, assistant superintendent, and superintendent of schools. A professional presenter for over twenty years, Ed has conducted seminars and workshops throughout the United States and Canada. He has developed programs for several school districts, colleges and universities, as well as Fortune 500 companies.

Ed has also served as a Corporate Director of Education and Training and has written and presented extensively on strategic planning, team building, organization development, executive coaching, and leadership.

Robert Atkinson, *The Life Story Interview*

James Autry, *Love and Profit*

Christina Baldwin, *Calling the Circle*

Rick Bass, *The Watch*

Sue Bender, *Plain and Simple*

Richard Bode, *Beachcombing at Miramar* and *First You Have to Learn to Row a Little Boat*

Frederick Buechner, *A Room Called Remember*, *The Longing for Home*, and *The Magnificent Defeat*

Richard Carlson, *Handbook For The Soul*

Pema Chodron, *When Things Fall Apart*

Deepak Chopra, *The Deeper Wound* and *The Seven Spiritual Laws of Success*

Forrest Church, *Life Lines: Holding On (And Letting Go)*

Alan Cohen, *I Had It All The Time*

Robert Coles, *The Spiritual Life of Children*

John Cowan, *The Common Table*

Annie Dillard, *Pilgrim at Tinker Creek*

W.E.B. DuBois, *Souls of Black Folk*

Wayne Dyer, *You'll See It When You Believe It*

Loren Eiseley, *The Immense Journey*

Marilyn Ferguson, *The Aquarian Conspiracy*

Victor Frankl, *Man's Search for Meaning*

Mark Gerzon, *Coming Into Our Own*

Dag Hammarskjold, *Markings*

Denise Hatcher, *Life History as a Way to Give Voice to Latinos*

James Hillman, *The Soul's Code*

Phil Jackson, *Sacred Hoops*

Nikos Kazantzakis, *The Saviors of God and Report to Greco*

Sam Keen & Ann Valley-Fox, *Your Mythic Journey*

Heinz Kohut, *The Analysis of the Self*

Harold Kushner, *When Bad Things Happen to Good People*, *How Good Do We Have to Be?* and *When All You've Ever Wanted Isn't Enough*

Gred Levoy, *Callings: Finding and Following an Authentic Life*

C.S. Lewis, *The Grief Observed*

Richard Lieder, *The Power of Purpose* and *Repacking Our Bags*

Edger Lee Masters, *Spoon River Anthology*

James Morgan, *If These Walls Had Ears*

Erich Newman, *The Child*

Sam Osherson, *Finding Our Fathers*

Scott Peck, *The Road Less Traveled*

Robert Raines, *Going Home* and *Living the Questions*

Shel Silverstein, *The Missing Piece*

Jane Smiley, *A Thousand Acres*

Studs Turkel, *May The Circle Be Unbroken*

Anne Wilson-Schaef, *The Addictive Organization*

Connie Zweig, *Meeting the Shadow*